I0810292

IMAGES
*of America*

# MARGARET CHASE SMITH'S SKOWHEGAN

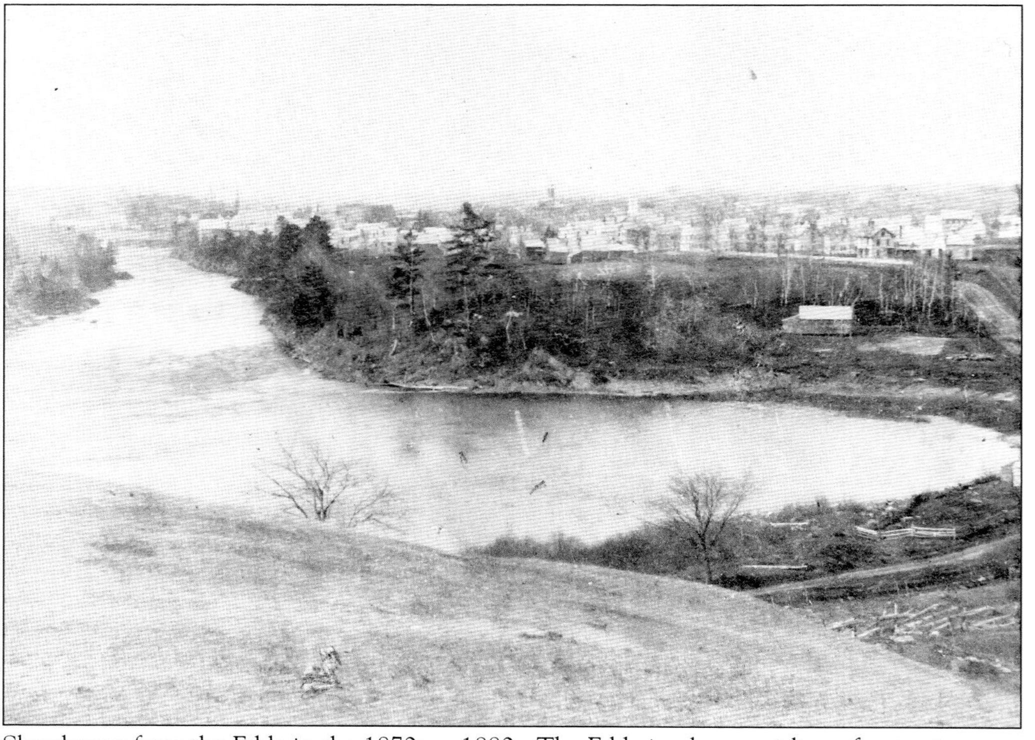

Skowhegan from the Eddy in the 1870s or 1880s. The Eddy is a large swirling of water in a part of the Kennebec River.

IMAGES
*of America*

# MARGARET CHASE SMITH'S SKOWHEGAN

Frank H. Sleeper
From the Collections of the
Margaret Chase Smith Library and Others

ARCADIA
PUBLISHING

ISBN 978-0-7385-6421-0

Published by Arcadia Publishing
Charleston, South Carolina

Printed in the United States of America

Library of Congress Control Number: 2009920441

For all general information, please contact Arcadia Publishing:
Telephone 843-853-2070
Fax 843-853-0044
E-mail sales@arcadiapublishing.com
For customer service and orders:
Toll-Free 1-888-313-2665

Visit us on the Internet at www.arcadiapublishing.com

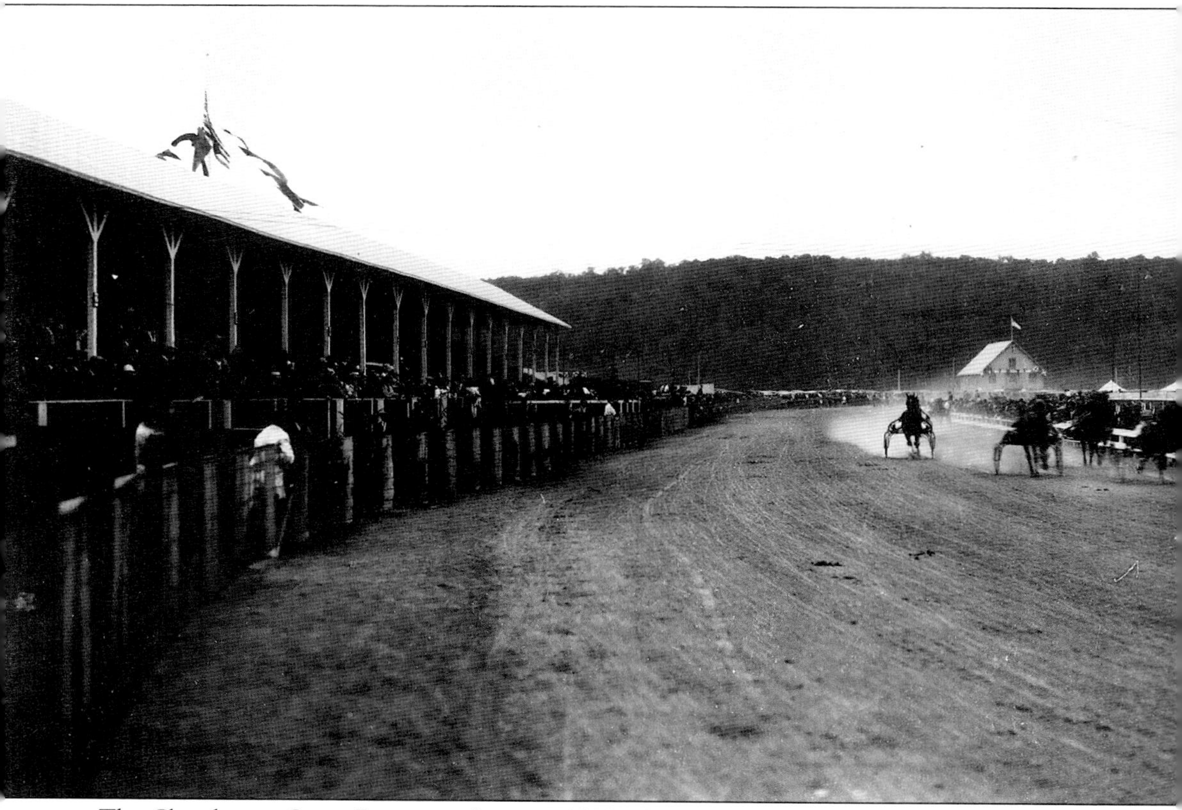

The Skowhegan State Fair at its best, *c.* 1930s. Harness racing was and is the highlight of Maine's oldest fair. The author's great uncle, Ralph Burrill of Canaan, may be one of the drivers in this race. He was one of Maine's best harness racers; eventually he went on to become a judge and ran a big inn in Canaan which was filled with harness racing memorabilia.

# Contents

# Introduction

Margaret Chase Smith has been called by her most recent biographer, Professor Patricia Wallace, "the most influential woman in the history of American politics." She was.

Every person, politician or otherwise, is influenced to some degree by his or her environment. And Senator Smith's environment until she was almost forty years old was the central Maine town of Skowhegan, where she was born, raised, went to school, held her first jobs, and where she met her future husband, Clyde Smith.

This is a town where much of the central business area lies in a historic district. There are several other Maine towns where this is true, where many buildings have survived for years. As a result, there is a certain sense of stability in Skowhegan and these other towns. When you return to Skowhegan, even if it is years later, you know that the central core of the town will not be greatly changed. I believe that some of this stability translated itself into the psyche of Senator Smith. It can be seen in her inclination against excess, against overdoing things—as the senator showed notably in her Declaration of Conscience against Senator Joseph McCarthy on June 1, 1950, four years before McCarthy was censored by the Senate.

Senator Smith brought many benefits (and is still bringing them through her library) to her community. This book starts with one of those benefits: President Dwight D. Eisenhower's trip to Skowhegan on June 26–27, 1955. It was the first time a president had ever been to the town while in office. Later on the Maine trip, Ike was to fish at Rangeley Lakes (Parmachenee) but Skowhegan had its day in the sun.

Possibly the greatest benefits Senator Smith brought to Maine were the defense installations that she worked to get here. Skowhegan didn't benefit directly from such installations, but the town very probably had much to do with Margaret Chase Smith's great interest in defense matters during the Cold War.

Her interest could well have started when the first boy she ever dated, Harry D. St. Ledger, was killed on July 18, 1918, at Belleau Wood, France. One of Senator Smith's sisters, Evelyn, married Rexford St. Ledger, Harry's brother.

Another incident that probably shaped the senator's strong attitude toward defense was the death of Lieutenant Commander John Edward French at Pearl Harbor on December 7, 1941. Commander French was a year behind Senator Smith at Skowhegan High. French graduated from the U.S. Naval Academy in 1922, married the daughter of a retired naval officer, taught at the Naval Academy, and was the navigation officer on the battleship *Arizona* when it was destroyed by the Japanese at Pearl Harbor. We have included French's picture here, along with the four Skowhegan boys killed on Iwo Jima, the boy who survived the Bataan Death March only to die four days after it ended, and some of the other thirty-three Skowhegan boys who died in World War II—and who must have influenced, at least to some degree, Senator Smith's tough stance on defense. It was not just her long-time administrative assistant, Brigadier

General William C. Lewis, who influenced her in this direction—Senator Smith, in good Maine tradition, was too independent to be influenced by just one source.

I once succeeded in getting a picture of the undefeated 1915–16 Skowhegan High girls' basketball team on which Mrs. Smith played into *Sports Illustrated* magazine. Included here, therefore, is a section on sports.

Finally, I have included photographs of Skowhegan taken before Senator Smith was born, to give a sense of the town's stability. As with any community, there has been change here as well, but not to the degree of most of urban America.

More work needs to be done on the local history of Skowhegan—and more will be done. Not enough emphasis has been placed in the past upon Skowhegan's influences on the attitudes of the "most influential woman in the history of American politics." It's to be hoped this book will help to correct this and that more research will be done on this important facet of Senator Smith's life.

This, my seventh book in the Images of America series, I dedicate to the young people of Skowhegan. I hope they will learn from it. I also hope it keeps them from their TV sets for at least an hour.

# *One*

# Ike's Visit

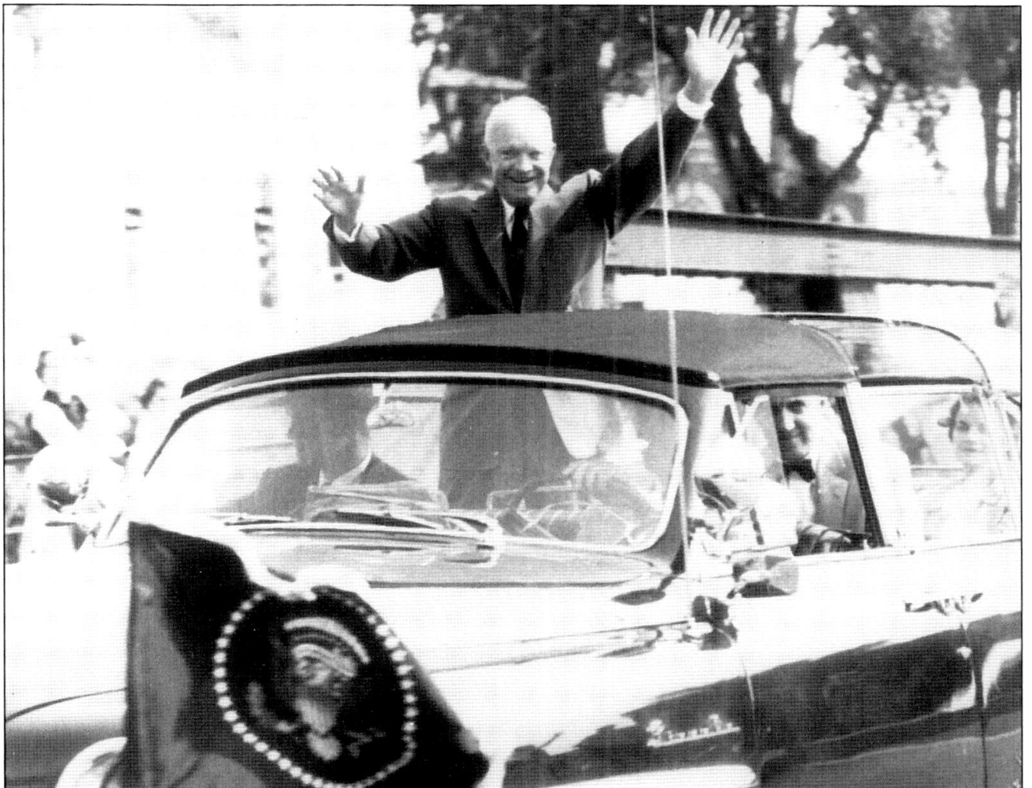

President Dwight D. Eisenhower's visit to Skowhegan, June 26–27, 1955. He is shown here with Governor Edmund S. Muskie and his wife Jane. Ike stayed overnight at the home of Senator Margaret Chase Smith. Their limousine is on the island in Skowhegan between the Centenary Methodist Church and the Skowhegan Fire Station.

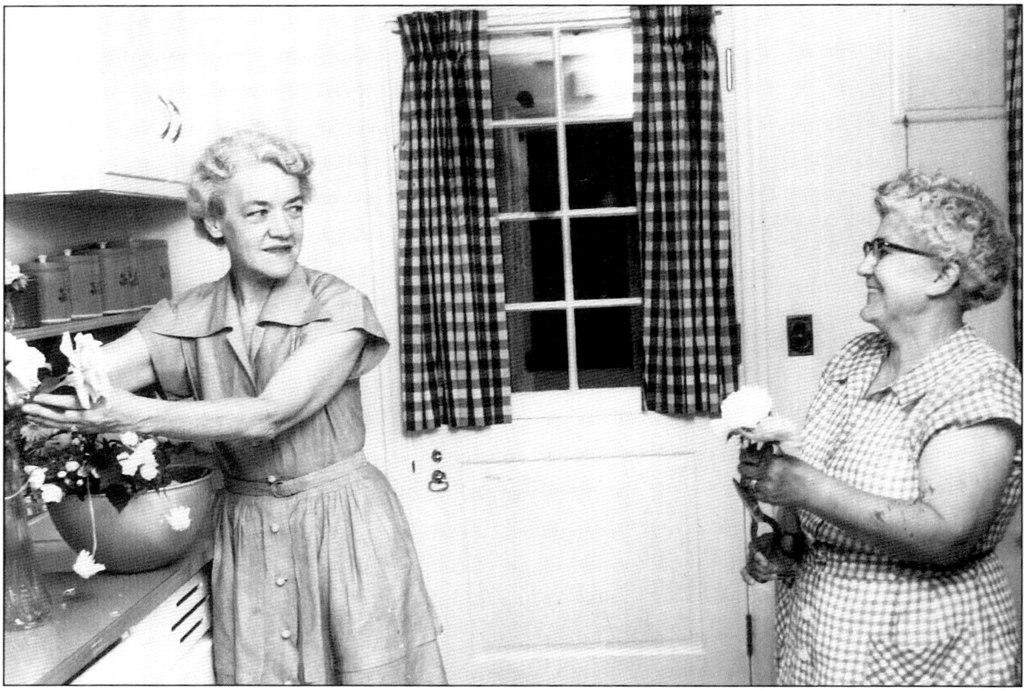

Senator Margaret Chase Smith helps her housekeeper, Agnes Staples, arrange some flowers for the Eisenhower visit.

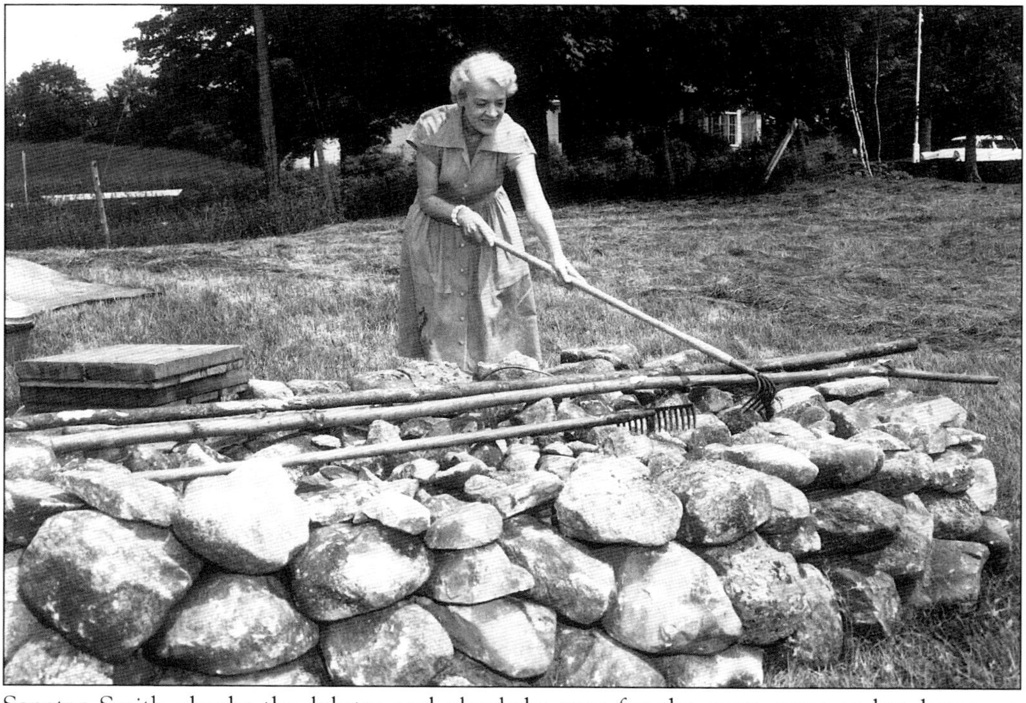

Senator Smith checks the lobster and clambake area for the press corps at her home on Norridgewock Avenue. President Eisenhower came there for lobster after he had his steak.

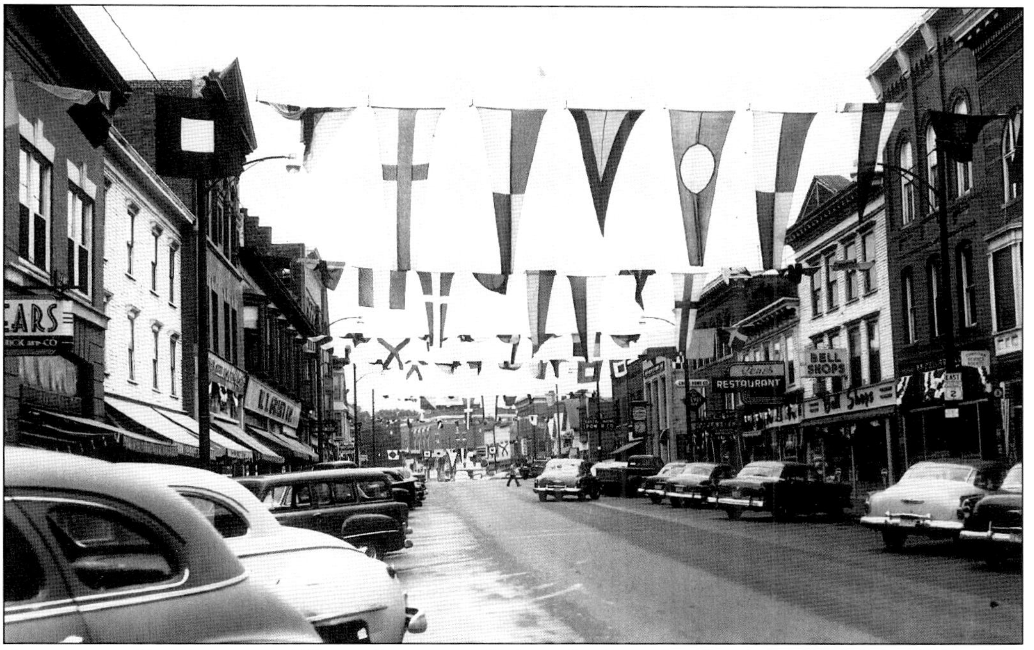

Downtown Skowhegan on Water Street just before the President's motorcade passed through.

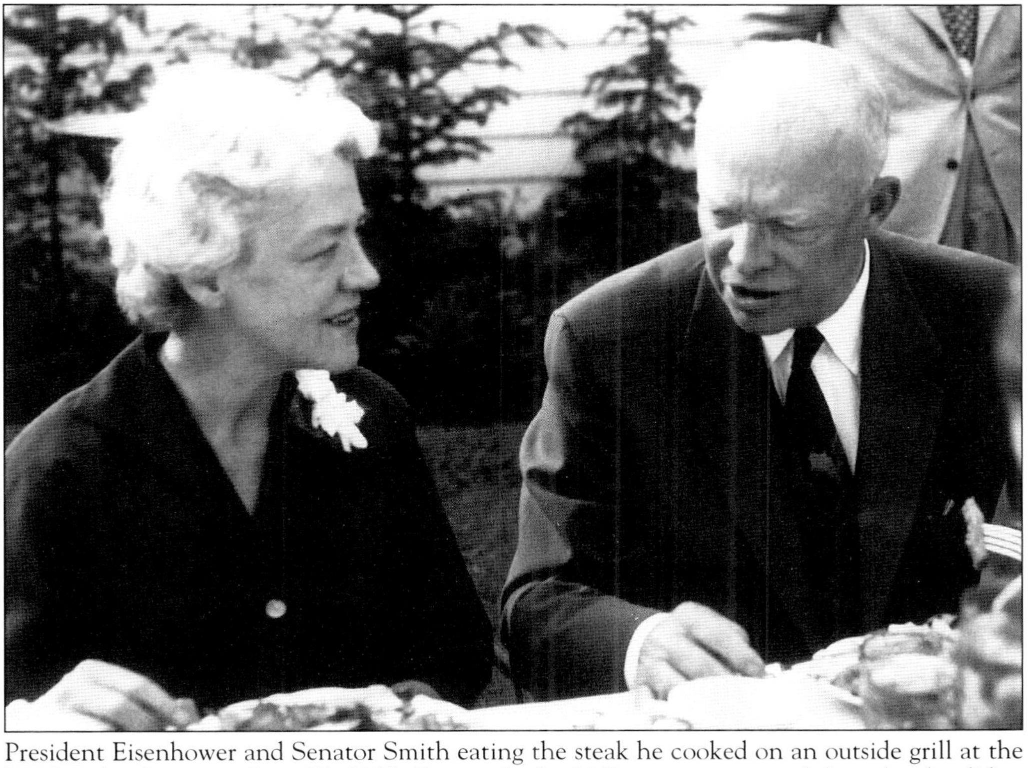
President Eisenhower and Senator Smith eating the steak he cooked on an outside grill at the lunch at her home on June 27, 1955. Doctors had told Ike not to eat any lobster but he did so and had no repercussions.

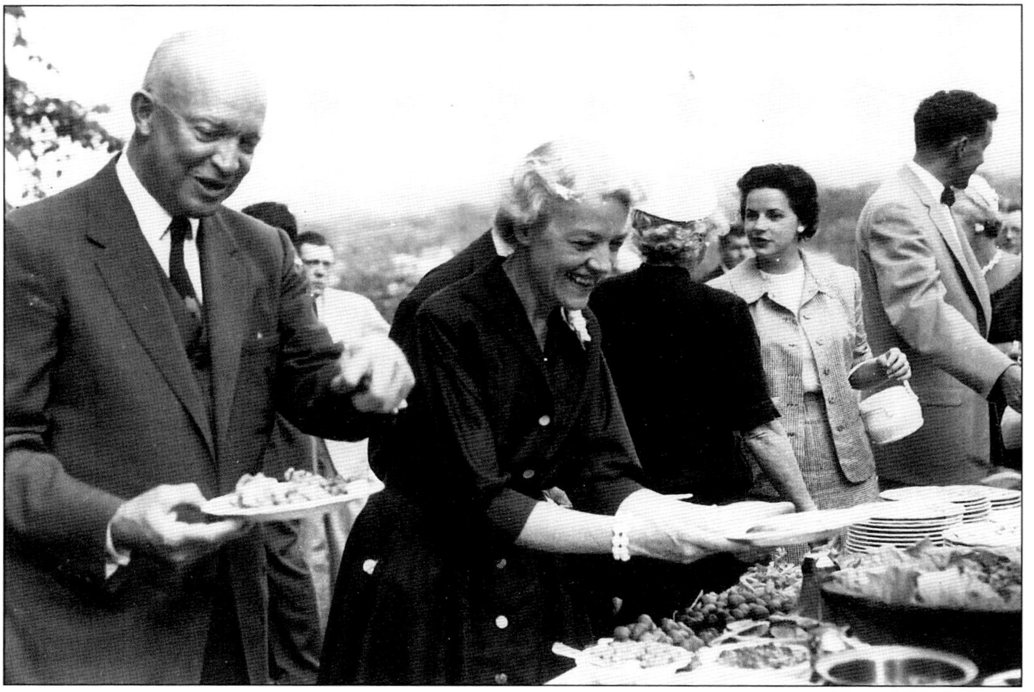

President Eisenhower, Senator Smith, an unidentified person, Jane Muskie, and Governor Edmund S. Muskie enjoy the steak dinner at the Smith home.

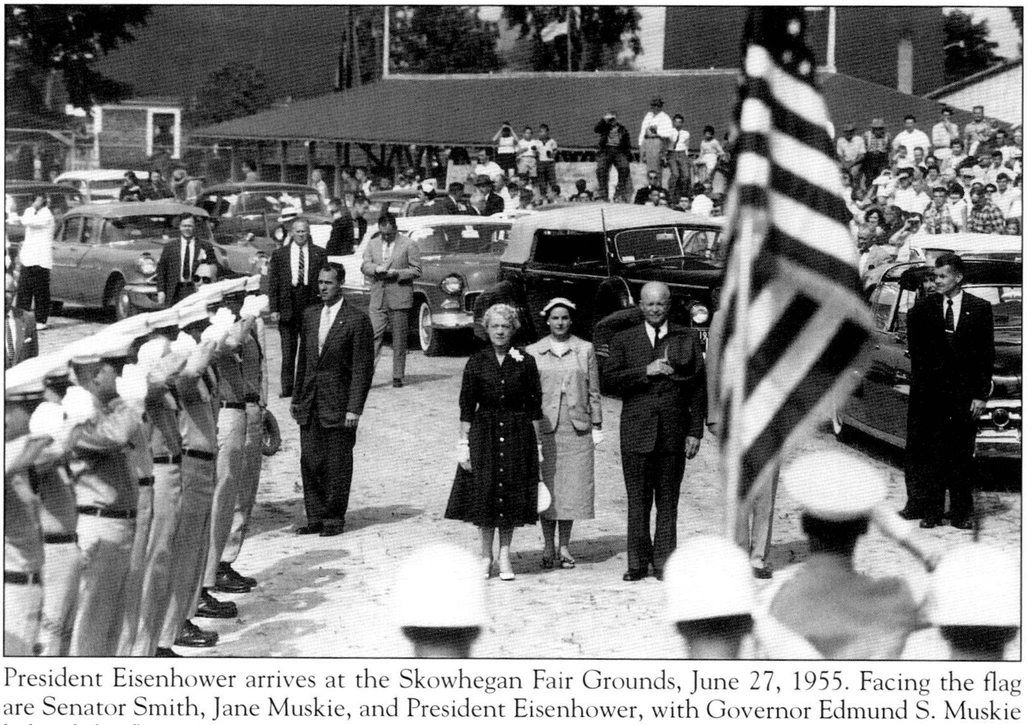

President Eisenhower arrives at the Skowhegan Fair Grounds, June 27, 1955. Facing the flag are Senator Smith, Jane Muskie, and President Eisenhower, with Governor Edmund S. Muskie behind the flag.

President Eisenhower and Senator Smith walking at the Skowhegan Fair Grounds where he spoke to several thousand Maine folk after his lunch at the Smith home.

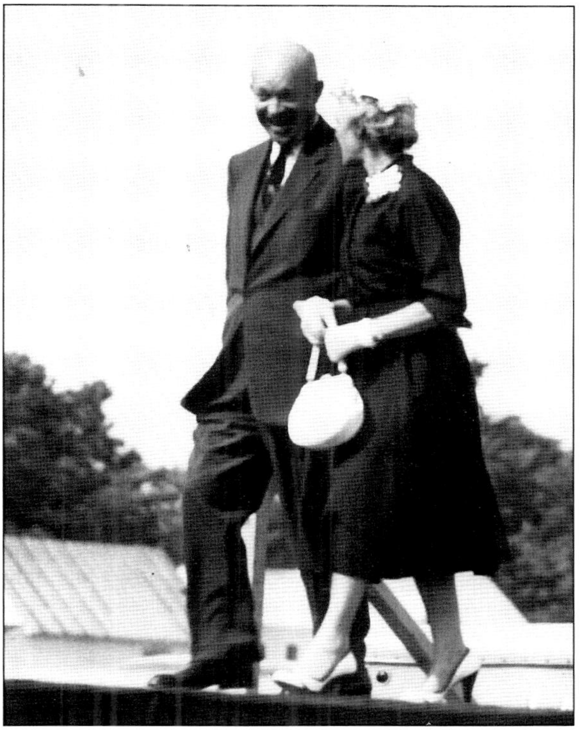

Proceeding to the speaker's platform are Senator Smith, President Eisenhower, James Hagerty (Eisenhower's press secretary), Governor Edmund S. and Jane Muskie, and Frederick G. Payne (Maine's other Senator). Hagerty is wearing sunglasses.

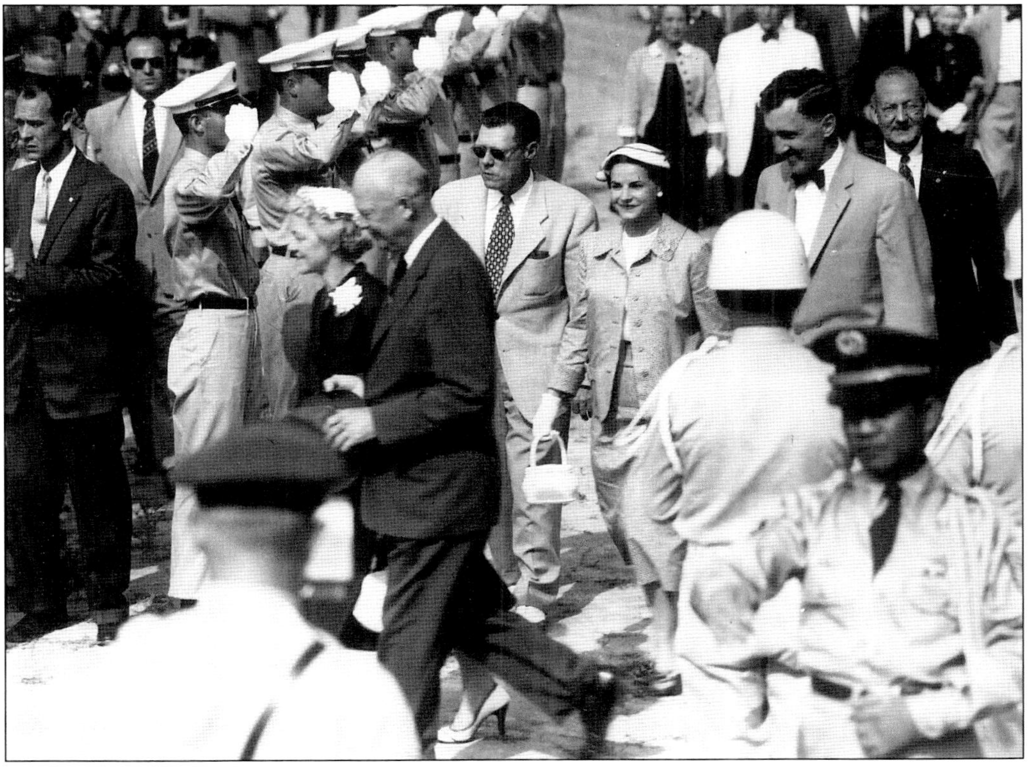

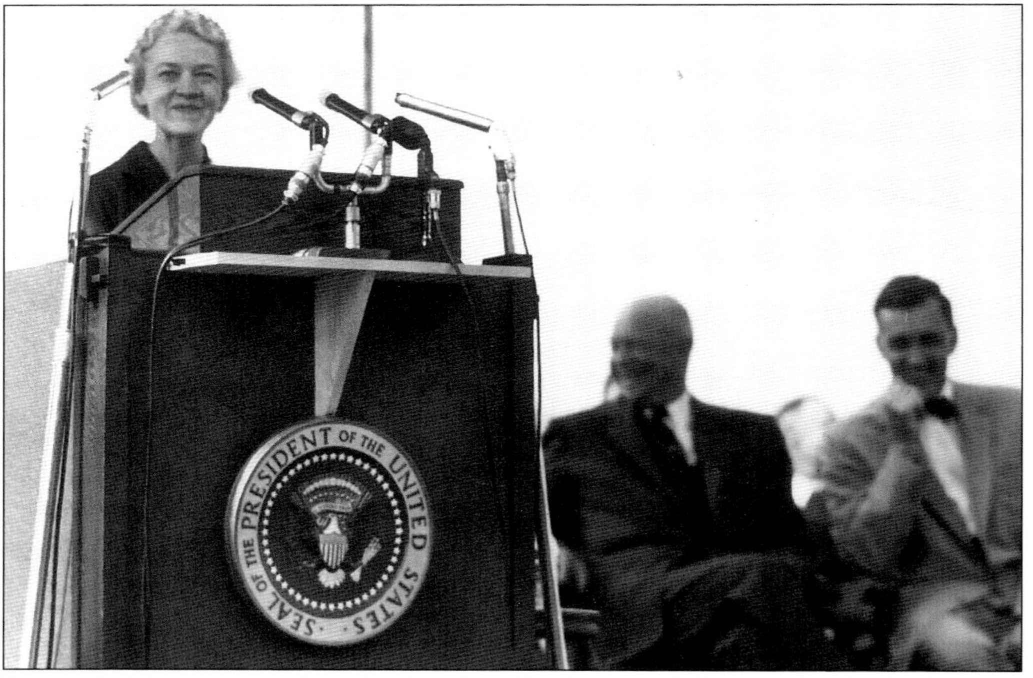


Senator Smith, in her speech, makes President Eisenhower and Governor Muskie laugh.

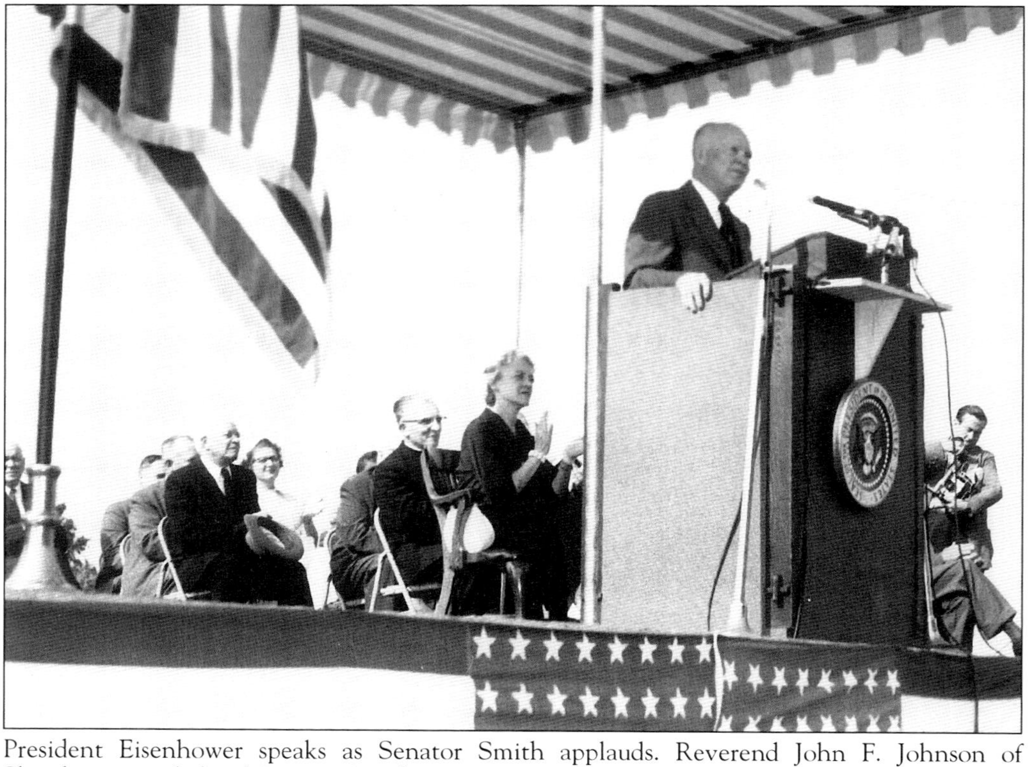

President Eisenhower speaks as Senator Smith applauds. Reverend John F. Johnson of Skowhegan sits behind Senator Smith.

# *Two*

# Margaret's Way

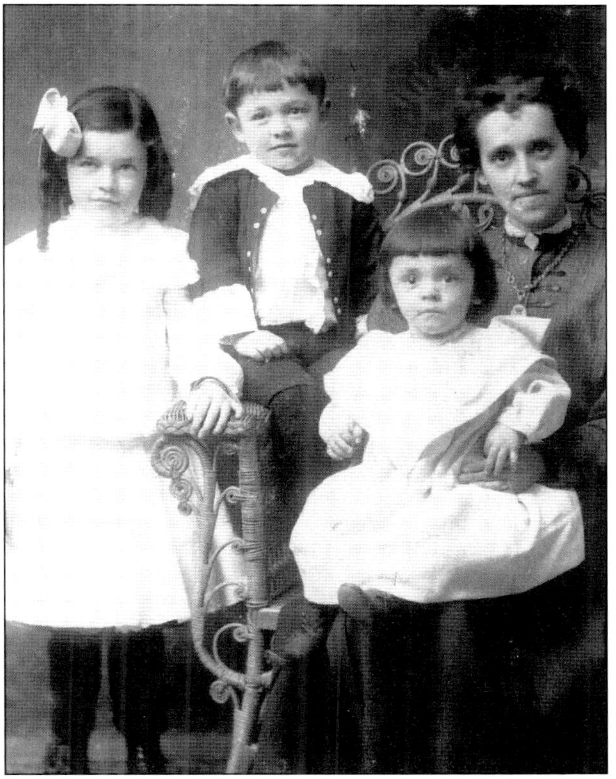

Margaret Madeline Chase at the age of six in 1903. Also in the photograph are Wilbur George Chase, Roland Murray, and Margaret's mother, Mrs. Carrie Chase.

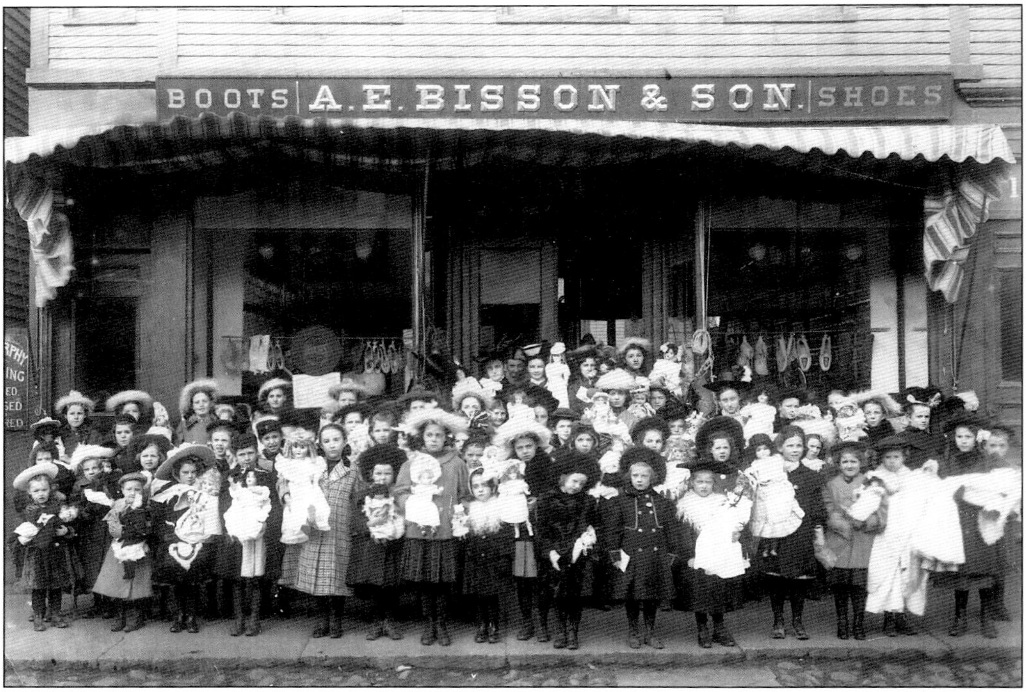


A doll contest in Skowhegan, *c.* 1906. Rosetta Roderick is in the third row, Roderick Perry and Margaret Chase are in the fourth row, and Ursula Roderick is in the back row.

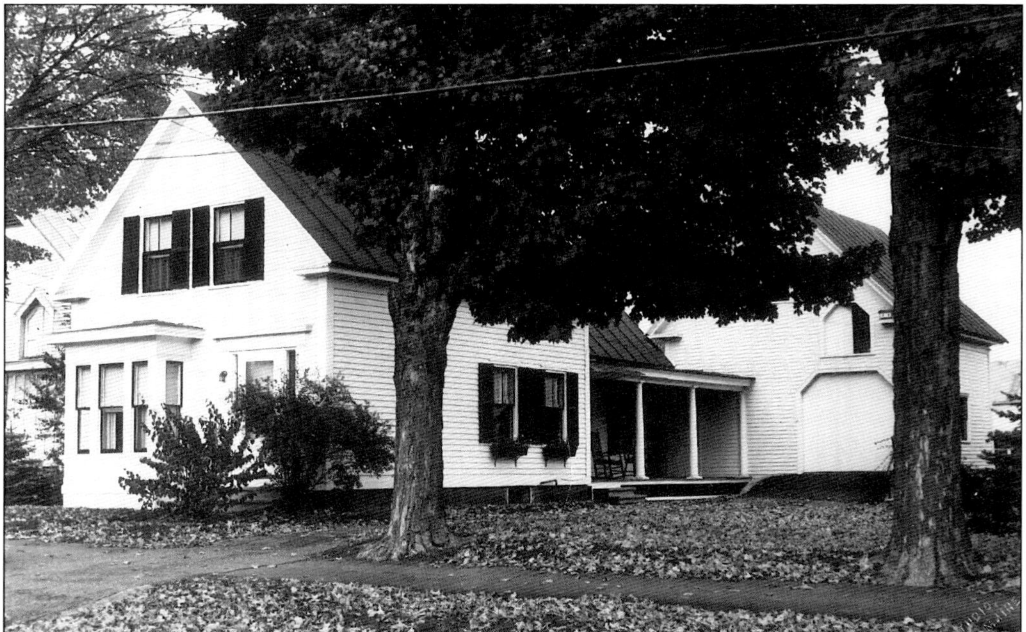

The John L. Murray home on North Avenue in Skowhegan. Margaret Chase Smith's mother and father, Carrie Murray and George Emery Chase, lived here, and all of the Chase children, including Margaret, were born here.

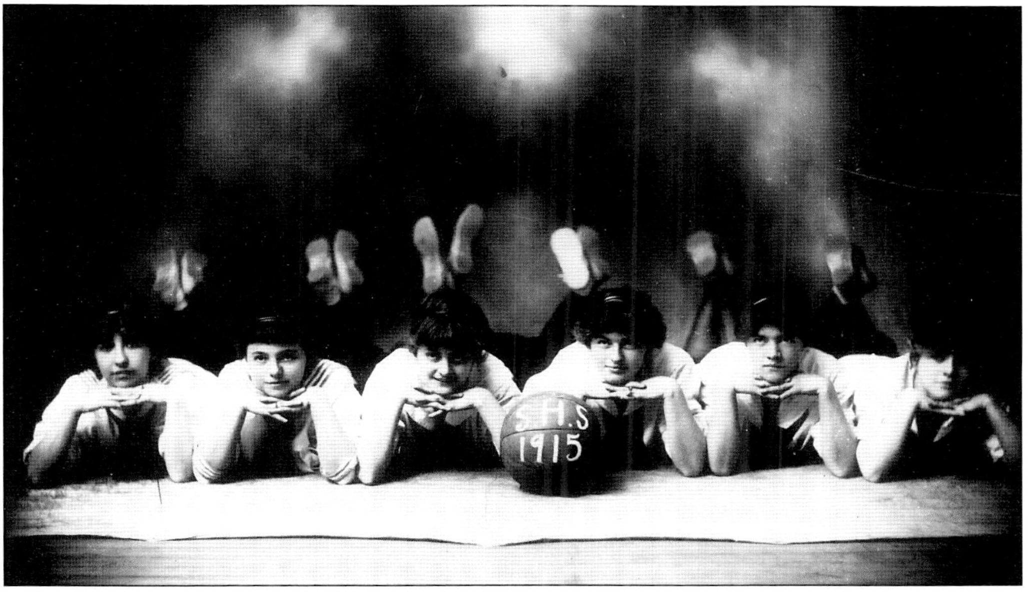


Margaret Chase was the manager of the girls' basketball team at Skowhegan High for four years and also played running center. From left to right are Corinne Salley, Gladys Pennell, Nell Gifford, Beatrice Smiley, Margaret Chase, and Helen White.

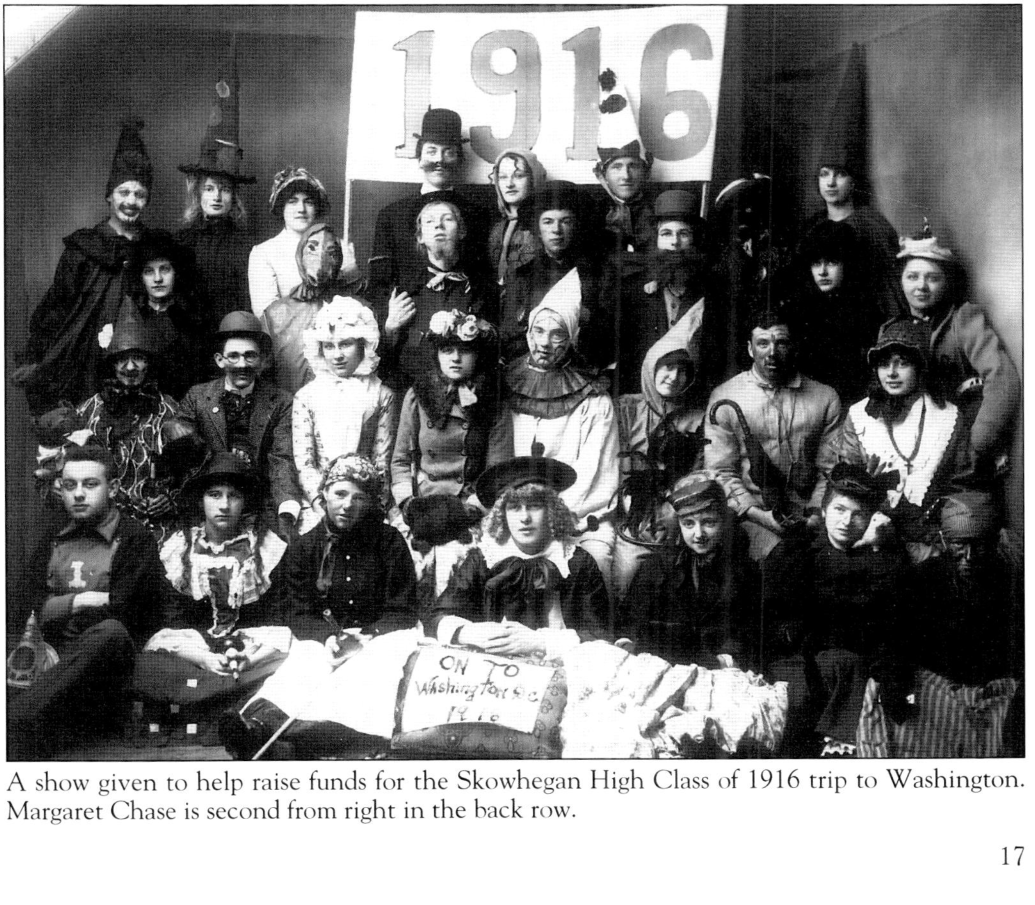


A show given to help raise funds for the Skowhegan High Class of 1916 trip to Washington. Margaret Chase is second from right in the back row.

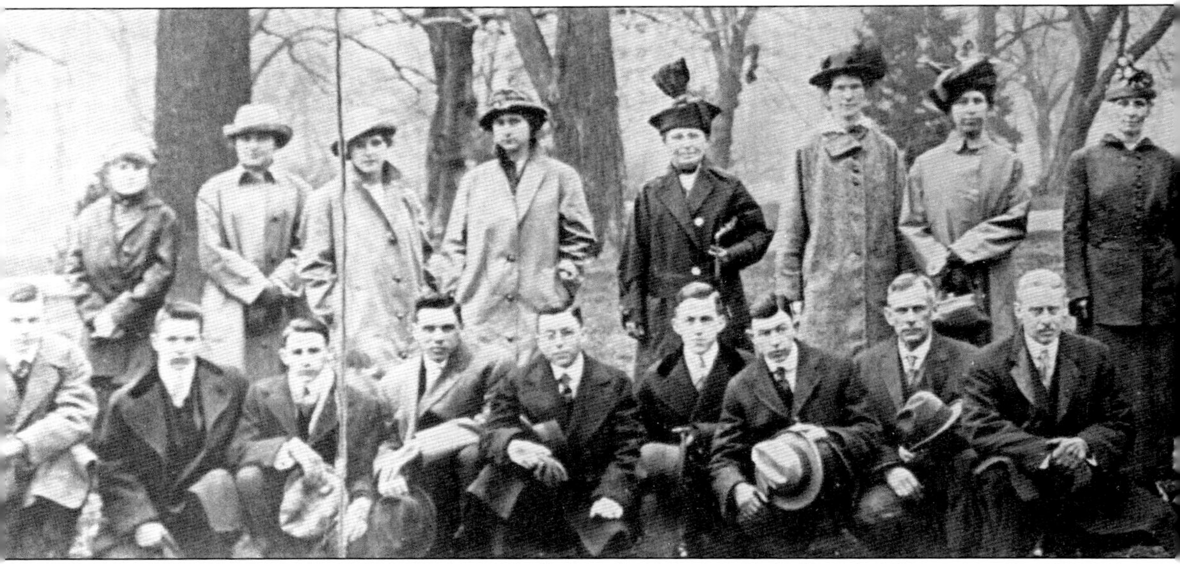

Margaret Chase Smith's first trip to Washington in 1916, with the Skowhegan High Class of 1916. Her $60 trip was financed by a loan at 6 percent interest by her grandfather, John Murray. The group went by train to Boston and Fall River, then by ship to New York City, and by train again to Philadelphia and Washington. The group shook hands with President Woodrow Wilson. From left to right are: (front row) Emery Dyer, Bruce White, Ralph Merriam, Harold Crosby, Peter Vincent, Adolph Bollier, Francis Friend, E.E. Greenwood, Representative John

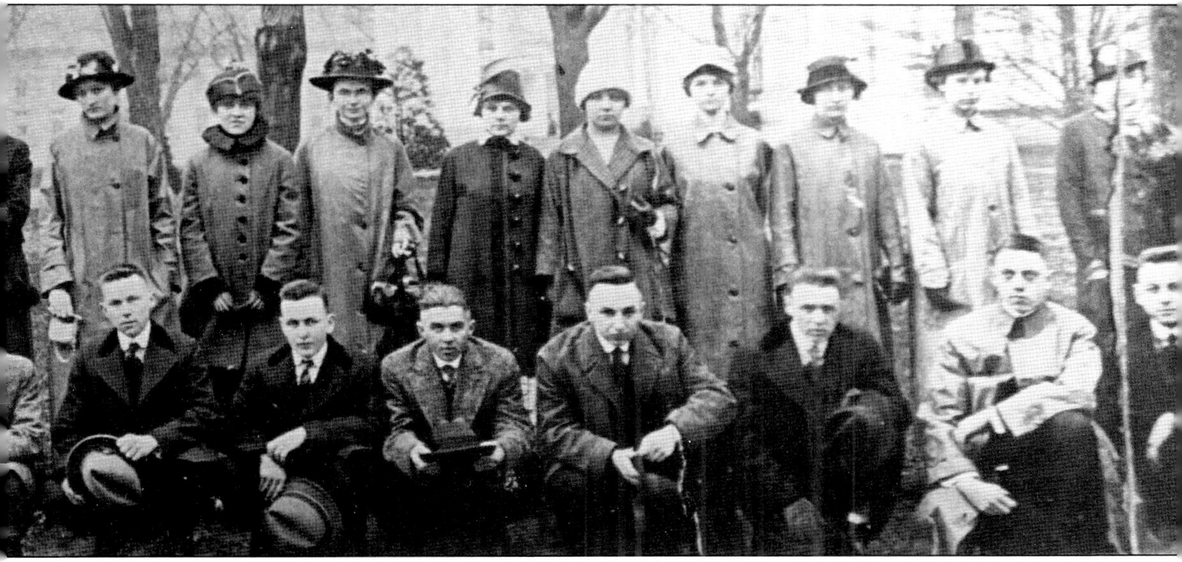

A. Peters of Maine, Bernard Bailey, Allan Wentworth, Lewis Brown, John Emery, Cassimere Bisson, Donald Dumont, Ray Parmenter, and Brooks Savage; (back row) Ruth Greenwood, Beatrice Smiley, Helen White, Geneva Smith, Mrs. E.E. Greenwood, Mrs. Martha Seaton of Massachusetts, Ratie Tozier, Miss Hoxie of Fairfield, Sarah Snow, Gertrude Groder, Margaret Chase, Jessie McGregor, Blanche Jewett, Marion Adams, Leora Foss, Lana Nottage, Pearl Harville, Theresa Bisson, and Nell Gifford.

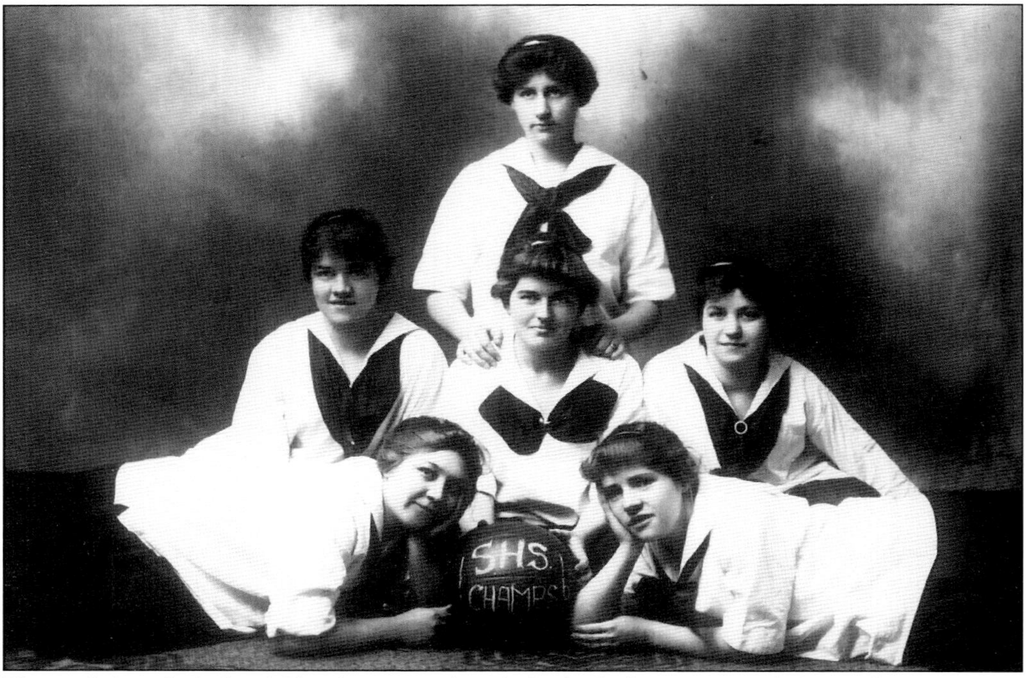


The undefeated 1915–16 Skowhegan High girls' basketball team. From left to right are: (front) Corinne Salley and Beatrice Smiley; (middle) Margaret Chase, Gladys Powell, and Helen White; (back) Nell Gifford.

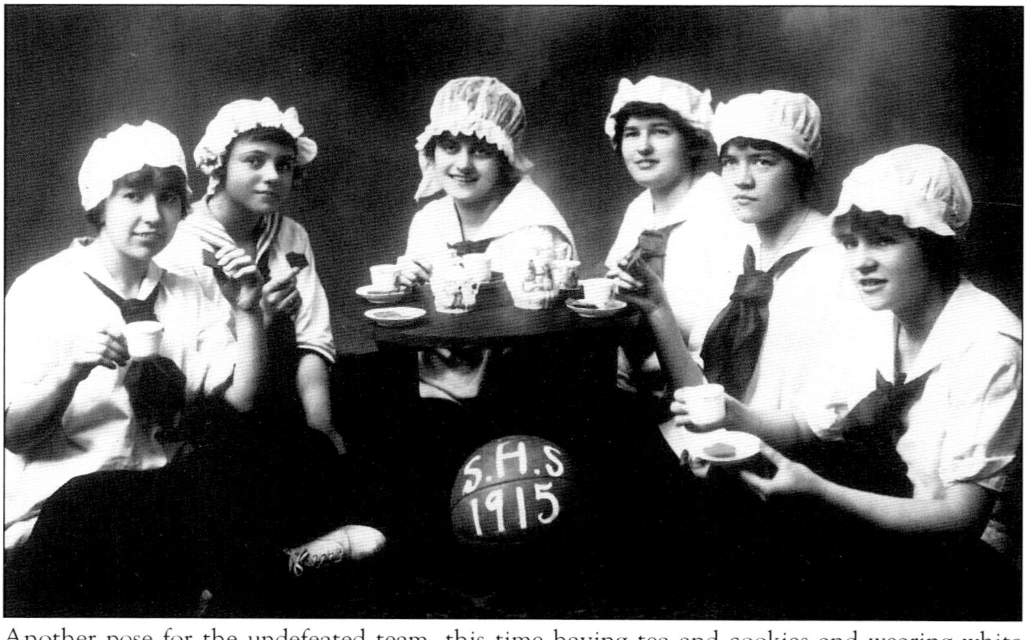


Another pose for the undefeated team, this time having tea and cookies and wearing white duster hats. Senator Smith would say later that the team spent almost as much time posing as it did playing. From left to right are Corinne Salley, Gladys Pennell, Nell Gifford, Beatrice Smiley, Margaret Chase, and Helen White.

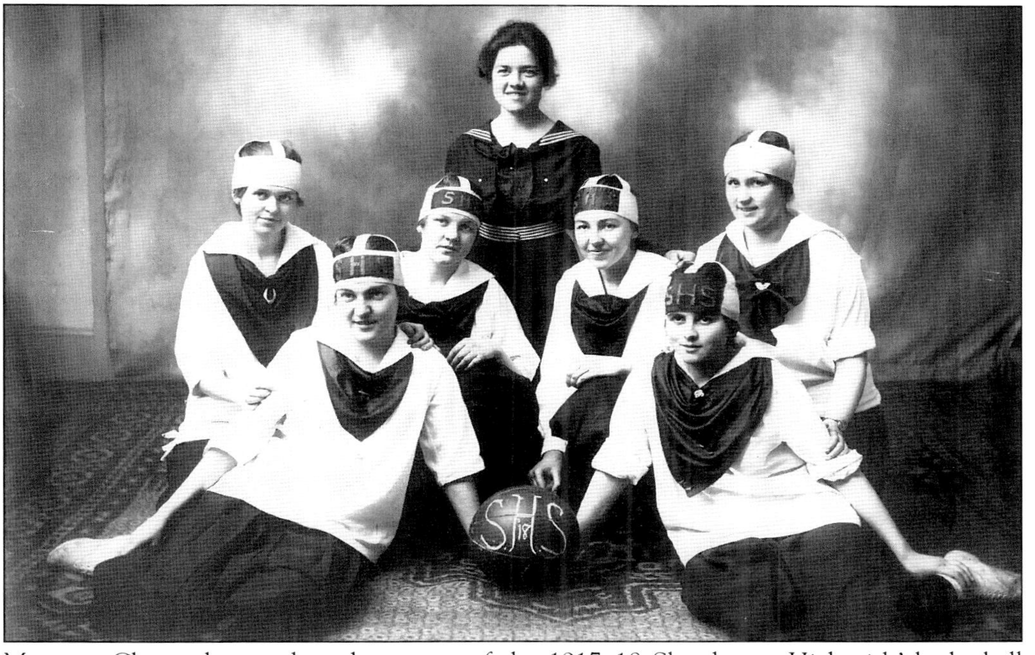

Margaret Chase, the coach and manager of the 1917–18 Skowhegan High girls' basketball team. Included are Lois Manor, Fedora Lessard, Martha Steward, May Friend, Lena Merrill, and Lovina Murray.

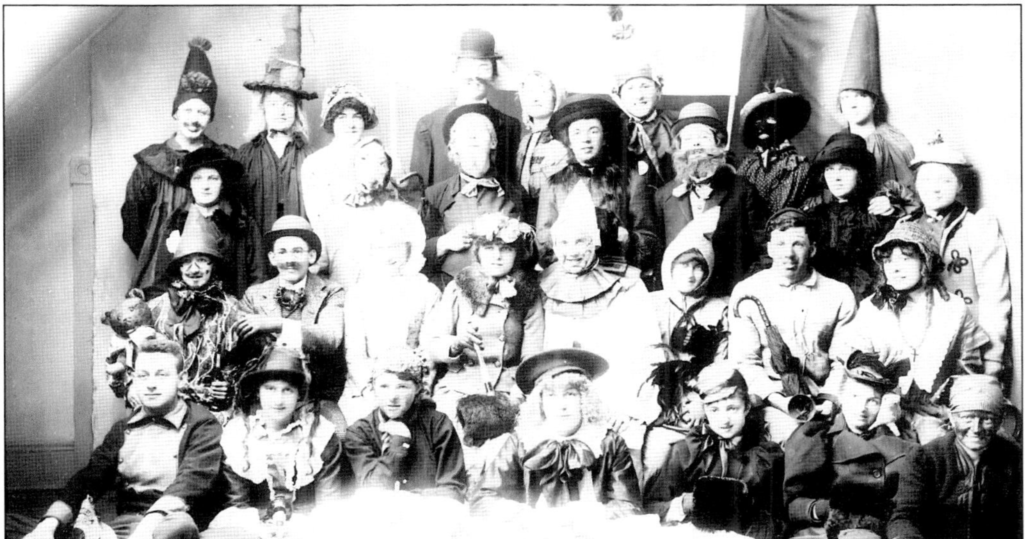

The Skowhegan High Class of 1916 curling party, where funny clothes and disguises were worn. From left to right are: (front row) Brooks Savage, Geneva Smith, Helen White, Lewis Brown, Theresa Bisson, Leora Foss, and Ruth Greenwood; (second row) Gail Chapman, Ralph Merriam, Lana Nottage, Verna Abbey, John Emery, unknown, Harold Crosby, and Margaret Churchill; (third row) Annie Scott, unknown, G. Allen Wentworth, Francis Friend, Emery T. Dyer, Florence Burrill, and Marion Adams; (back row) Donald Dumont, Eva Withee, Mary Hayden, Ray Parmenter, Gertrude Groder, Ray Boynton, unknown, and Myra Akeley.

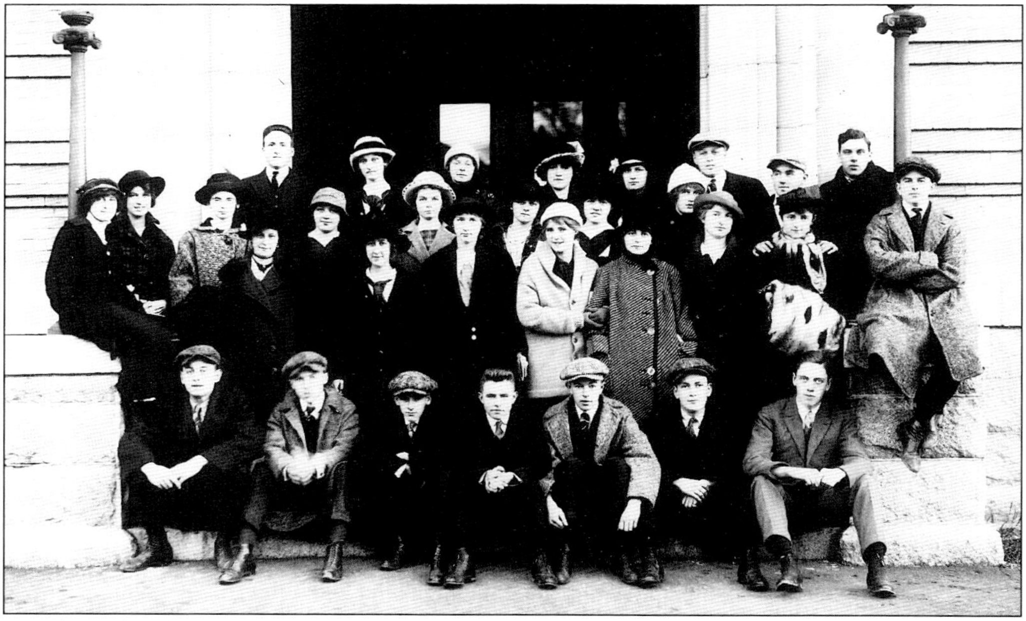

Another Skowhegan High Class of 1916 group, this time with Margaret Chase in it. From left to right are: (front row) Brooks Savage, G. Allen Wentworth, Ralph F. Mziam, Bernard Bailey, Francis Friend, Lewis W. Brown, and Ray Parmenter; (second row) Annie Scott, Gail Chapman, Geneva Smith, Helen White, Ruth Greenwood, Eva Withee, and Theresa Bisson; (third row) Myra Akeley, Jessie McGregor, Marion Adams, Lenora Foss Jones, Verna Abbey, Margaret Chase, Florence Burrill, and Emery Dyer; (back row) Ray Boynton, Gertrude Groder, Margaret Churchill, Mary Hayden, Lana Nottage, Donald Dumont, John Emery, and Harold Crosby.

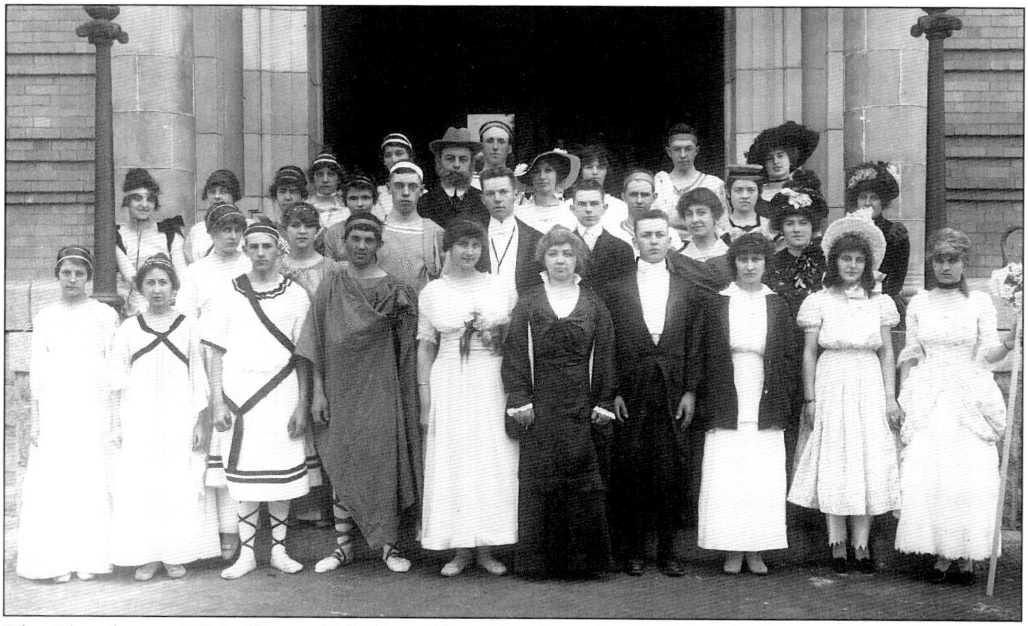

The Skowhegan High Class of 1916 on Thursday, June 3, 1915, just before its junior exhibition.

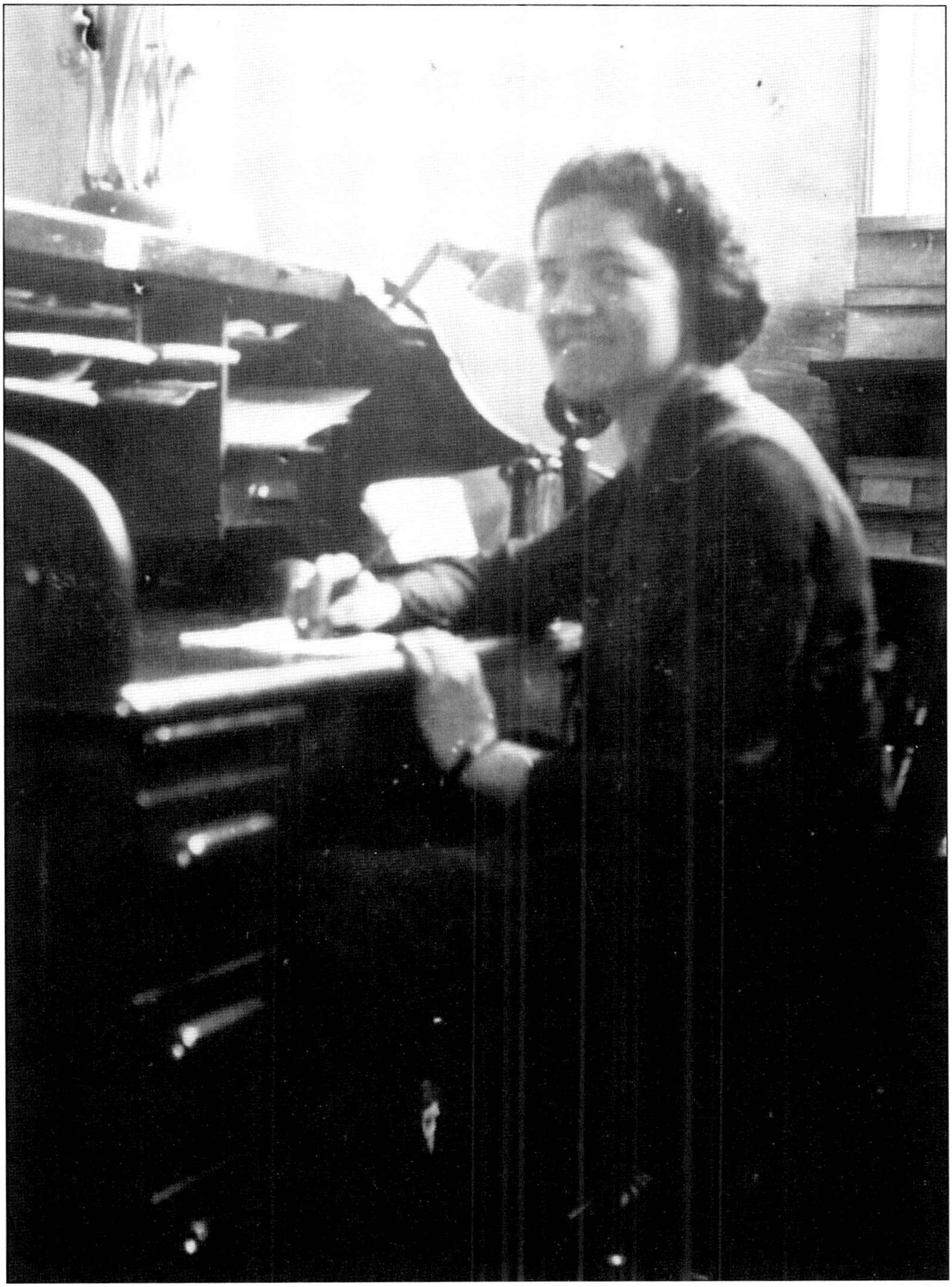

Miss Margaret M. Chase at a roll-top desk while she was the circulation manager at the *Independent Reporter*, the Skowhegan weekly newspaper, *c.* 1925. The future senator was with the paper from 1919 to 1928 and even wrote for it a couple of years. Roland Patten was the owner and her boss.

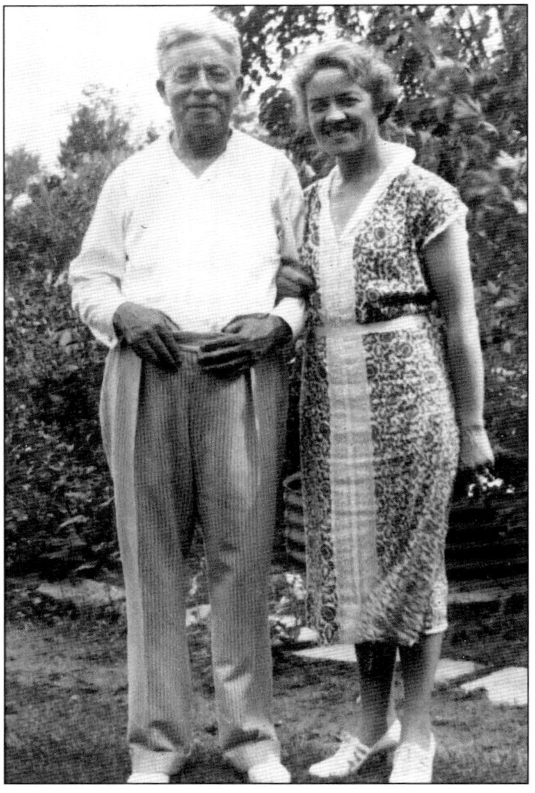

Mr. and Mrs. Clyde H. Smith at home on Fairview Avenue, c. 1936. Margaret and Clyde were married on May 14, 1930.

The home of Mr. and Mrs. Clyde H. Smith on Fairview Avenue in 1939. It was also known as the "Big House."

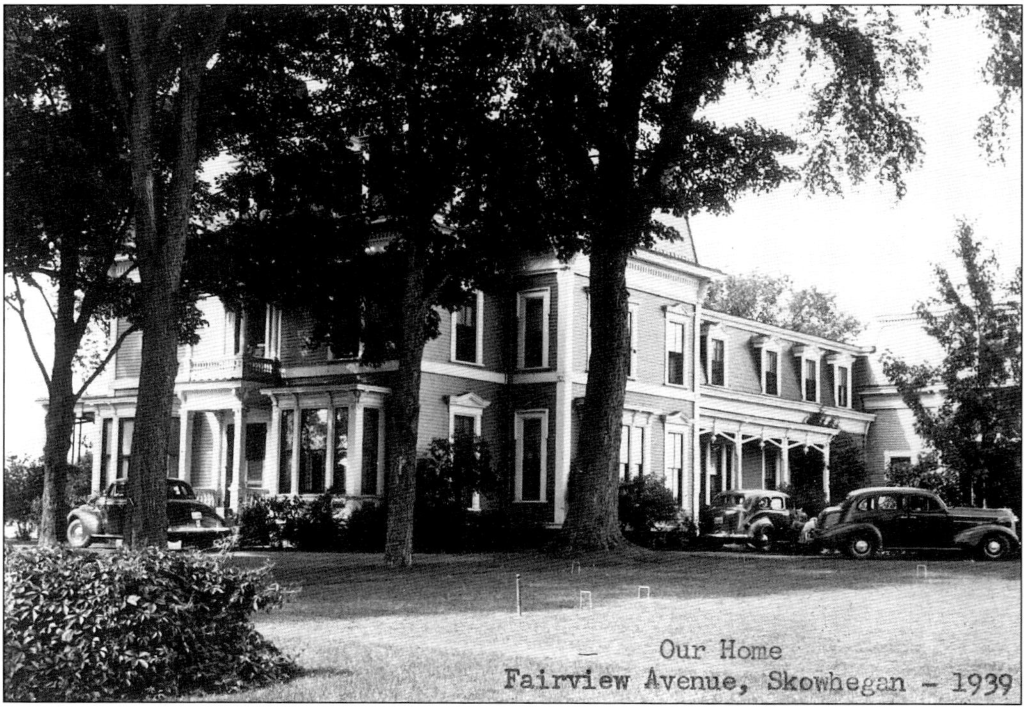

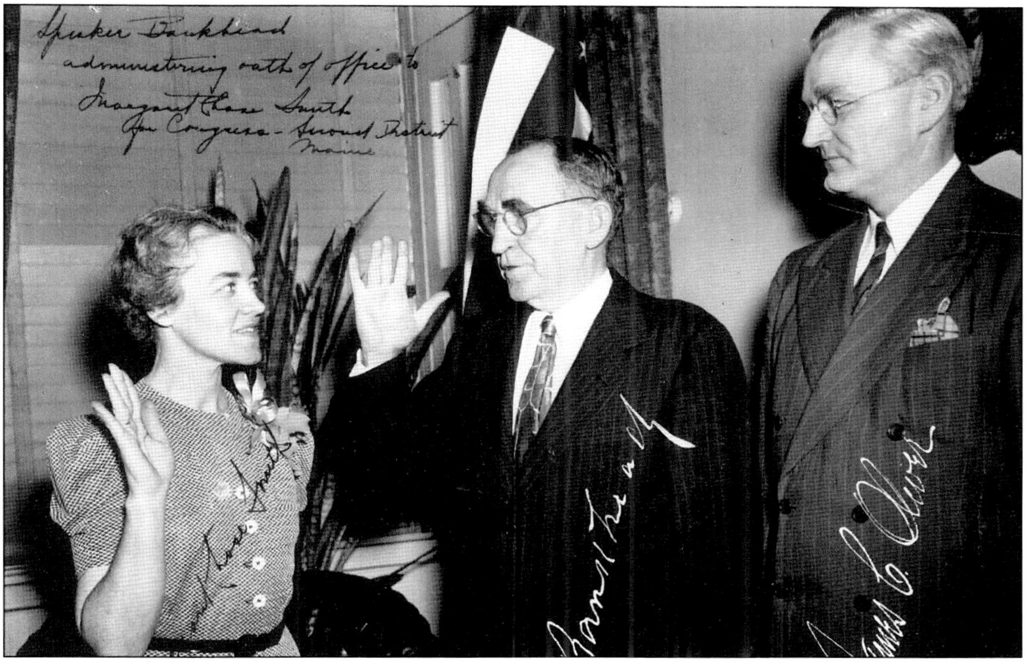


Representative Margaret Chase Smith is administered the oath of office by Speaker William B. Bankhead on June 10, 1940, after winning the special election to succeed her husband, who had died in office. Representative James C. Oliver of Maine witnessed the ceremony.

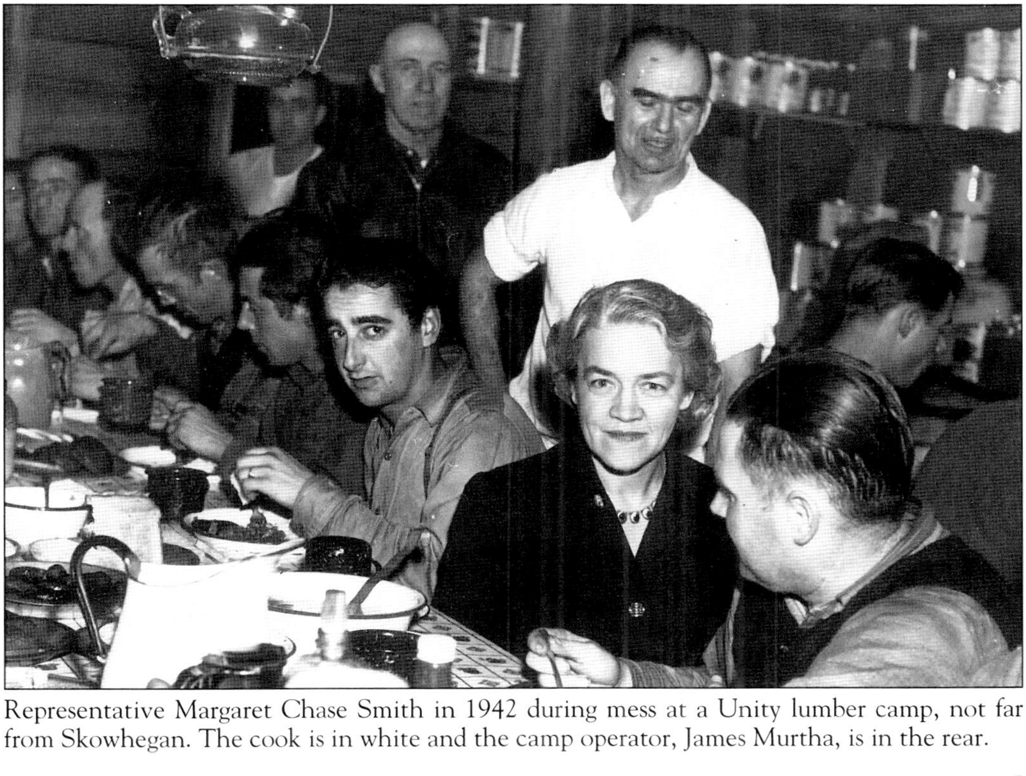

Representative Margaret Chase Smith in 1942 during mess at a Unity lumber camp, not far from Skowhegan. The cook is in white and the camp operator, James Murtha, is in the rear.

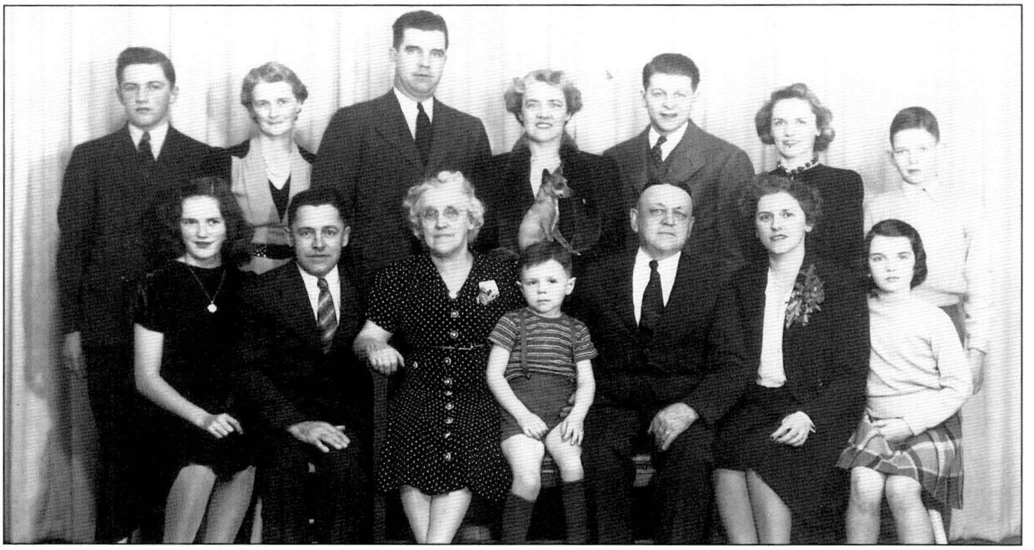

A 1945 photograph of the family of Mr. and Mrs. George Emery Chase, parents of the future senator. From left to right are: (front row) Mary Margaret Chase, Wilbur G. Chase, Mrs. George Emery Chase (Carrie Matilda Murray), John Murray Bernier, George Emery Chase, Evelyn Chase St. Ledger, and Anne St. Ledger; (back row) Richard W. Chase, Mrs. Wilbur G. Chase (Carolyn Crocker), Rexford St. Ledger, Margaret Chase Smith and her dog Minnix, Joseph A. Bernier, Laura Chase Bernier, and Bruce St. Ledger.

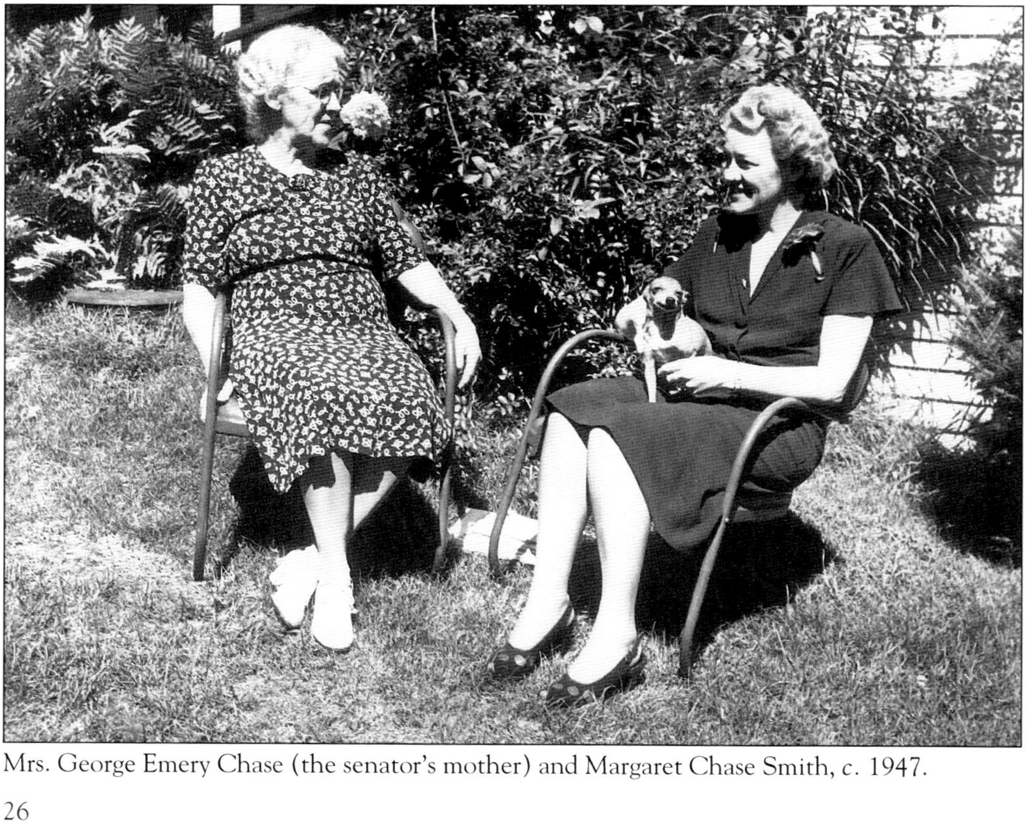

Mrs. George Emery Chase (the senator's mother) and Margaret Chase Smith, *c.* 1947.

May Craig, Guy Gannett Publishing Company's Washington reporter, in Skowhegan, c. 1947, with Senator Wallace H. White and Representative Margaret Chase Smith.

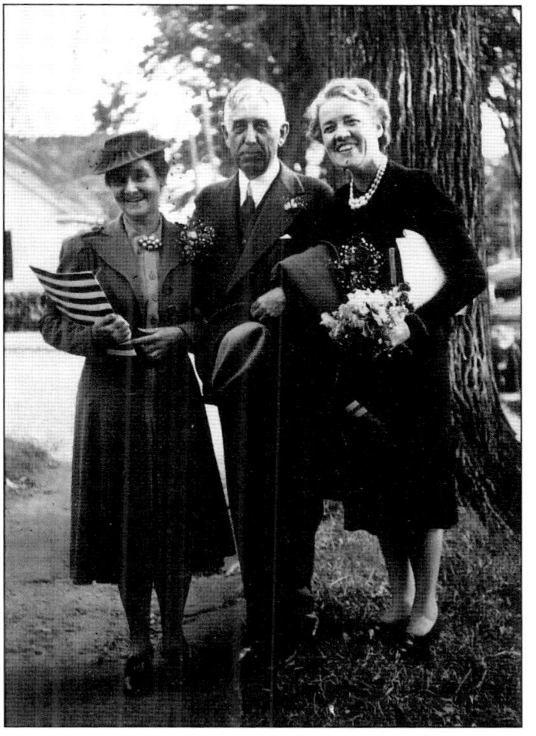

A Skowhegan family home photograph. Representative Margaret Chase Smith and her mother, Carrie Murray Chase, stand in their driveway on North Avenue in 1948.

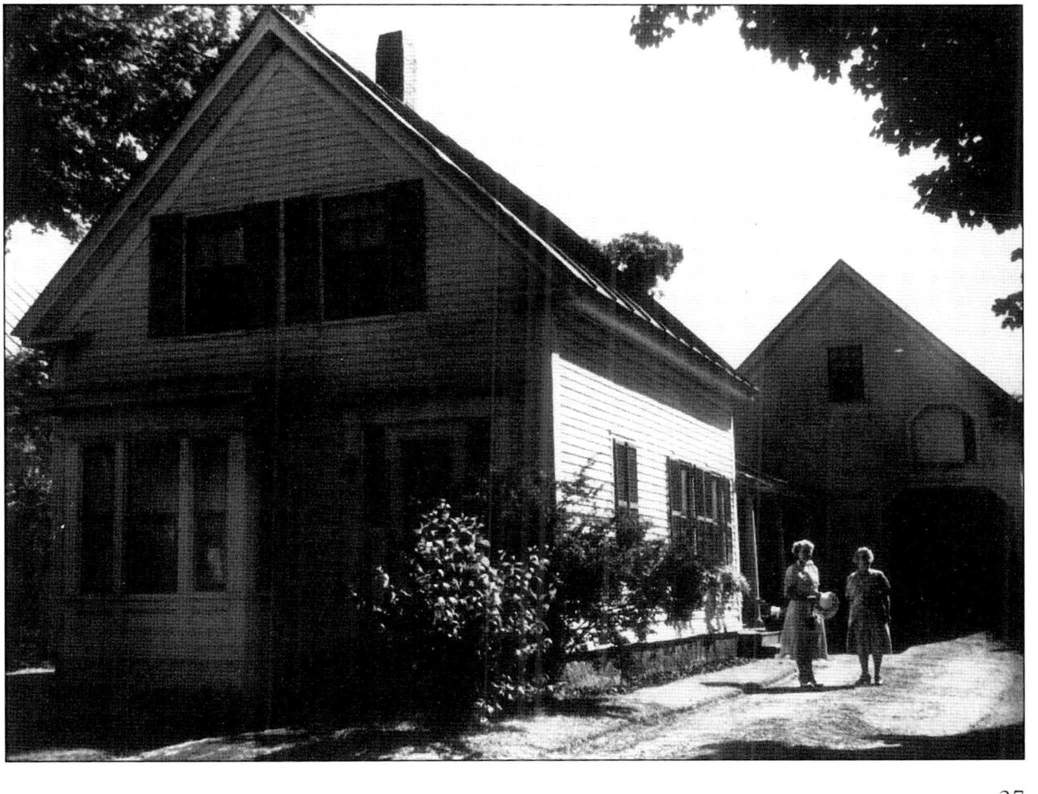

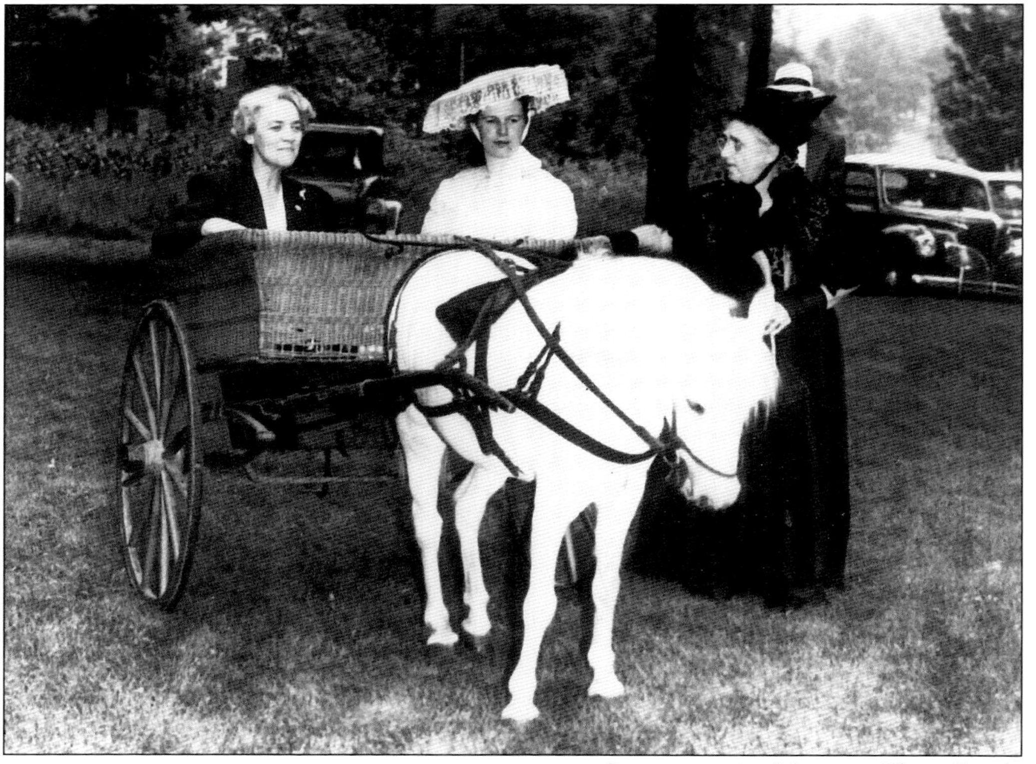

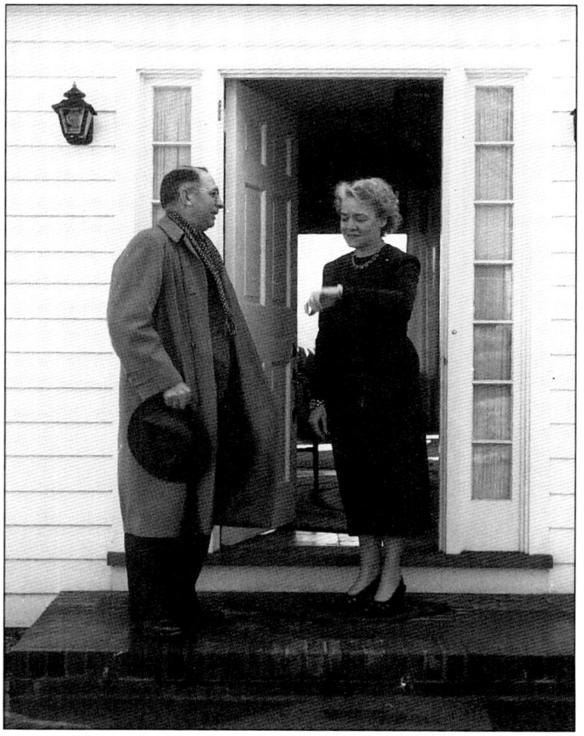

Representative Margaret Chase Smith attends the Skowhegan Centennial Celebration, July 11–13, 1948. From left to right are Representative Smith, Mrs. Fred March, and Mrs. Lawrence Hall.

Alonzo Harriman of Auburn, architect of Margaret Chase Smith's home, visits with the senator in 1949.

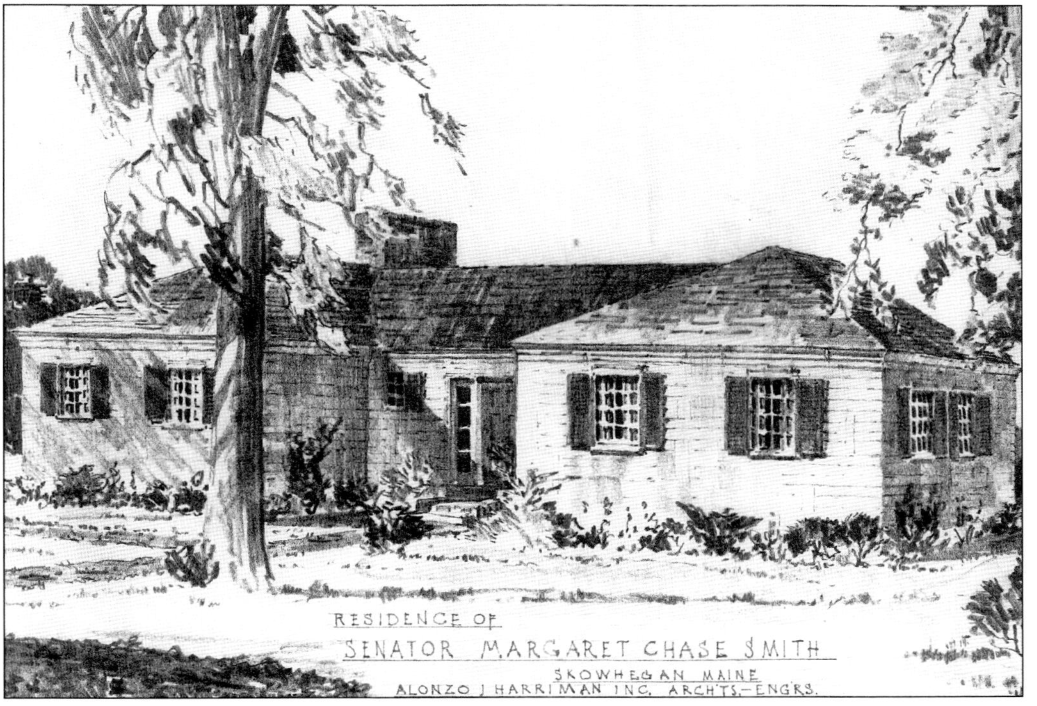


An architect's drawing of the new Smith home in 1949.

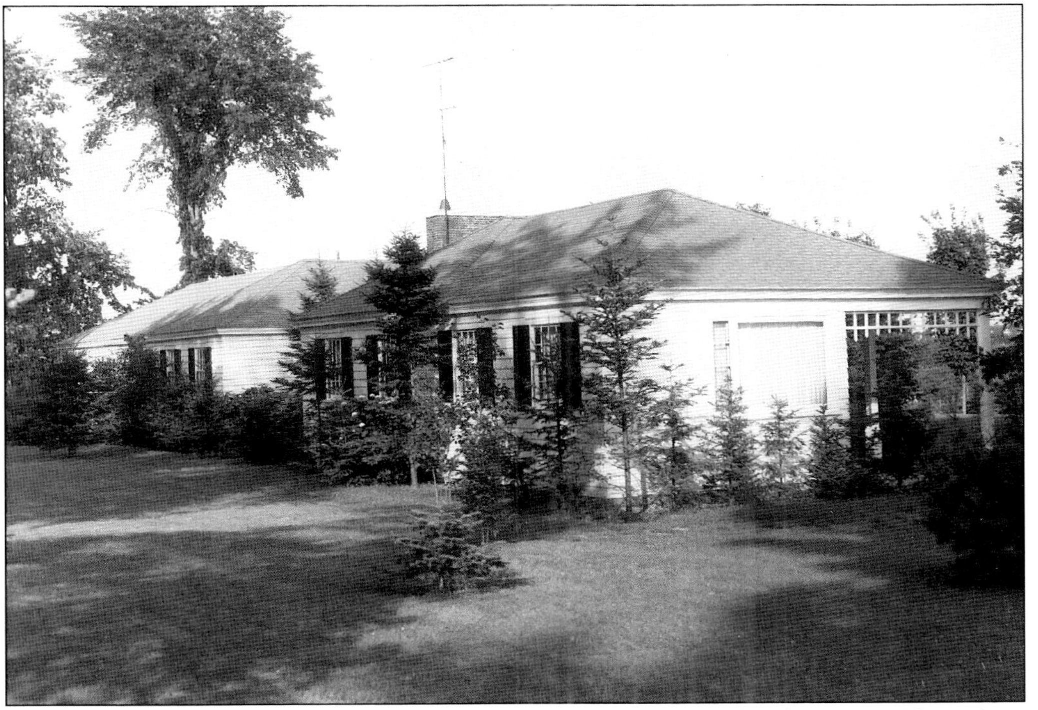

The Margaret Chase Smith home on Norridgewock Avenue, completed in 1949. This is how it looked in 1959.

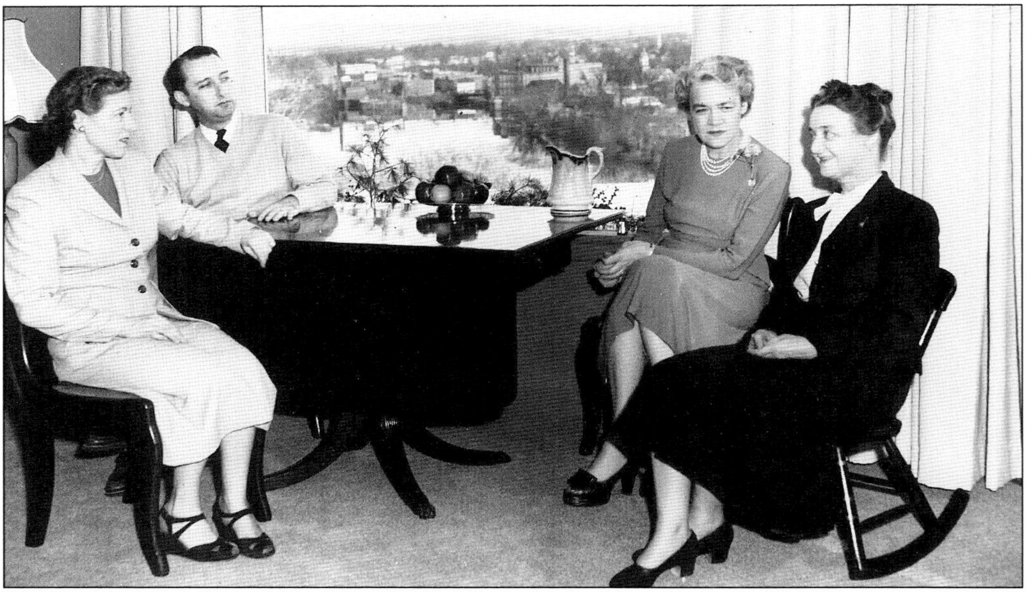

May Craig's first visit to the senator's new home in Skowhegan in 1949. From left to right are: Mrs. Blanche Bernier, the senator's secretary; William C. Lewis Jr., her administrative assistant; Senator Smith; and May Craig.

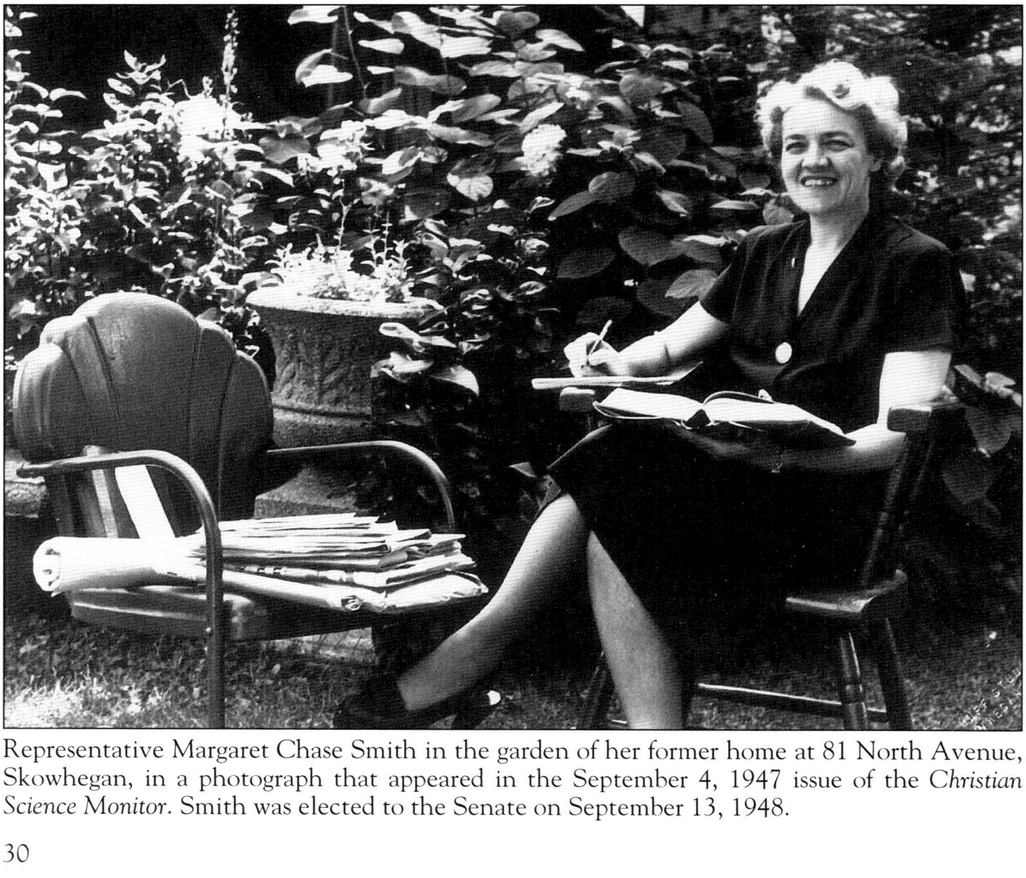

Representative Margaret Chase Smith in the garden of her former home at 81 North Avenue, Skowhegan, in a photograph that appeared in the September 4, 1947 issue of the *Christian Science Monitor*. Smith was elected to the Senate on September 13, 1948.

*Three*

# A Folio

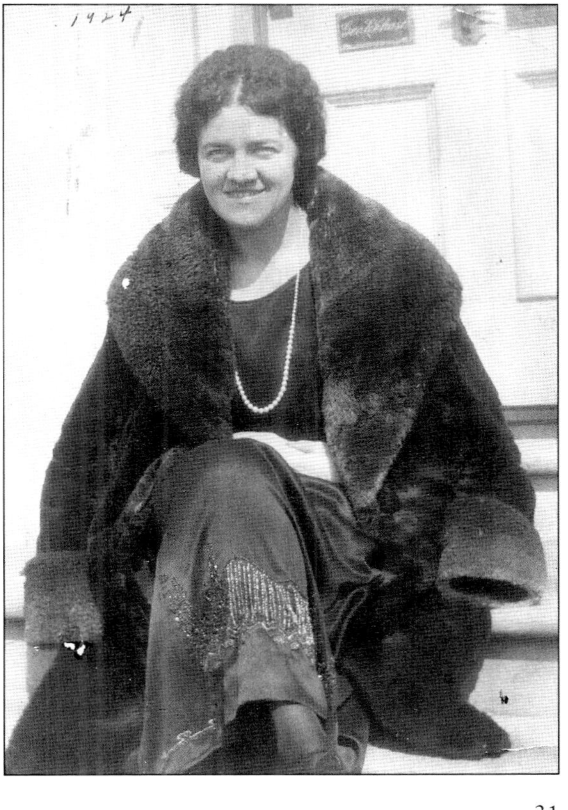


Miss Margaret M. Chase, once the president of the Skowhegan Business and Professional Women's Club, is shown here *c.* 1924.

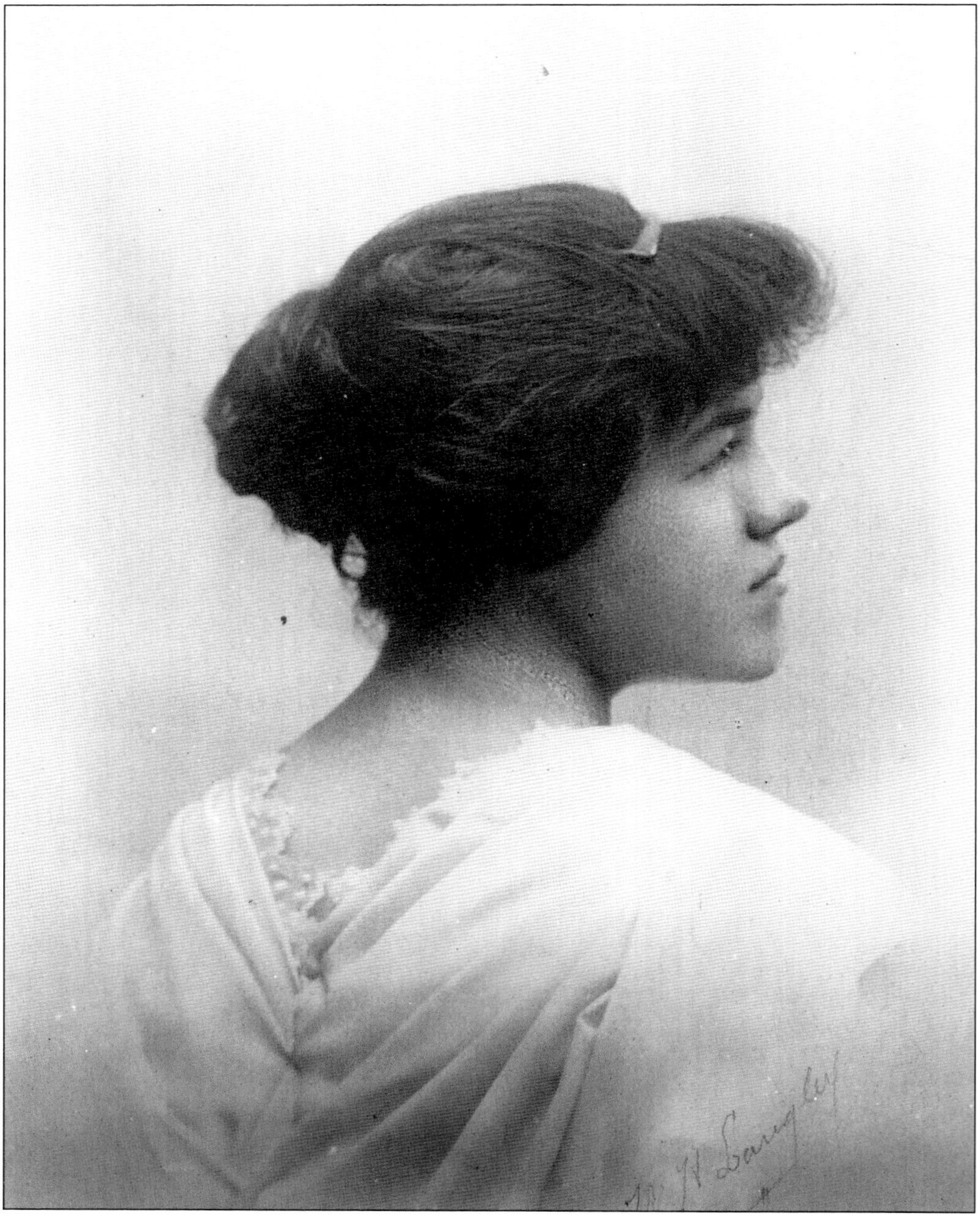

Miss Margaret M. Chase's 1916 Skowhegan High School graduation photograph.

Mrs. Margaret Chase Smith tries on a new hat in the hallway of the Smiths' large Fairview Avenue home in Skowhegan, *c.* 1938.

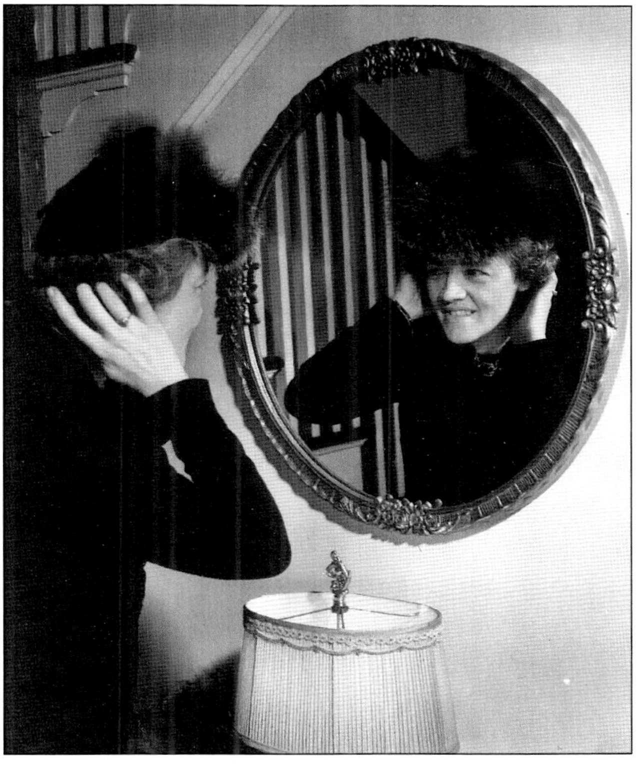

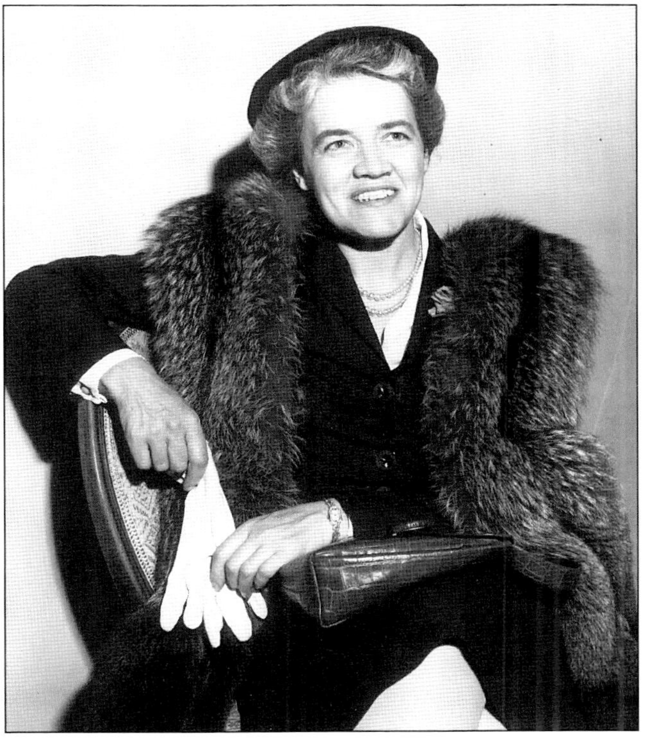

Representative Smith seated at home, wearing white gloves and a stole, November 18, 1943.

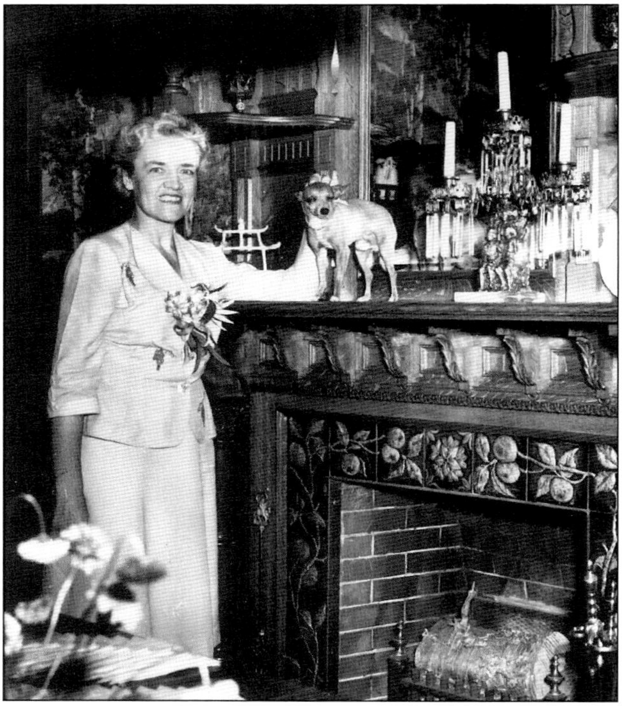

Representative Smith with her dog Minnix. The dog is standing on the mantle at her home on Fairview Avenue, Skowhegan, on September 13, 1944.

Margaret Chase Smith, at fifty-one years old, is shown here at her parents' home, surrounded by flowers and telegrams from friends. On June 22, 1948, she became the first Republican woman to win a Senate primary in Maine.

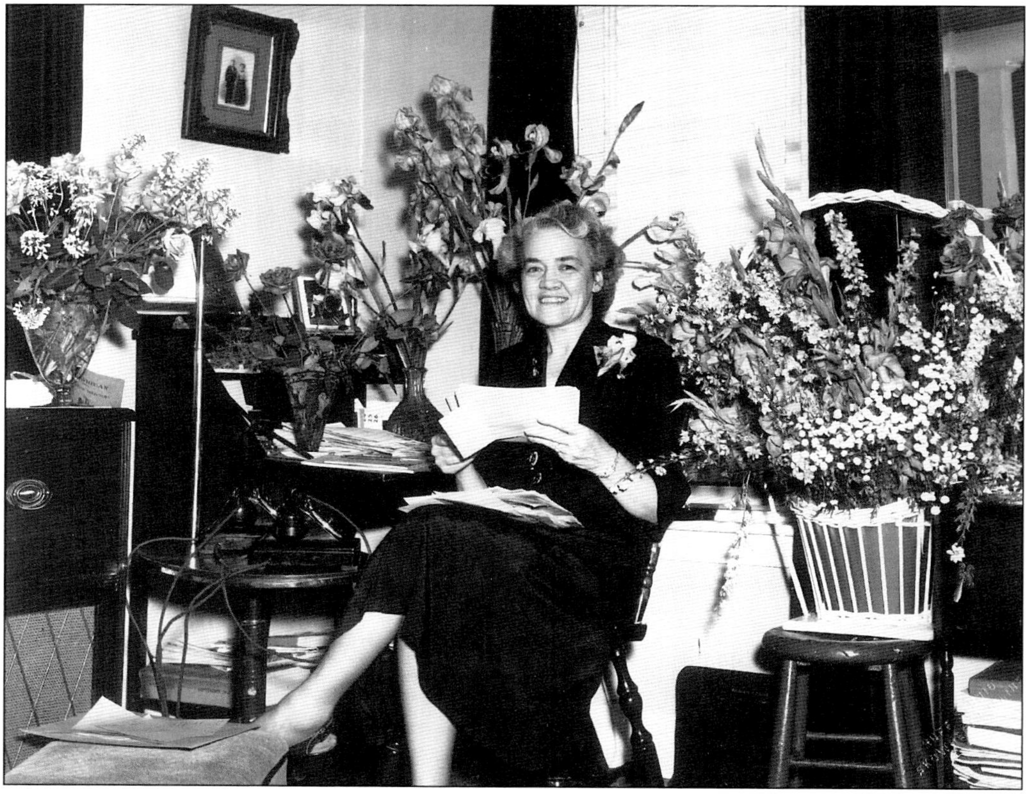

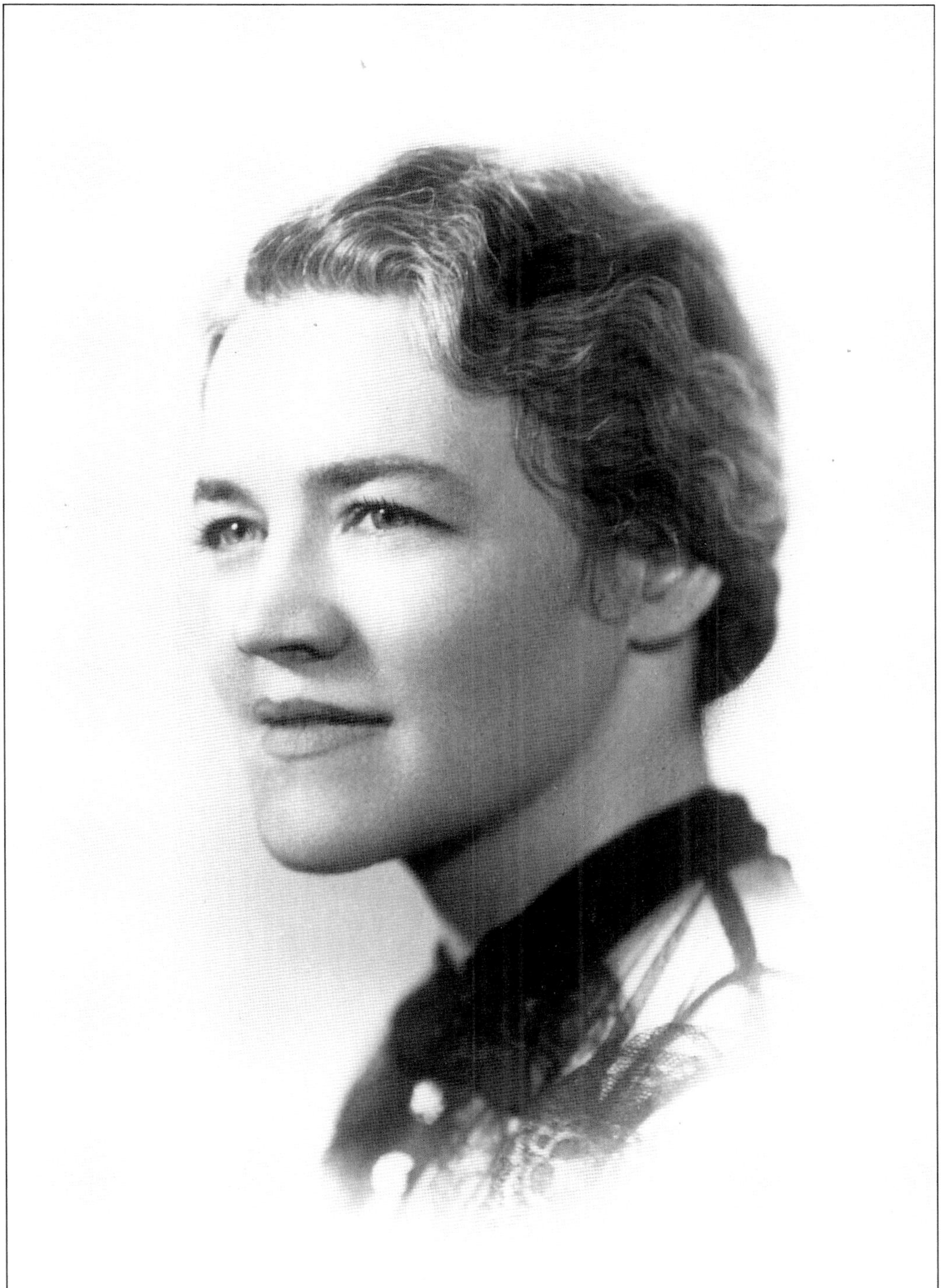

Margaret Chase Smith, c. 1942.

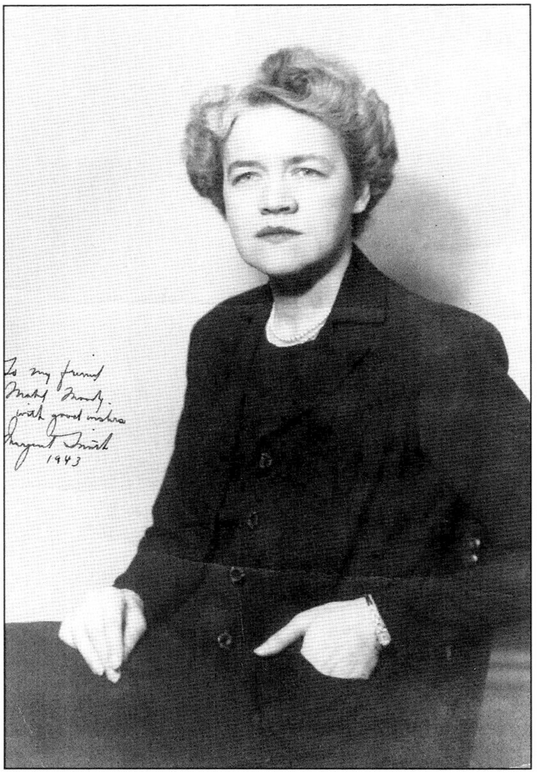

Margaret Chase Smith in 1943. The note on the photograph reads: "To my friend Mabel Moody, with good wishes, Margaret Smith."

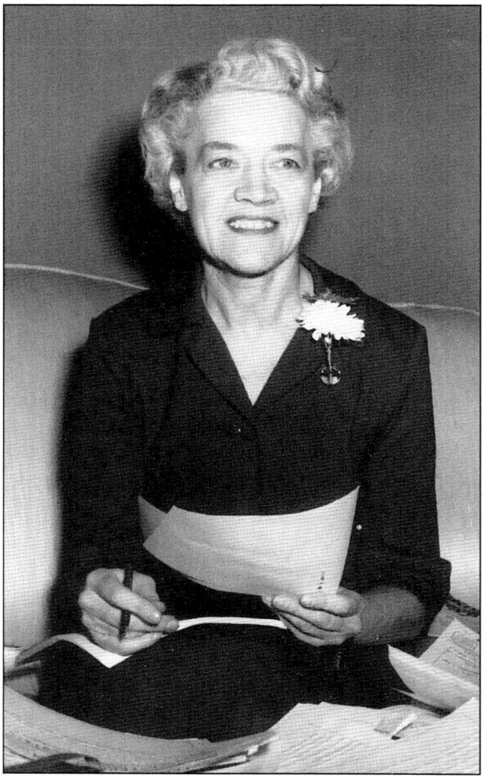

Senator Smith reads telegrams about her 1960 reelection win, November 9, 1960. As this photograph shows, Senator Smith aged extremely gracefully.

# *Four*

# A Walk in the Early 1900s

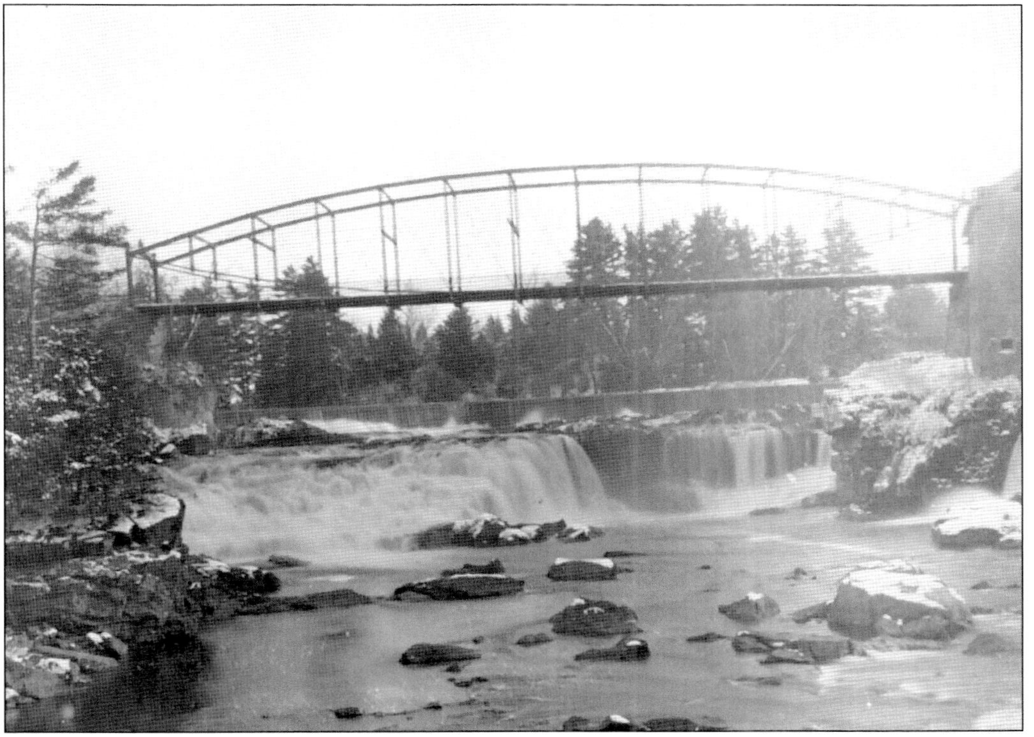

When Margaret Chase was a young girl, she would have seen this bridge over the Kennebec River at Skowhegan. Now, the two bridges in the center of the town are both named after her.

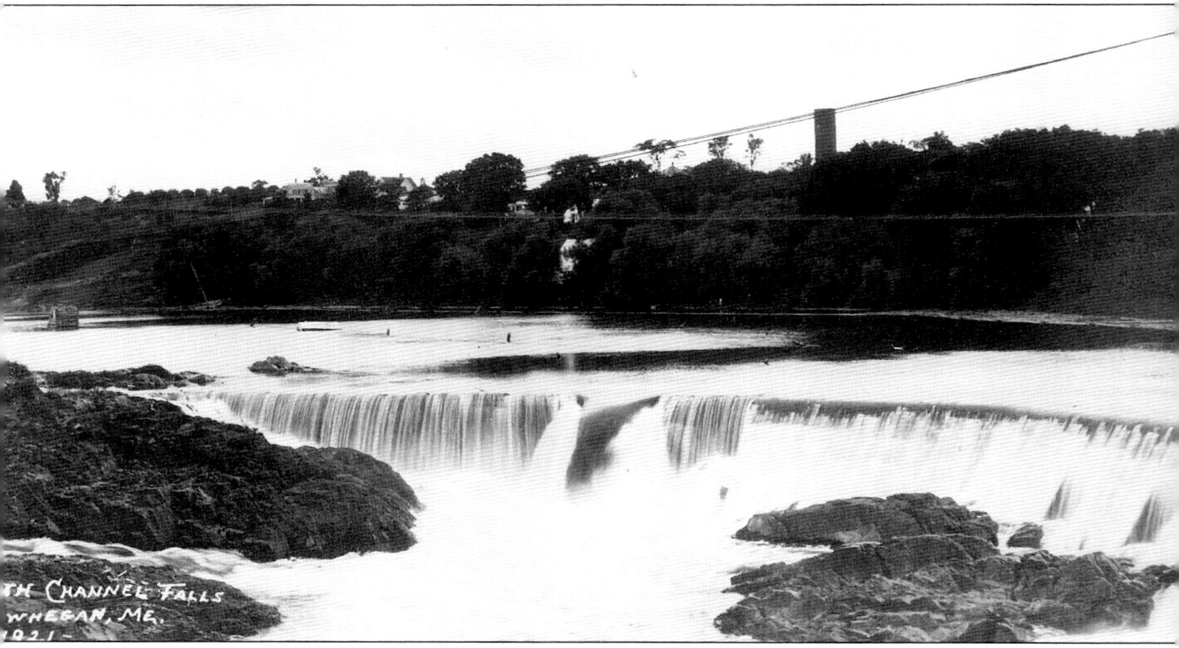


This is how the North Channel Falls on the Kennebec River at Skowhegan looked when Margaret Chase Smith was young. Changes have not always been existent in the Skowhegan environment.

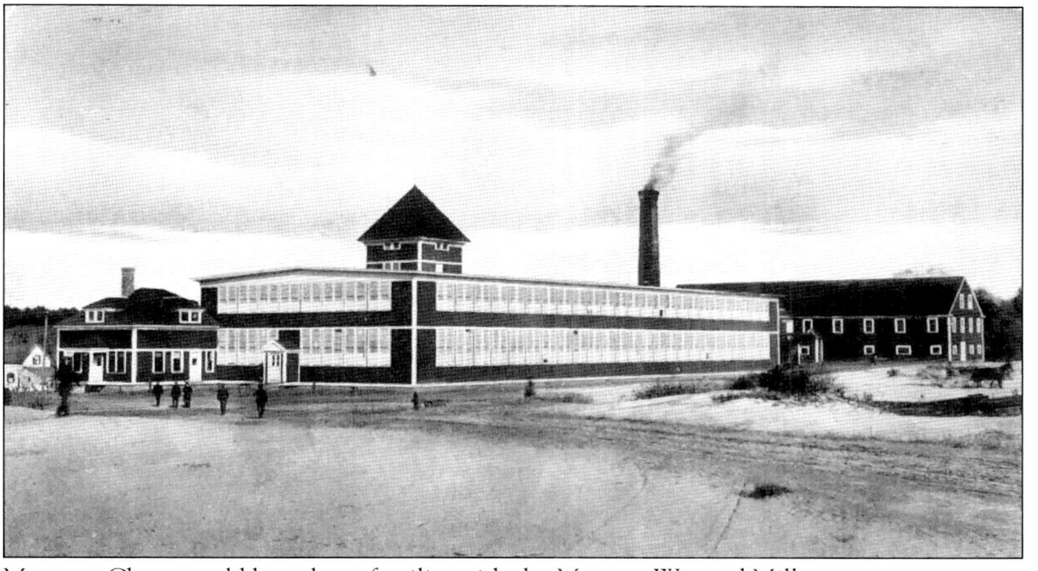

Margaret Chase would have been familiar with the Marston Worsted Mills as a youngster.

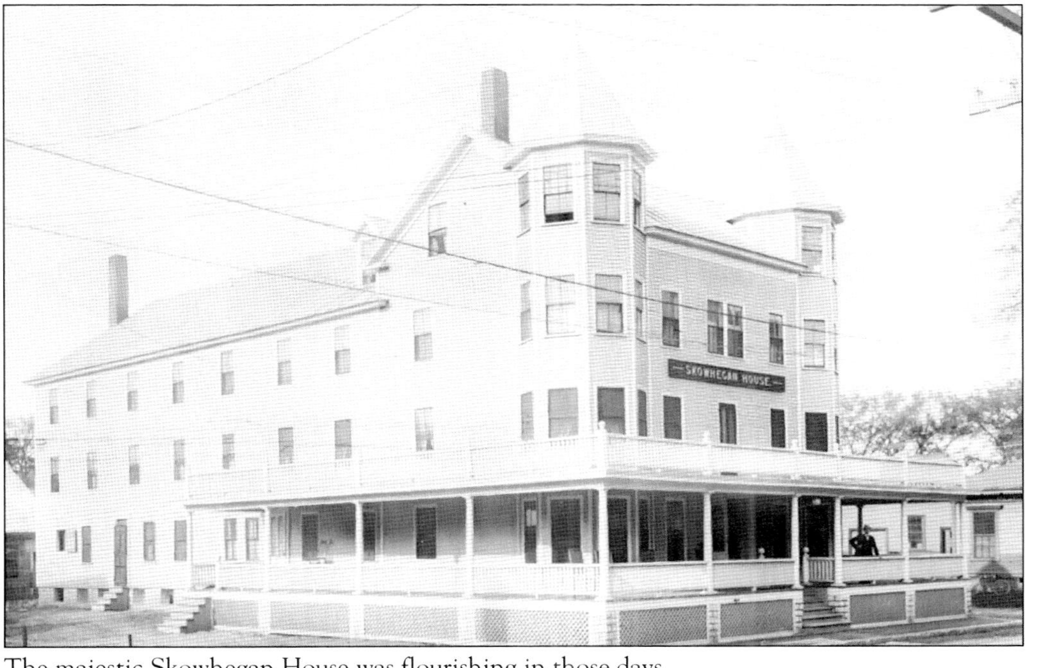



The majestic Skowhegan House was flourishing in those days.

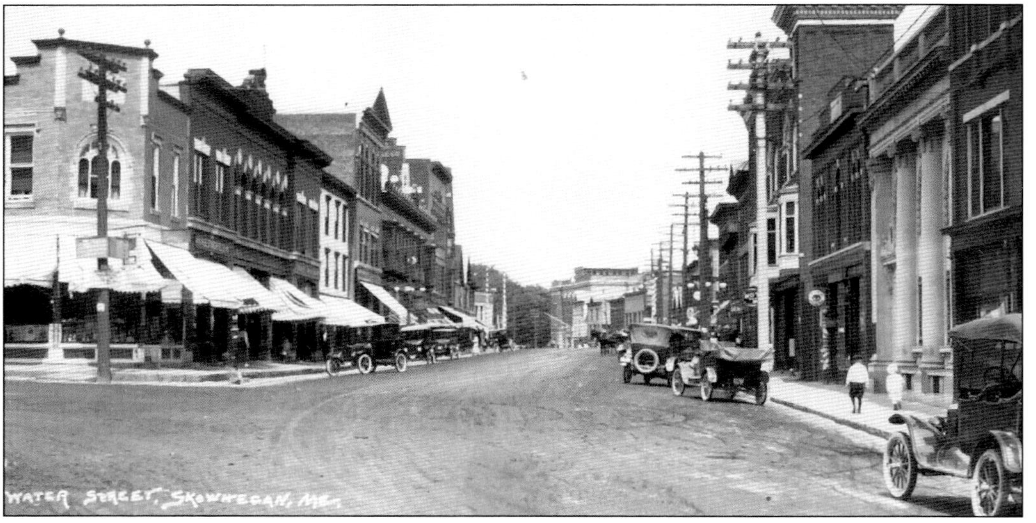


Water Street, shown here when Margaret Chase was young, remains one of the busiest streets in Skowhegan.

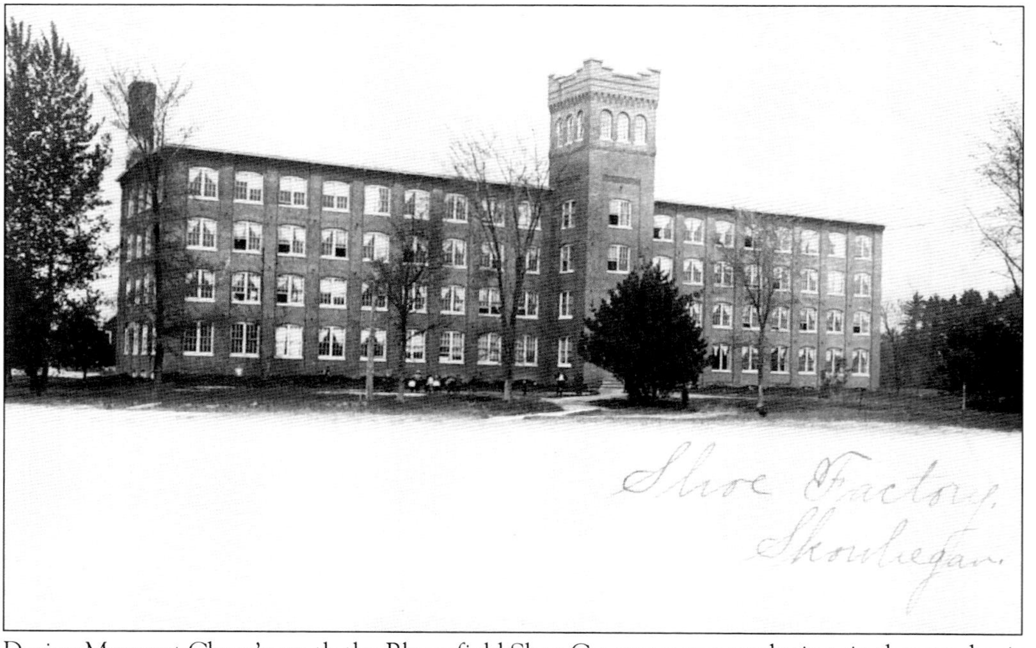


During Margaret Chase's youth the Bloomfield Shoe Company was producing six thousand pair of shoes daily.

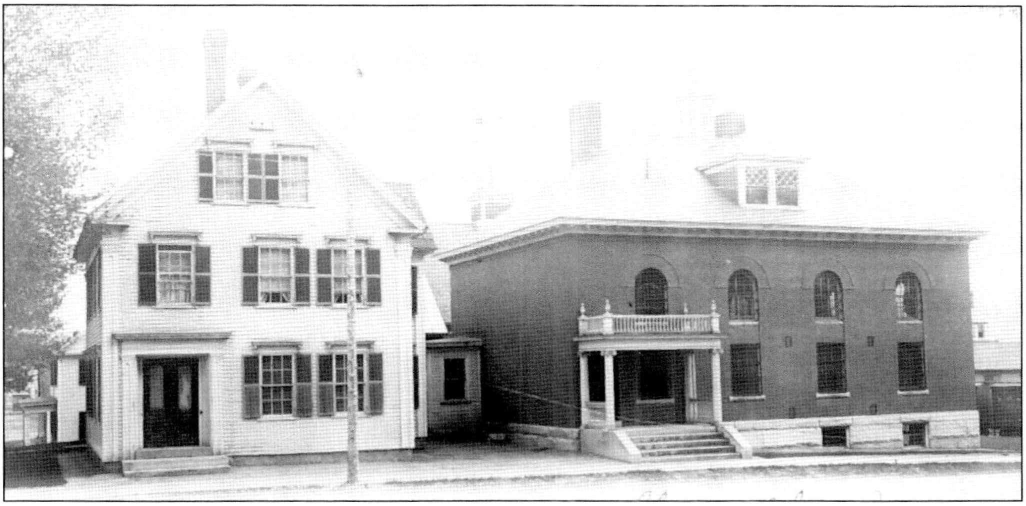

As with most of us, Margaret Chase never saw the inside of the sheriff's residence and jail for Somerset County.

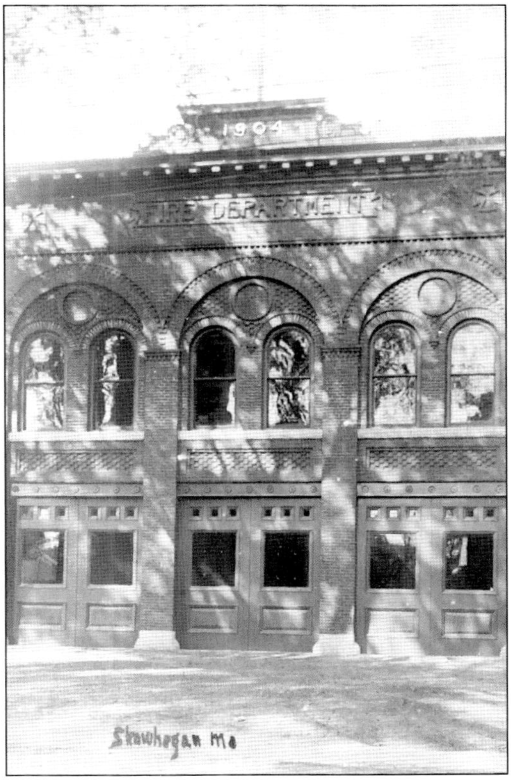


The fire department station in Skowhegan in the 1910s or '20s.

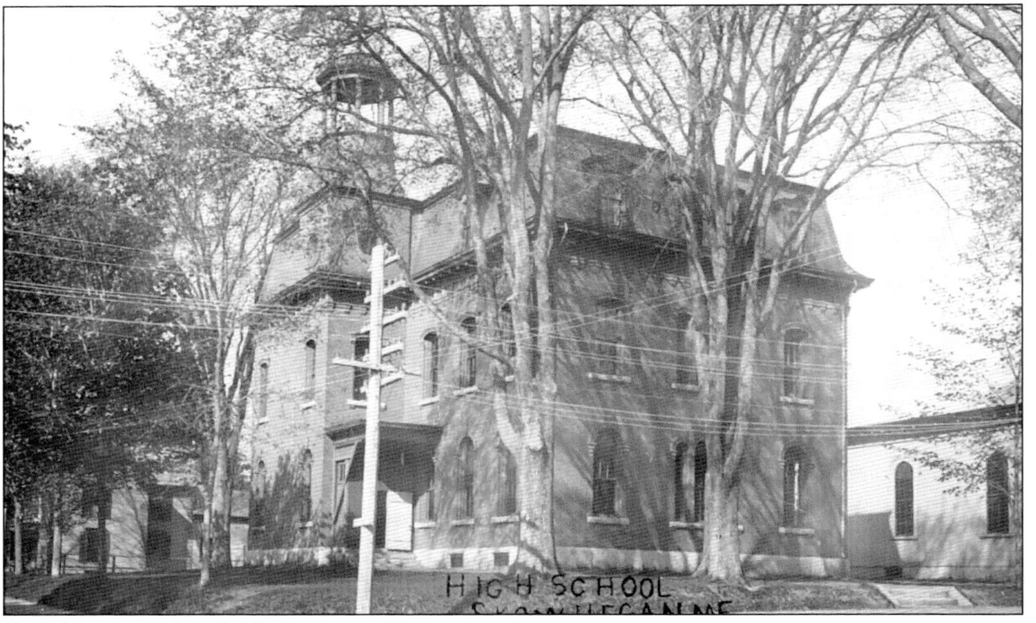


Skowhegan High, which Margaret Chase attended, was an impressive structure.

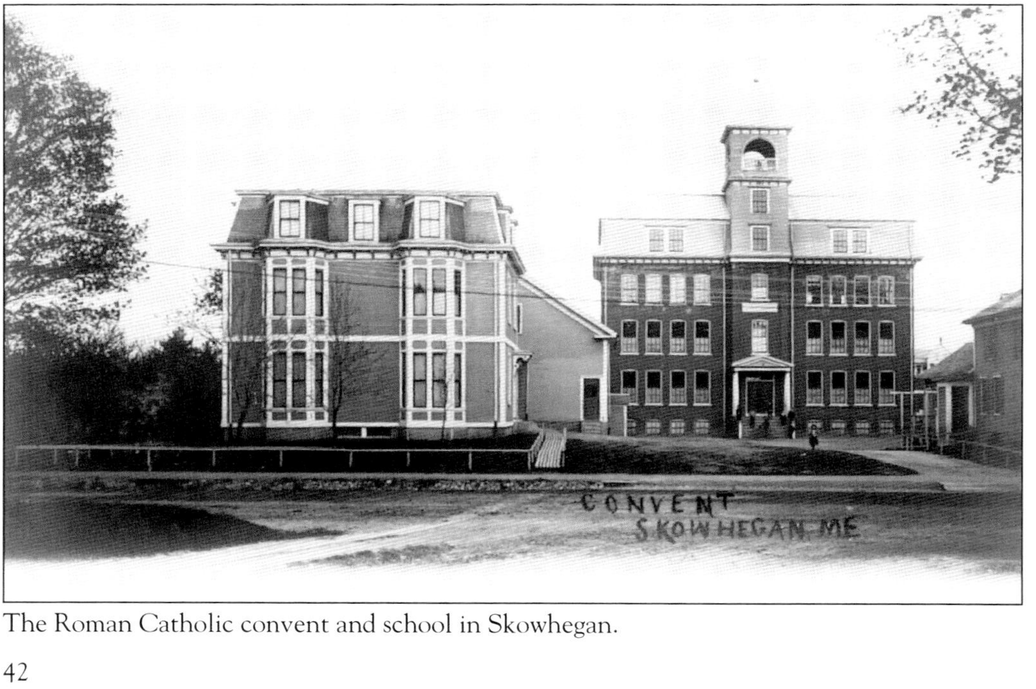


The Roman Catholic convent and school in Skowhegan.

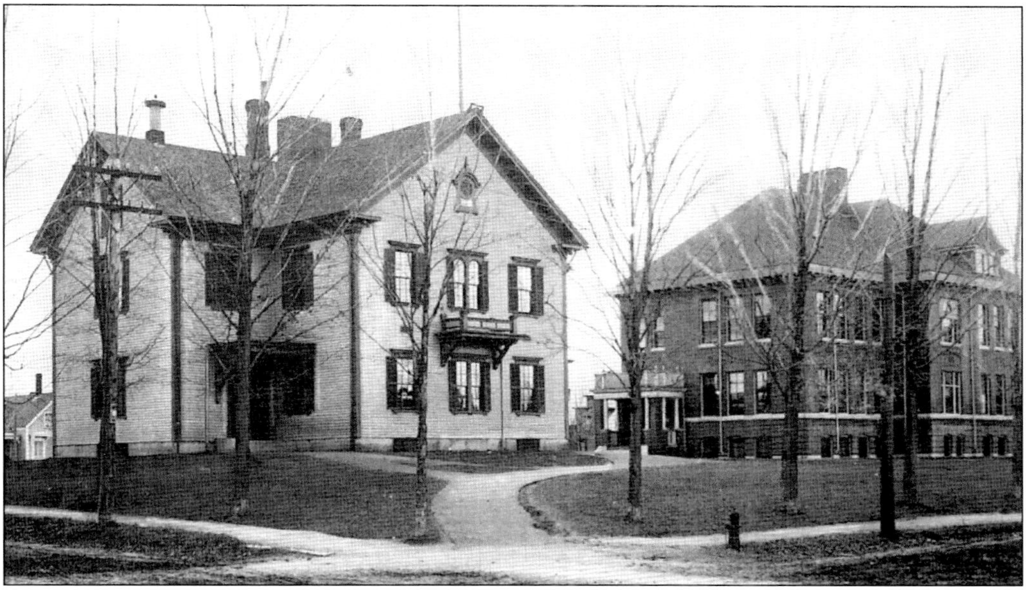
The Garfield and Lincoln Schools are shown here around the time Margaret Chase was attending them.

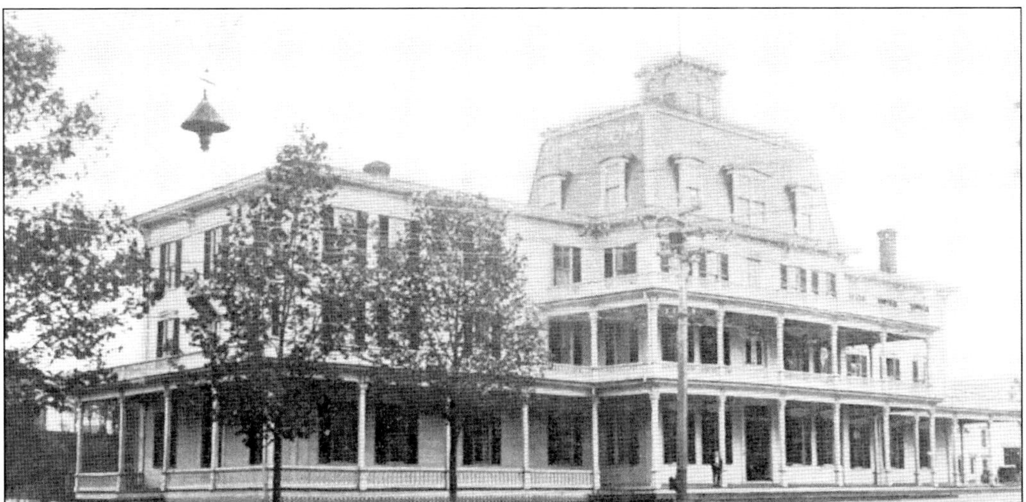
Hotel Heselton at the turn of the century. It burned to the ground on December 17, 1905. Margaret Chase was eight years old at the time.

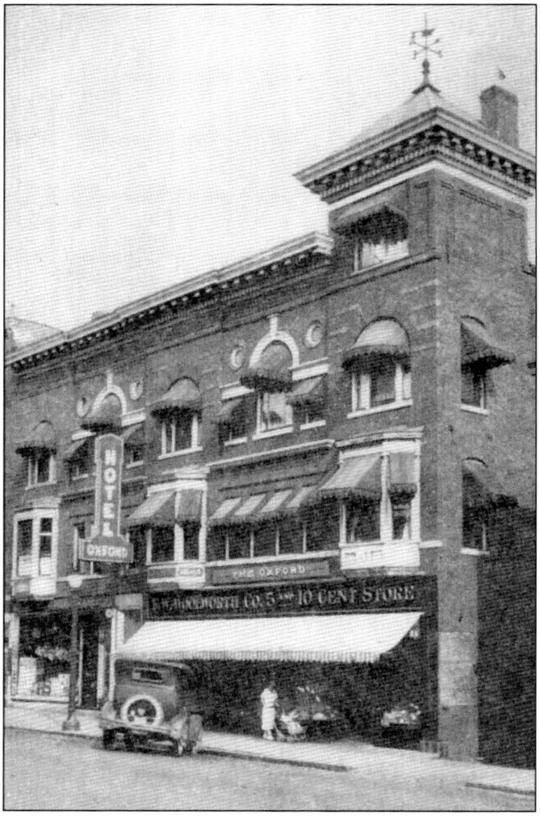


The Hotel Oxford didn't fare much better—it burned on December 31, 1908. Many of the grand hotels of this era met similar fates.

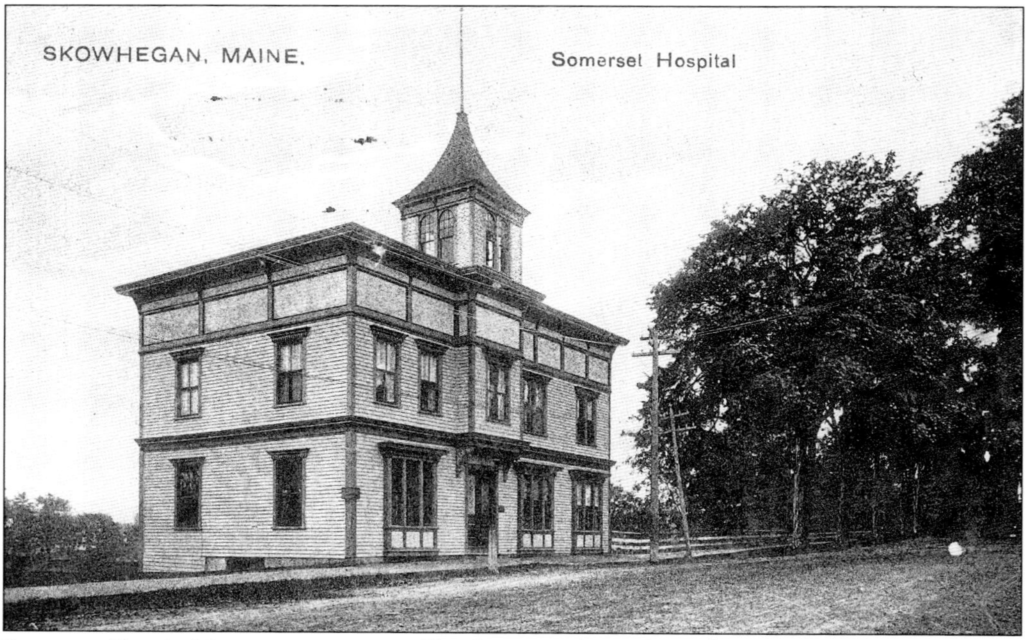


Somerset Hospital began operating on Elm Street in the early in the twentieth century.

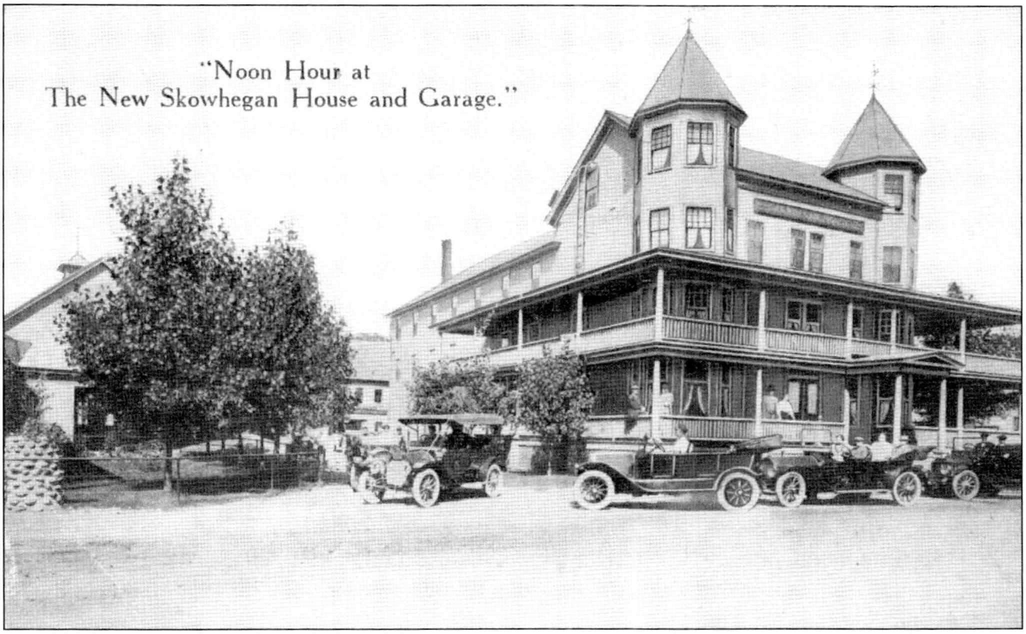

Noon at the "new" Skowhegan House and Garage, early in the twentieth century. Margaret Chase would have seen it in operation.

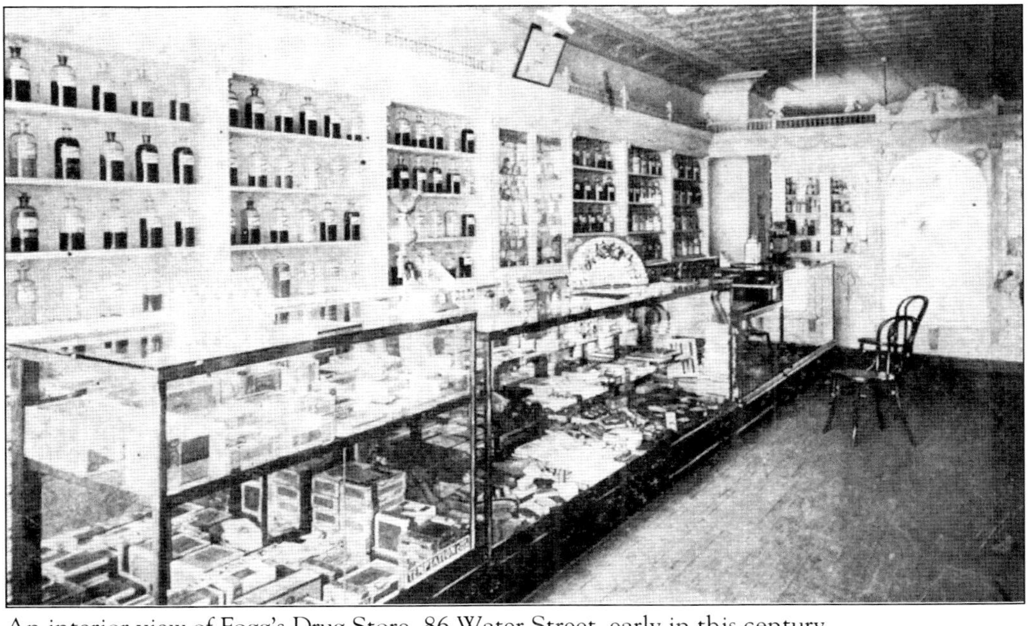
An interior view of Fogg's Drug Store, 86 Water Street, early in this century.

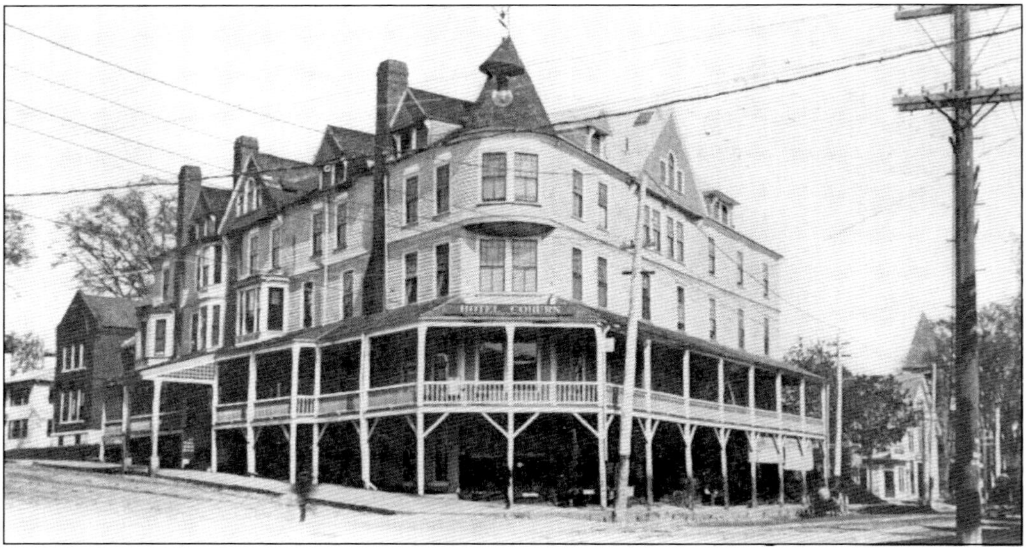


Hotel Coburn was operating when Margaret Chase was young.

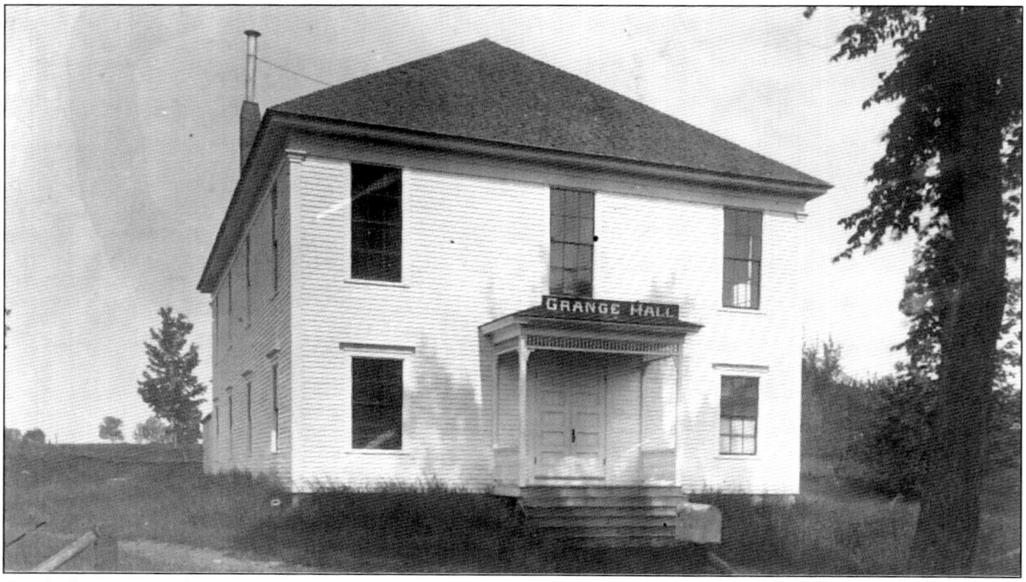


And there was the Grange. Senator Smith always aimed to get the Grange vote, which was quite strong in Maine. This is the Grange Hall in Skowhegan.

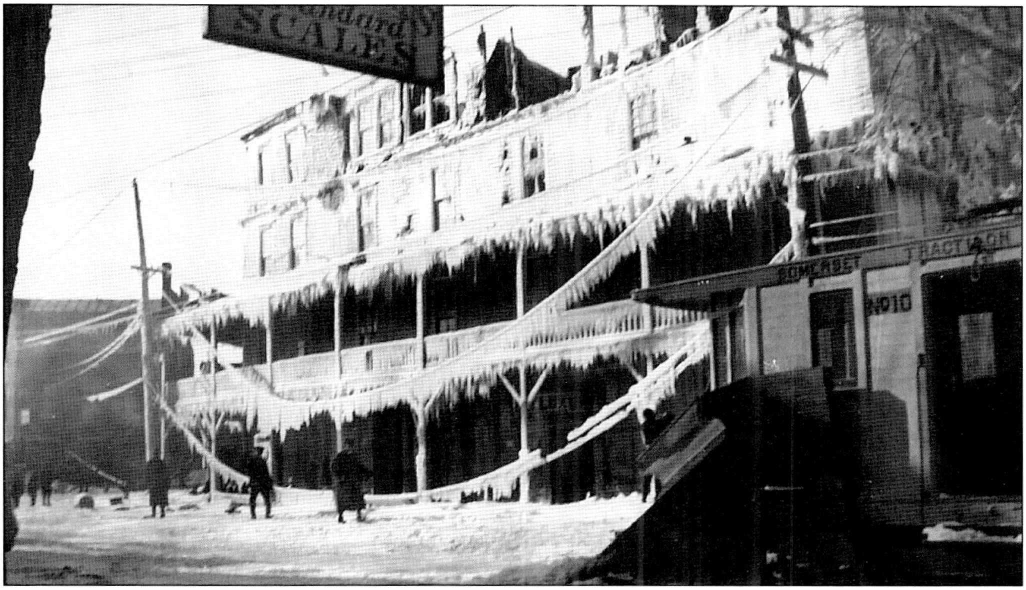


Like the Heselton and Oxford Hotels, Hotel Coburn didn't last. It was destroyed by fire on March 3, 1918.

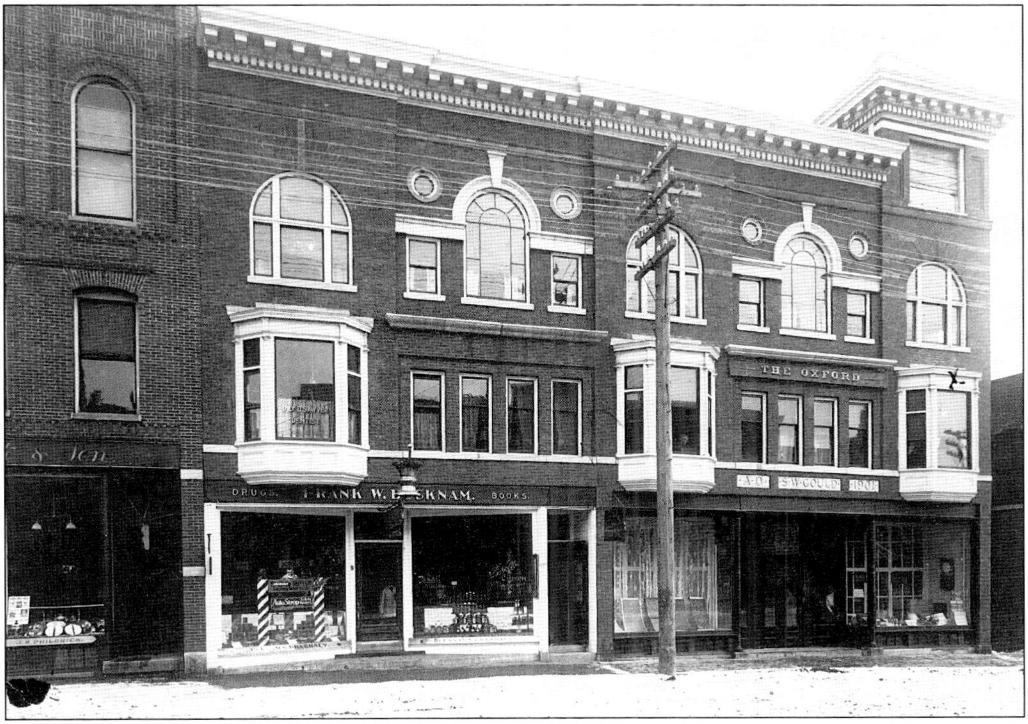


The Oxford Hotel, on the second floor, attracted other businesses to its building. Frank Bucknam's Drug and Book Store was on the first floor, as was S.W. Gould's law firm. The Oxford moved into this building owned by Gould after the fire of December 31, 1908.

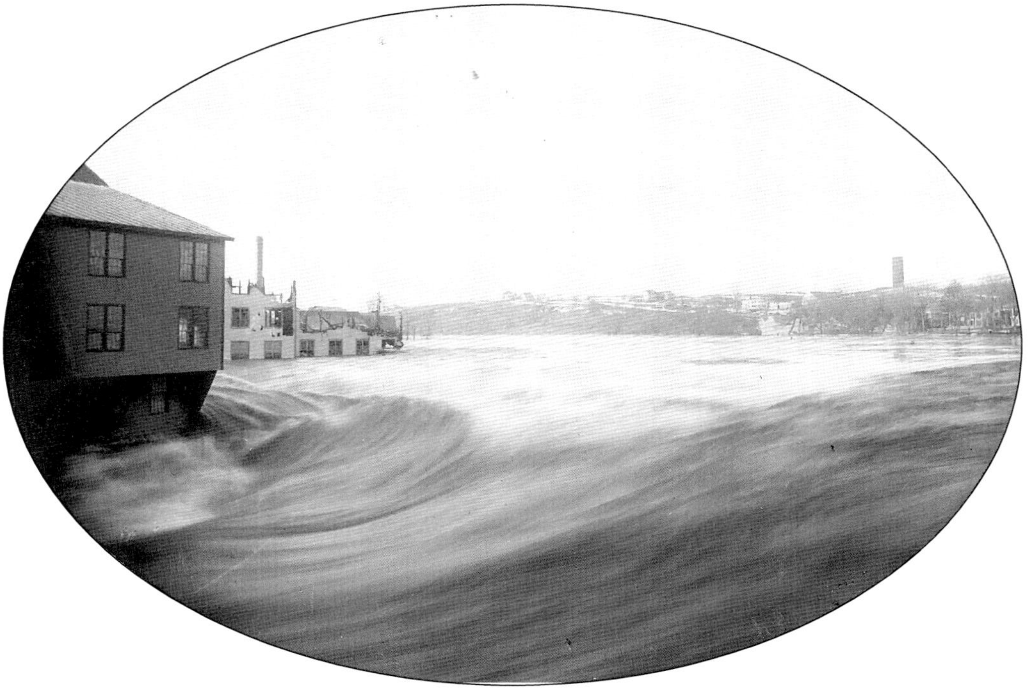

The Skowhegan flood after the turn of the century. You could never trust the Kennebec during the spring flood season.

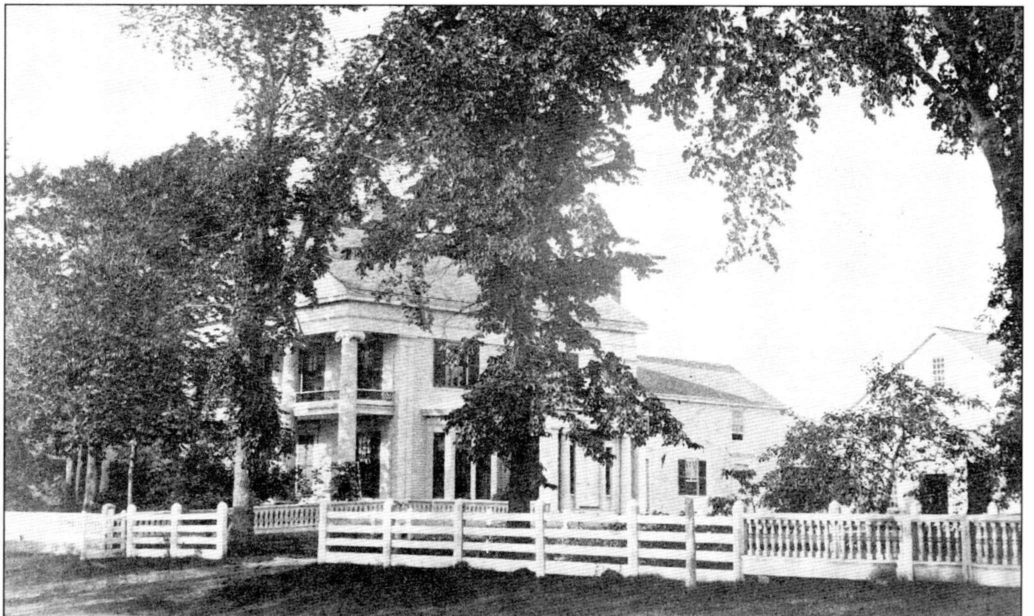

Governor Abner Coburn's residence. The Skowhegan resident died on January 4, 1885, at the age of eighty-two. He was governor from 1862 to 1863. Built in 1848 on Baptist Hill, the Greek-columned home has fallen into disrepair.

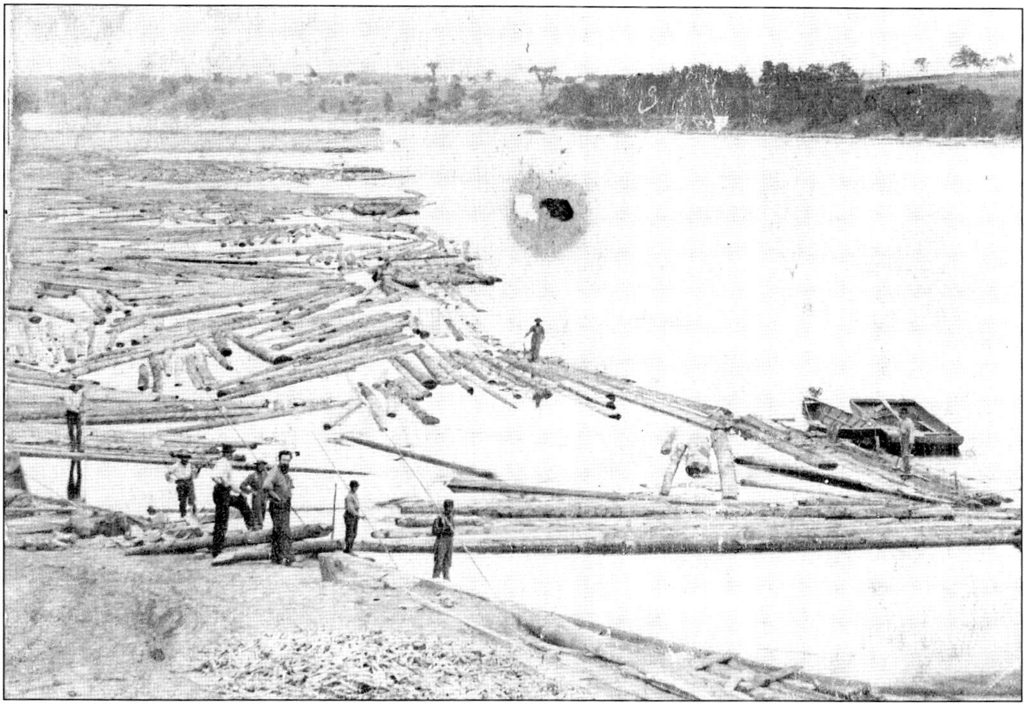

Logs in the Kennebec River in the early 1900s. This was a frequent sight for Margaret Chase, as log drives were at their height at this time.

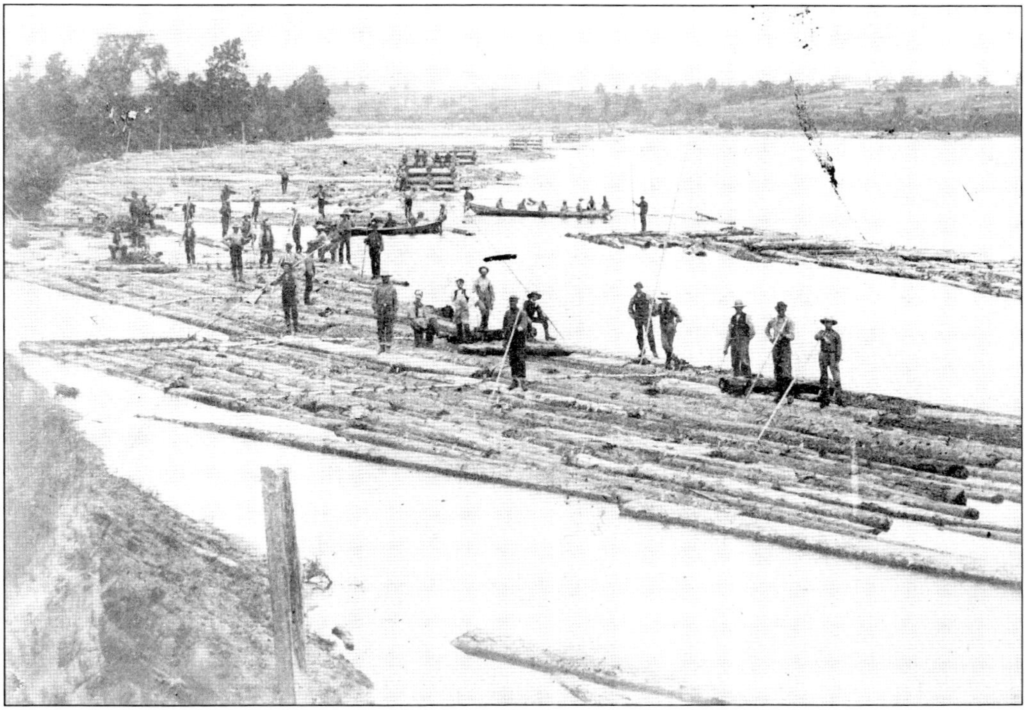

Working a log drive just after the turn of the century.

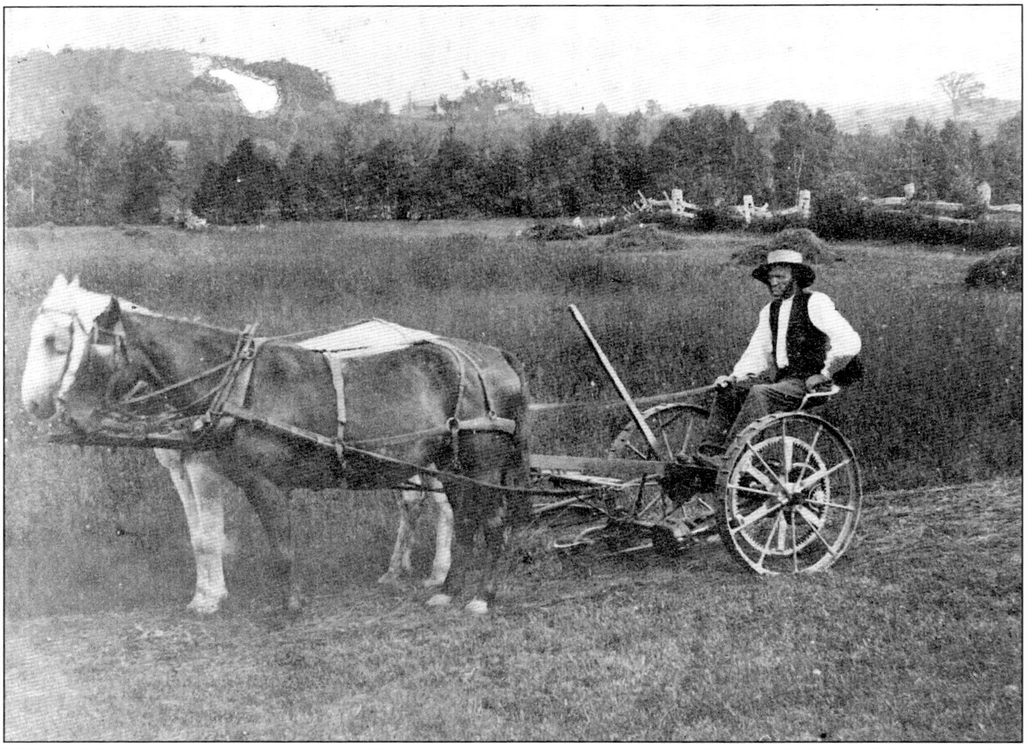

When Margaret was young agriculture was an important part of people's lives. Using scythes drawn by horses was a common technique in the area for cutting hay.

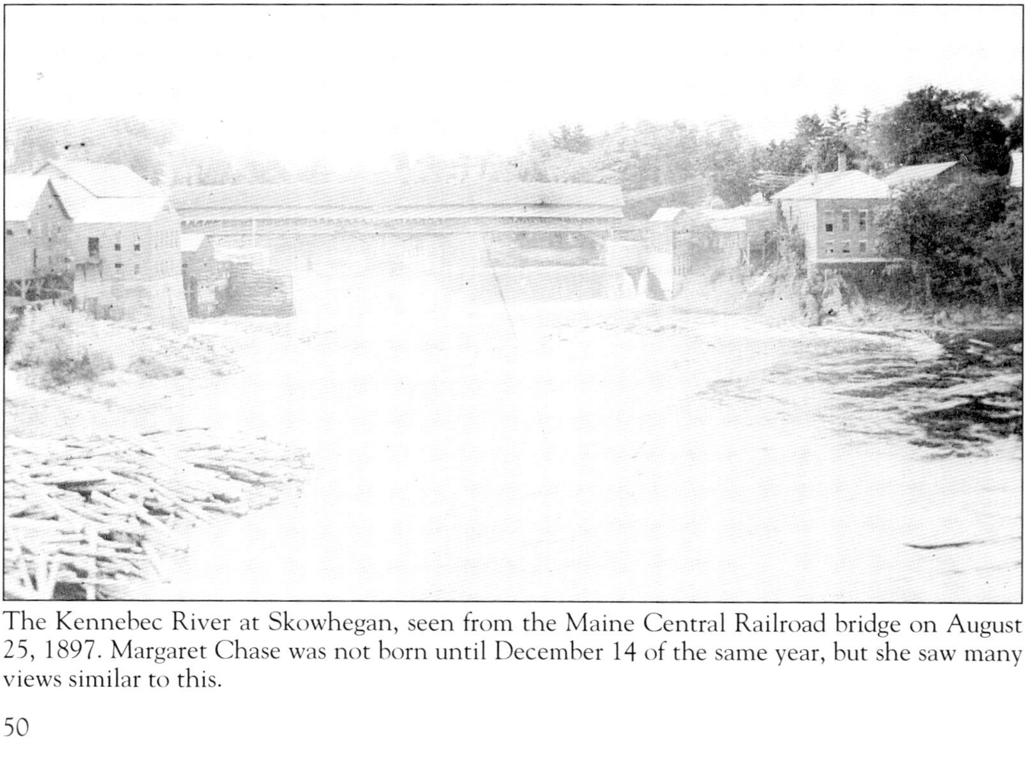

The Kennebec River at Skowhegan, seen from the Maine Central Railroad bridge on August 25, 1897. Margaret Chase was not born until December 14 of the same year, but she saw many views similar to this.

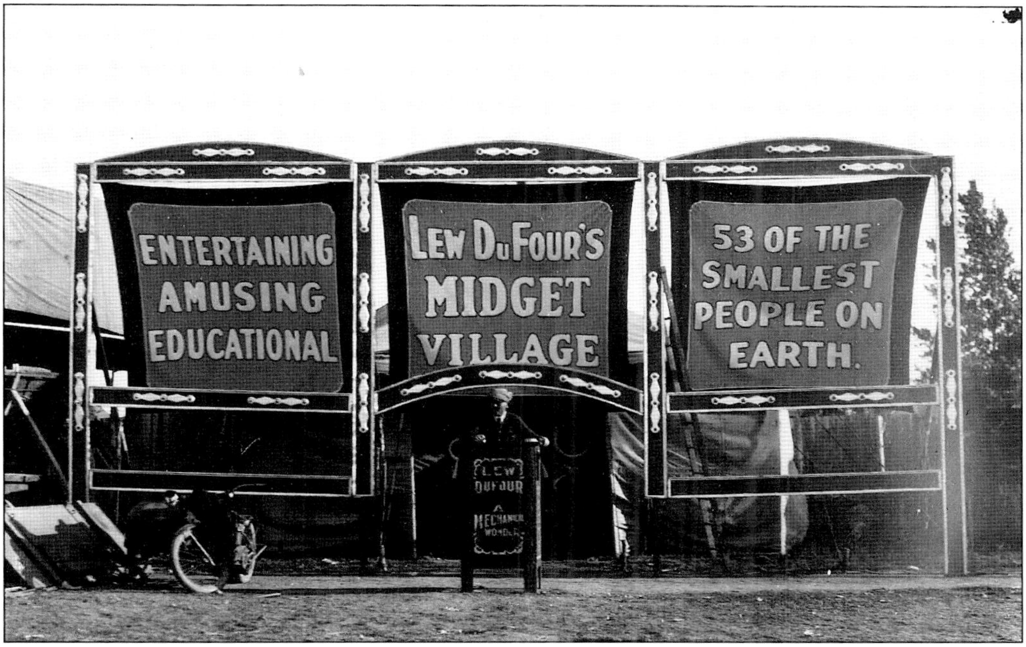


The Skowhegan Fair, when Lew DuFour's company was there, claimed to showcase fifty-three of the smallest people on earth.

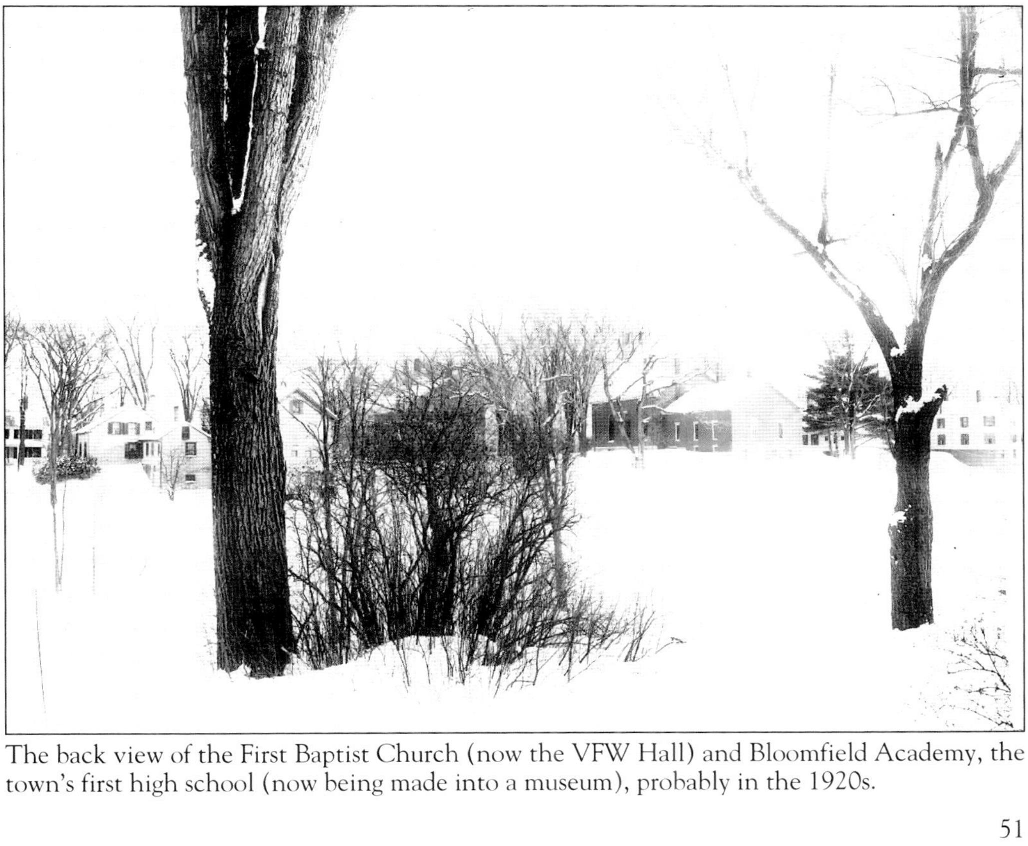

The back view of the First Baptist Church (now the VFW Hall) and Bloomfield Academy, the town's first high school (now being made into a museum), probably in the 1920s.

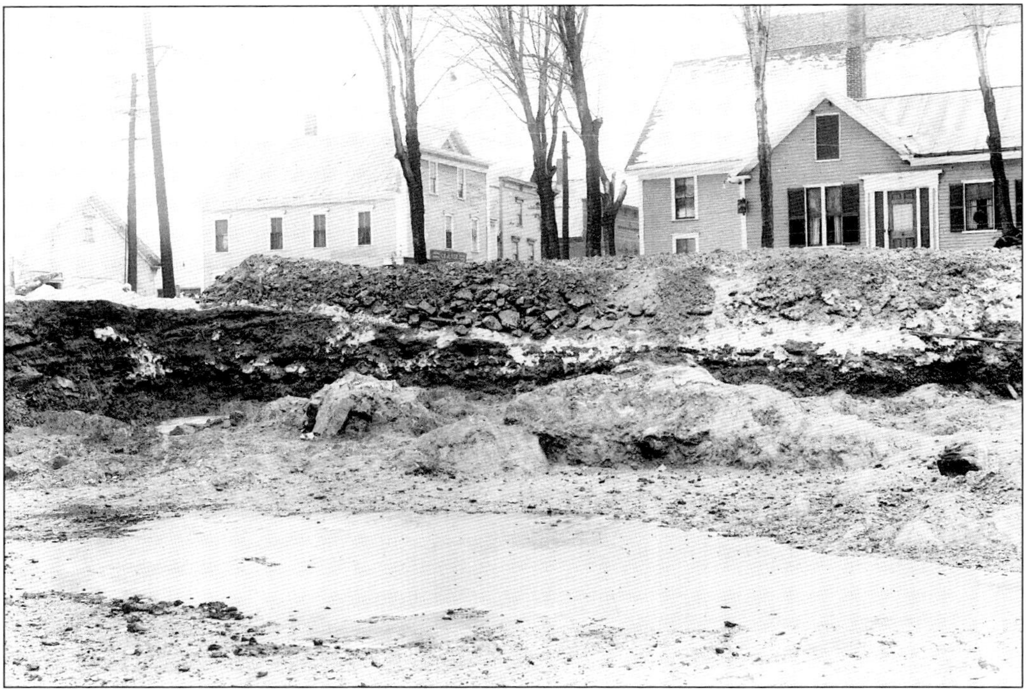

Margaret Chase watched as a new post office at the corner of Water and North Streets was being constructed from November 1916 (Margaret had graduated from Skowhegan High in June) to July 1, 1918. The finished post office looks quite angular from the air.

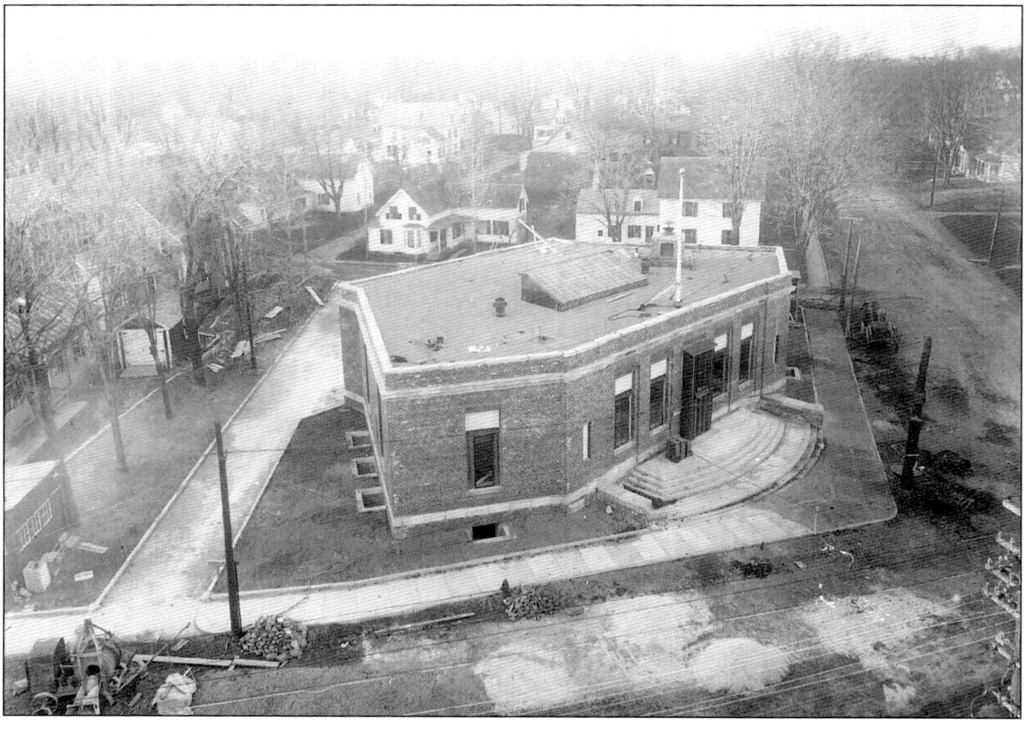

A window display in a Skowhegan store during World War I. There were frequent displays of patriotism in Skowhegan during the war. Margaret Chase had graduated from Skowhegan High several years before this picture was taken.

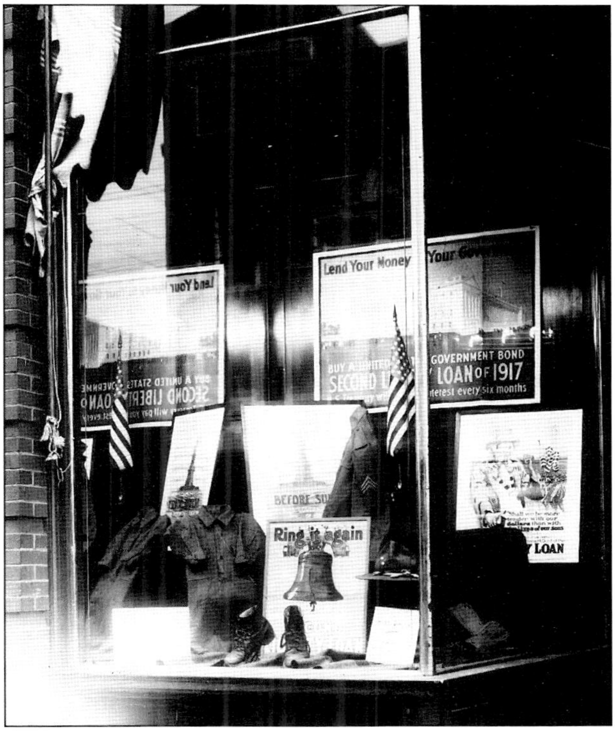


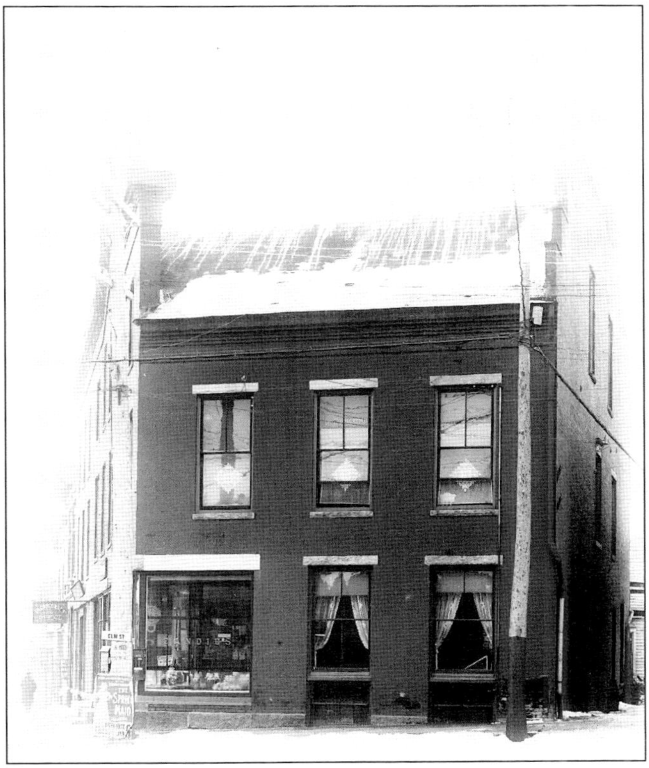

The corner of Elm Street and Madison Avenue in downtown Skowhegan, c. 1910s. *The Spring Maid* was showing at the Opera House. The office of Dr. Leander Almarin Dascombe is on the left.

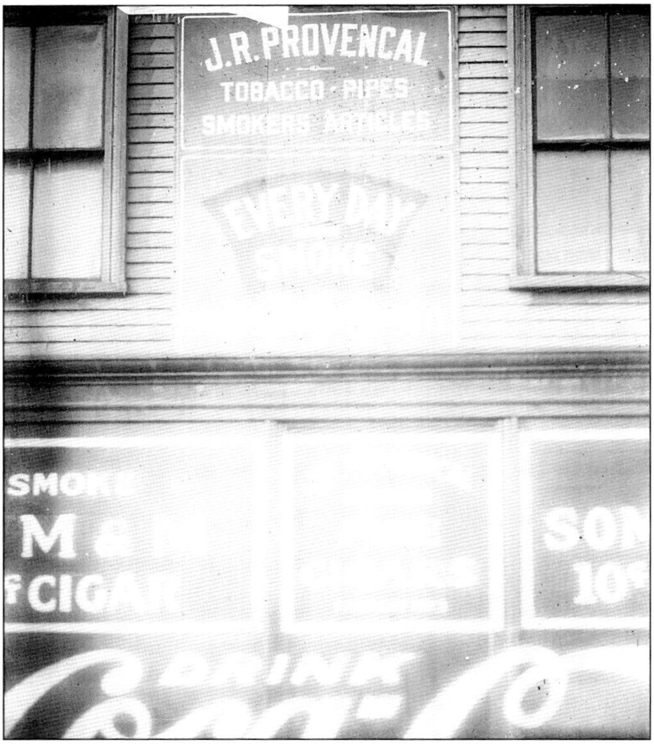


J.R. Provencal, tobacco, pipes, and smokers' articles, in downtown Skowhegan in the 1910s or '20s. Margaret Chase didn't smoke so this didn't probably fall into her vision.

The Western Union and the Great Atlantic and Pacific Tea Co. were in what is now the Candlelight Restaurant in downtown Skowhegan.

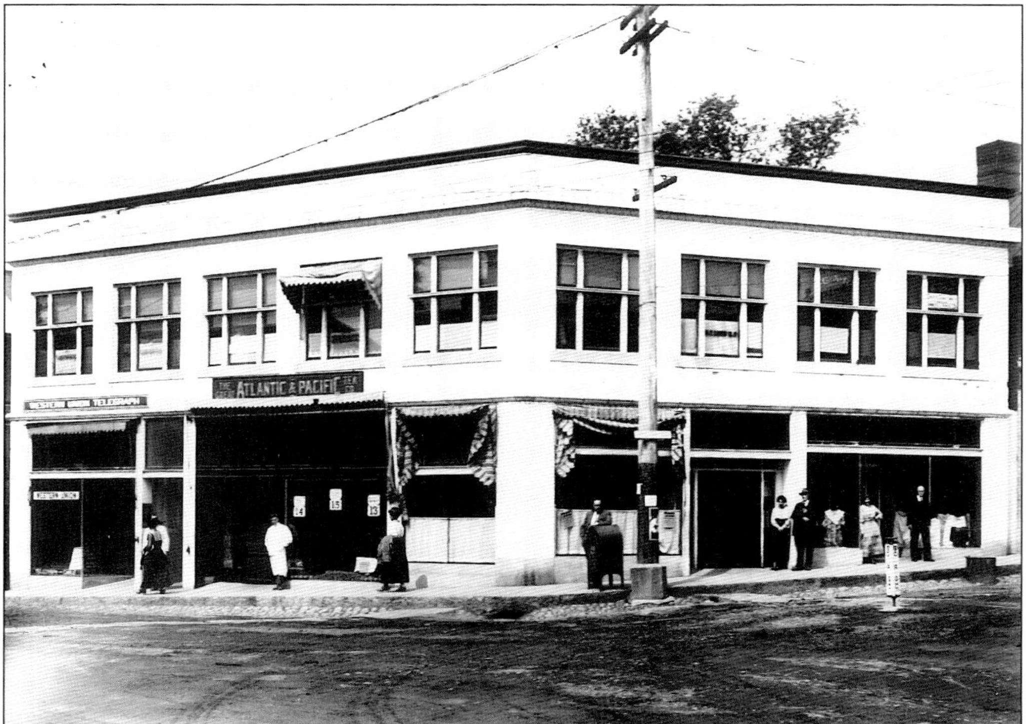

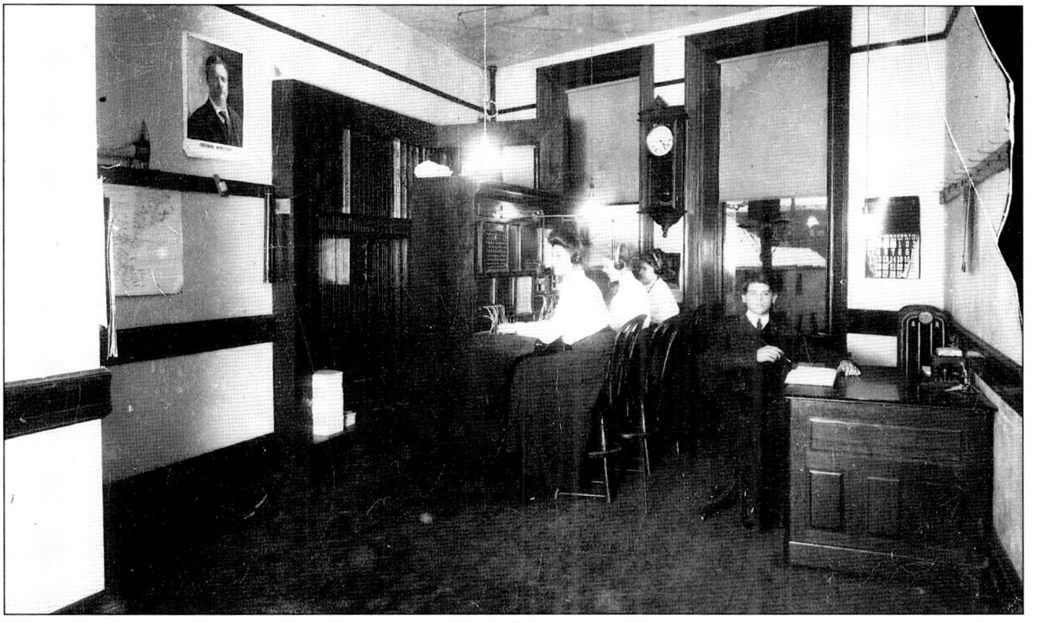

The telephone office in Skowhegan, *c.* 1920. Margaret Chase was a part-time operator here while in high school and worked in the office collecting phone bill money from 1917 to 1919.

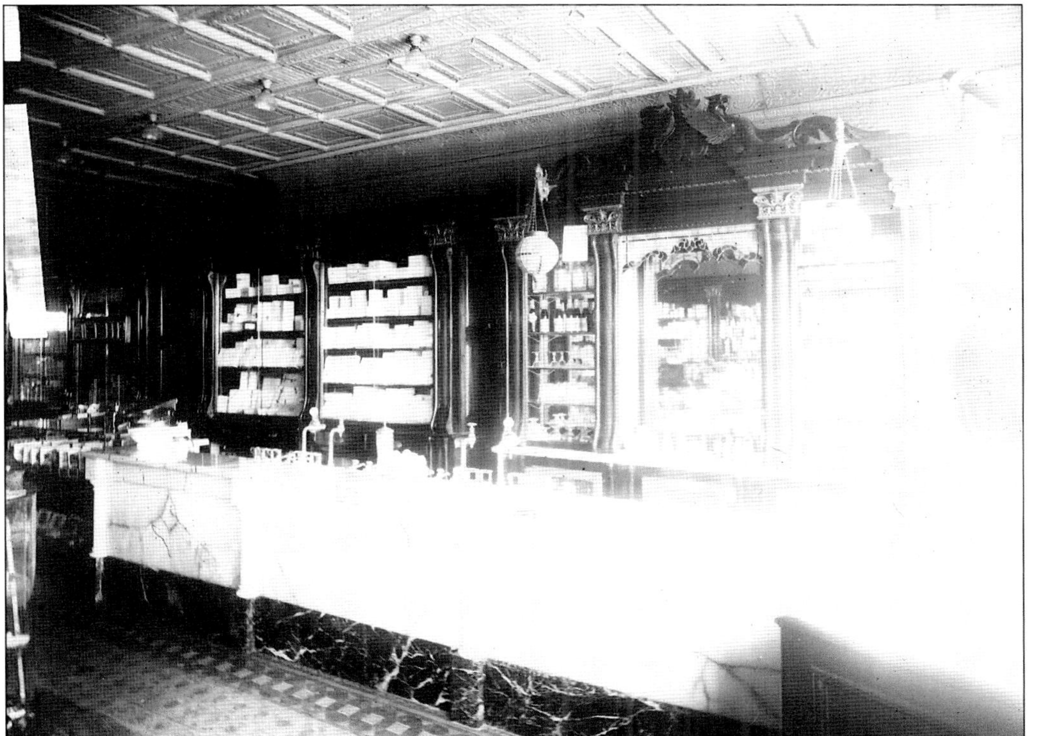

The soda fountain at Bucknam's Drug Store, *c.* 1920s. Margaret Chase no doubt patronized this often, as did many other area youth.

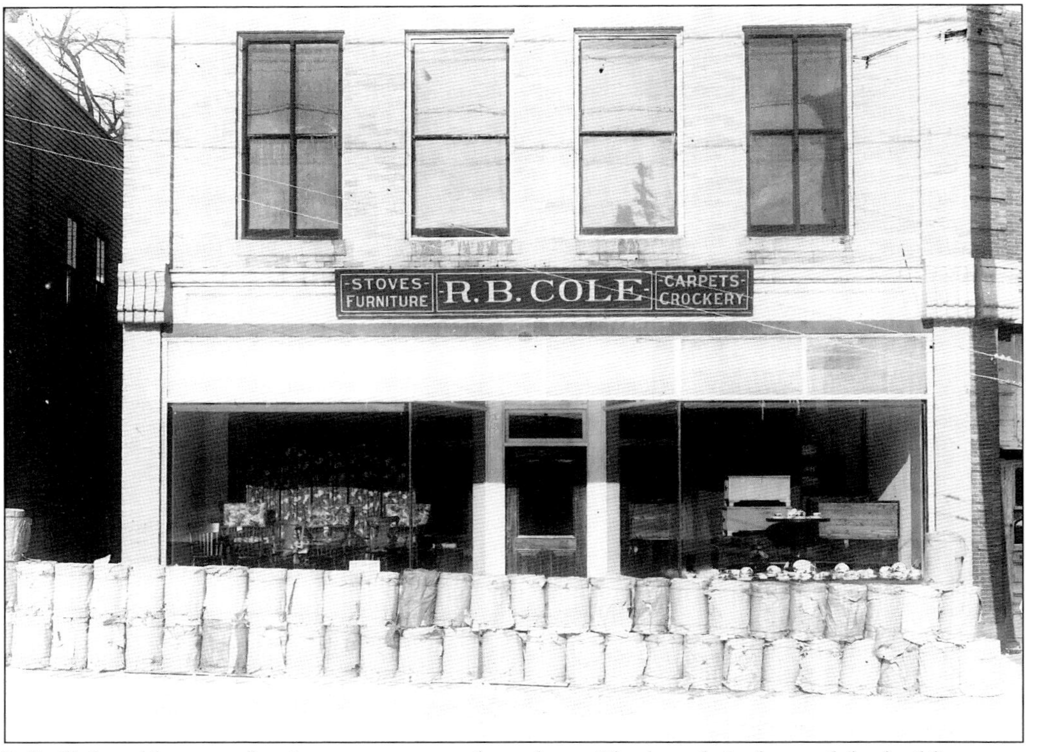


R.B. Cole sold stoves, furniture, carpets, and crockery. The barrels in front of the building may contain crockery.

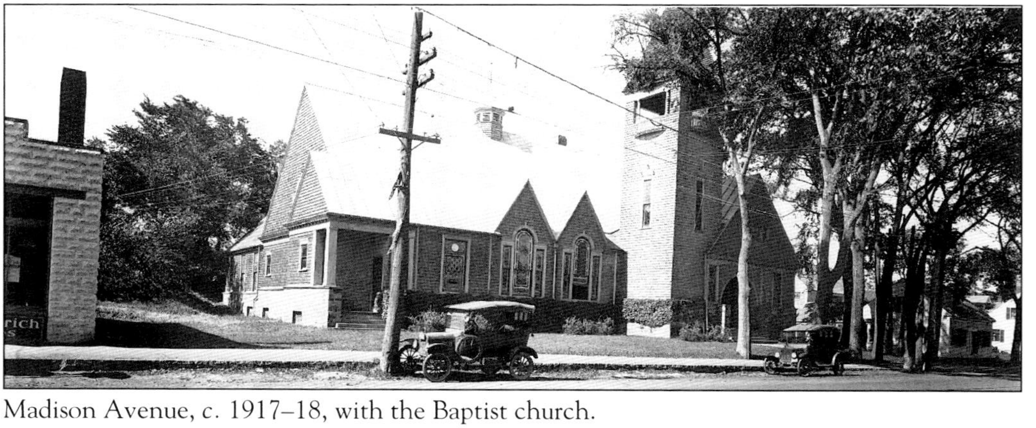

Madison Avenue, *c.* 1917–18, with the Baptist church.

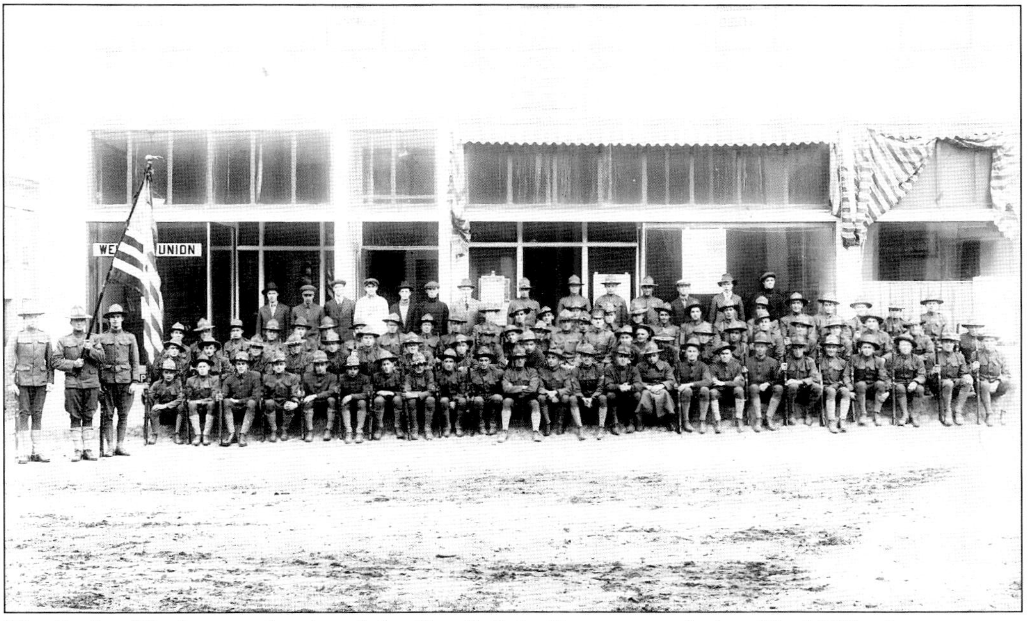

The Dodge Block, now the site of the Candlelight Restaurant, during World War I.

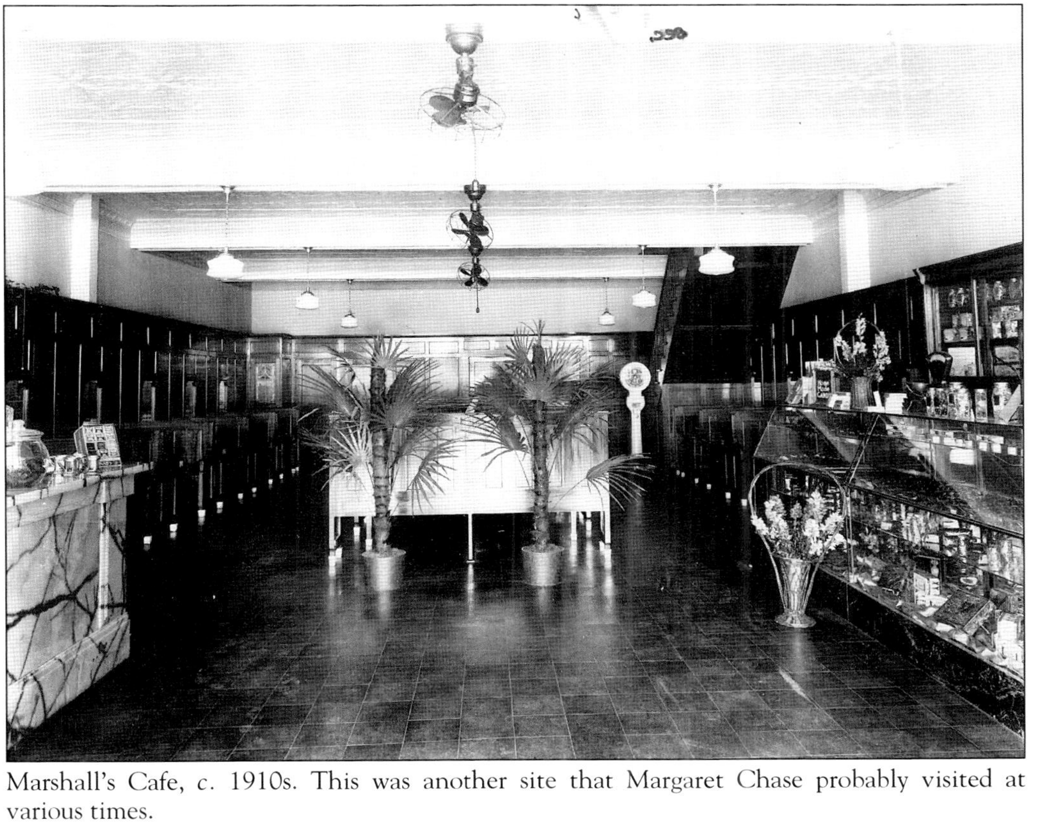
Marshall's Cafe, *c.* 1910s. This was another site that Margaret Chase probably visited at various times.

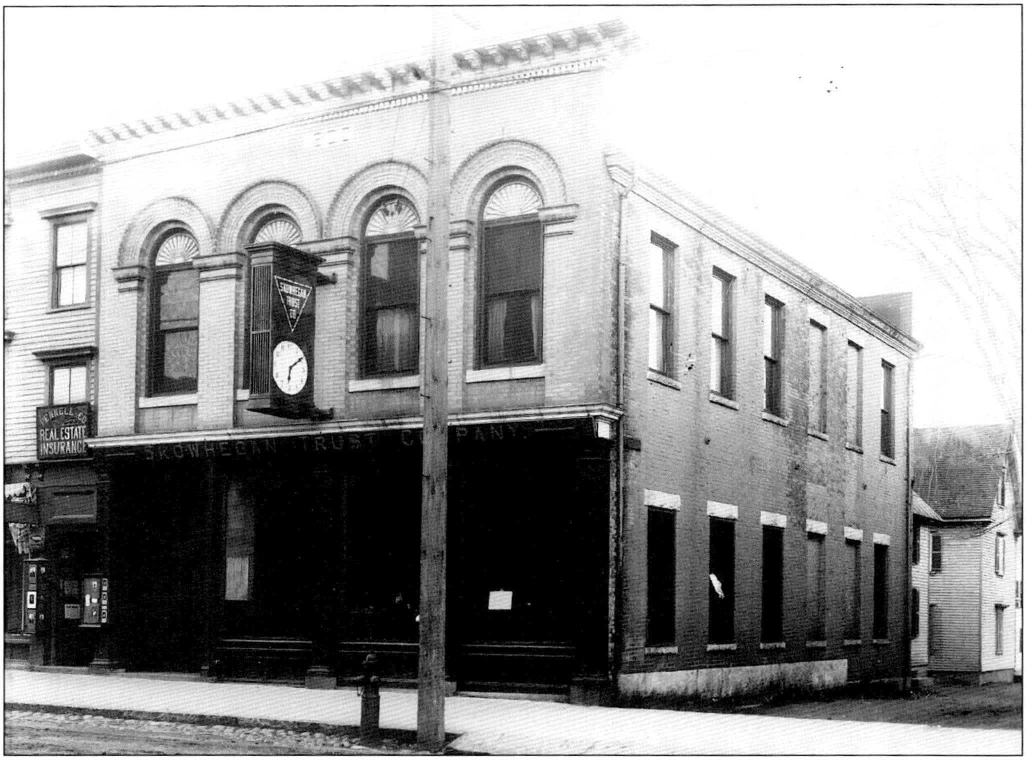


The Skowhegan Trust Co., now McMichael's Law Firm, in the 1910s or '20s. The bank was organized in February 1911, and operated until 1931.

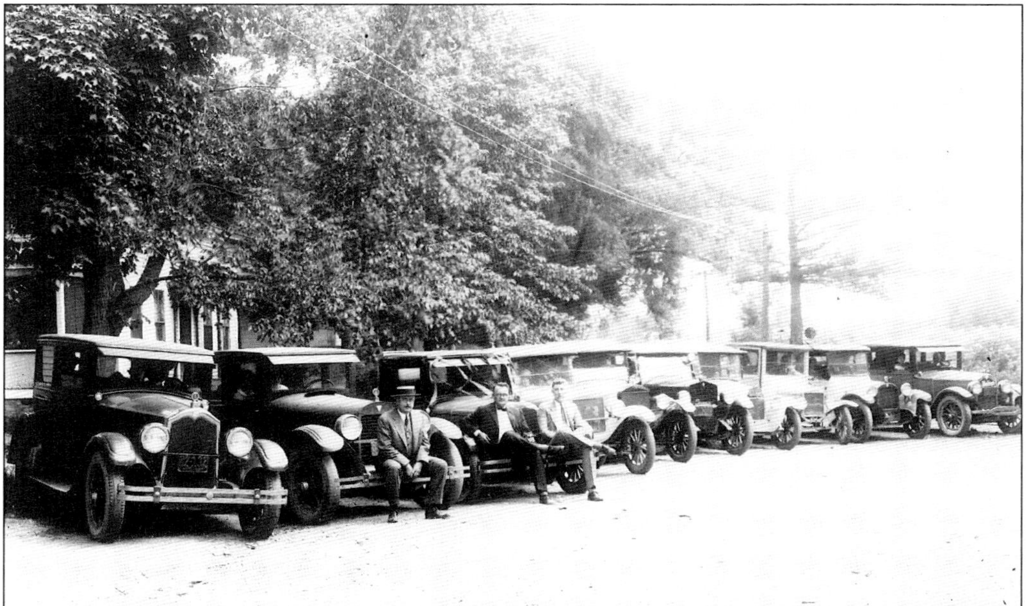

A lineup of Fords in Skowhegan in the 1920s. There's no record that Margaret Chase ever owned a Ford.

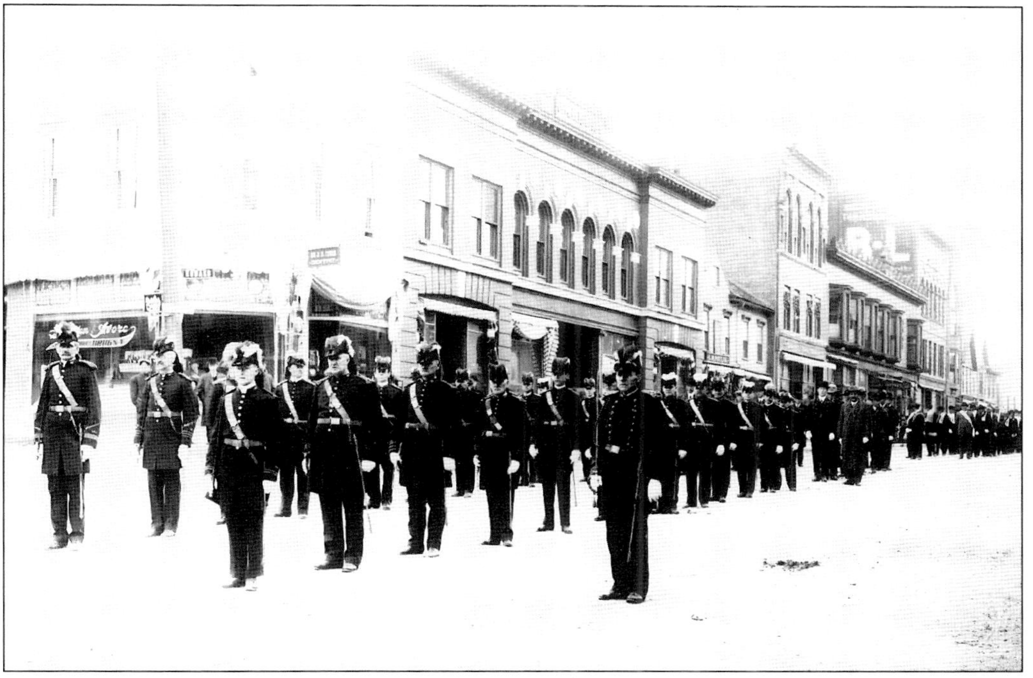

A Masonic parade on Water Street, Skowhegan, in the 1920s. Margaret Chase, like most other people of her time, probably looked forward to and enjoyed the Skowhegan parades.

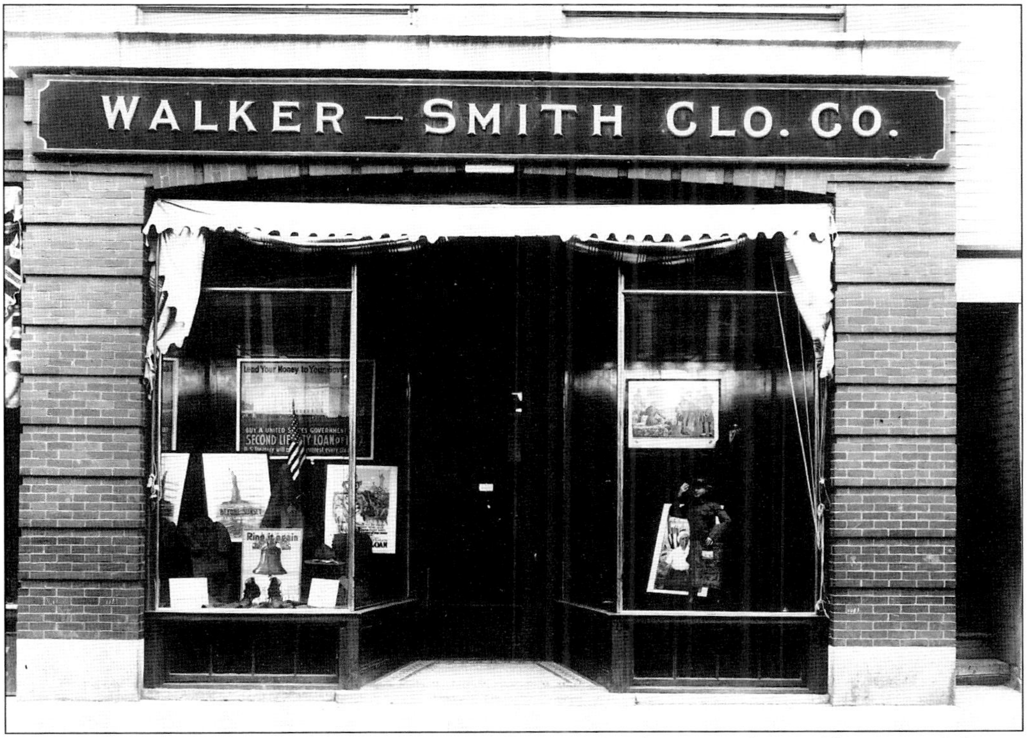


The Walker-Smith Clothing Company in downtown Skowhegan with World War I exhibits.

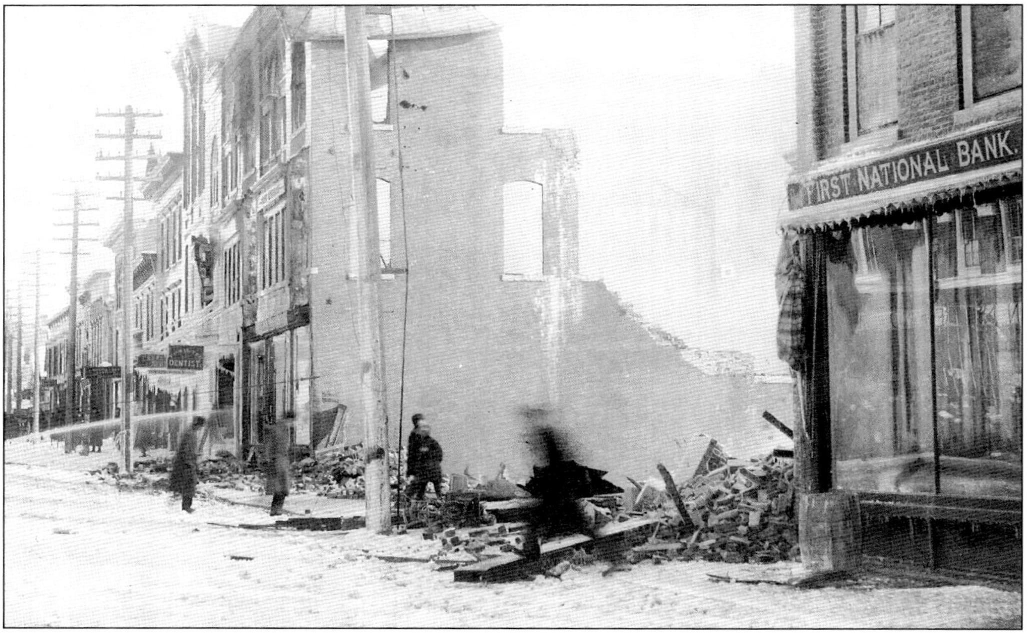


A fire next to the First National Bank, *c.* early 1900s.

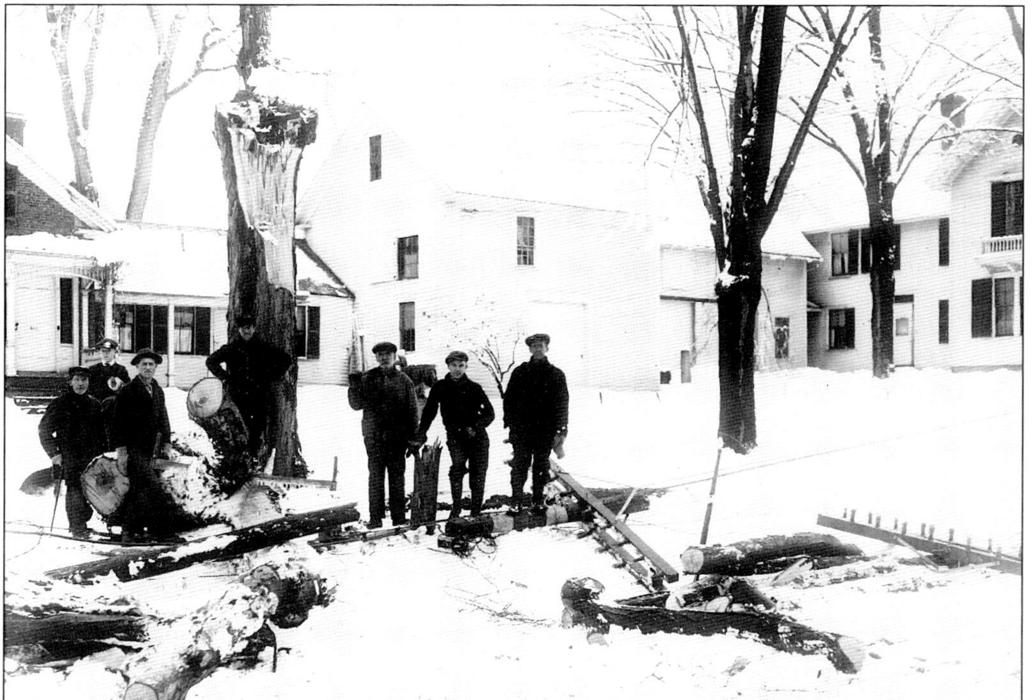

A 1920 photograph of the results of a snowstorm in Skowhegan. Bert Hopkins owned the house on the left and Dr. Oliver J. Caza that on the right.

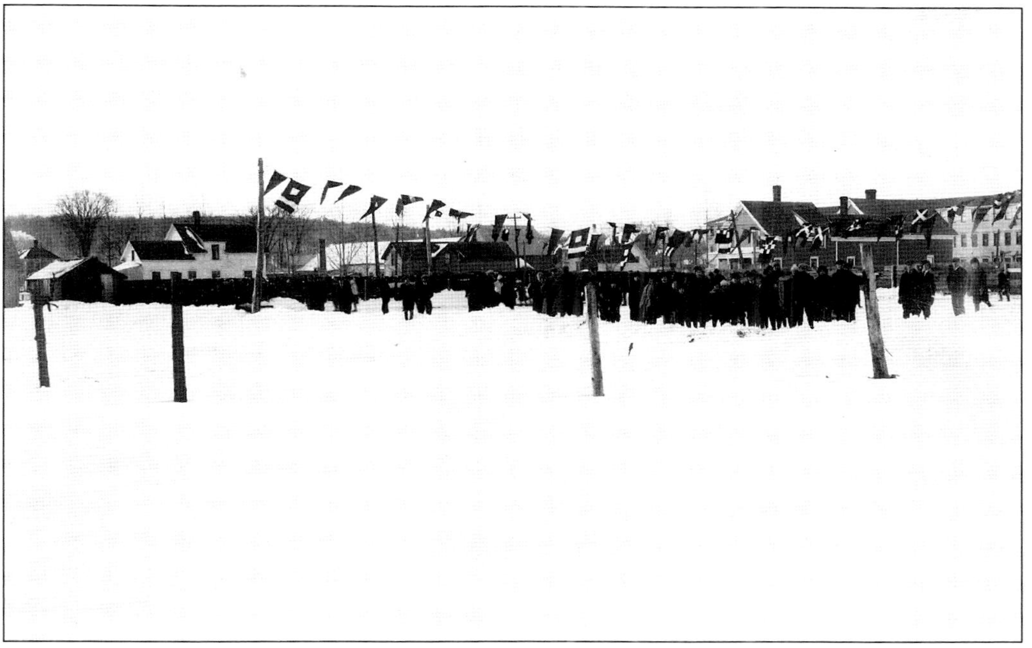
The skating rink on Jewett Street.

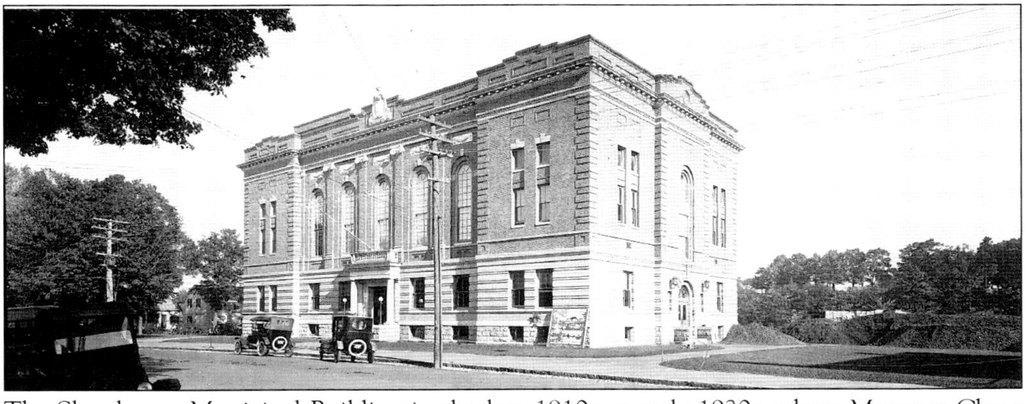
The Skowhegan Municipal Building in the late 1910s or early 1920s, where Margaret Chase may have worked part-time for awhile.

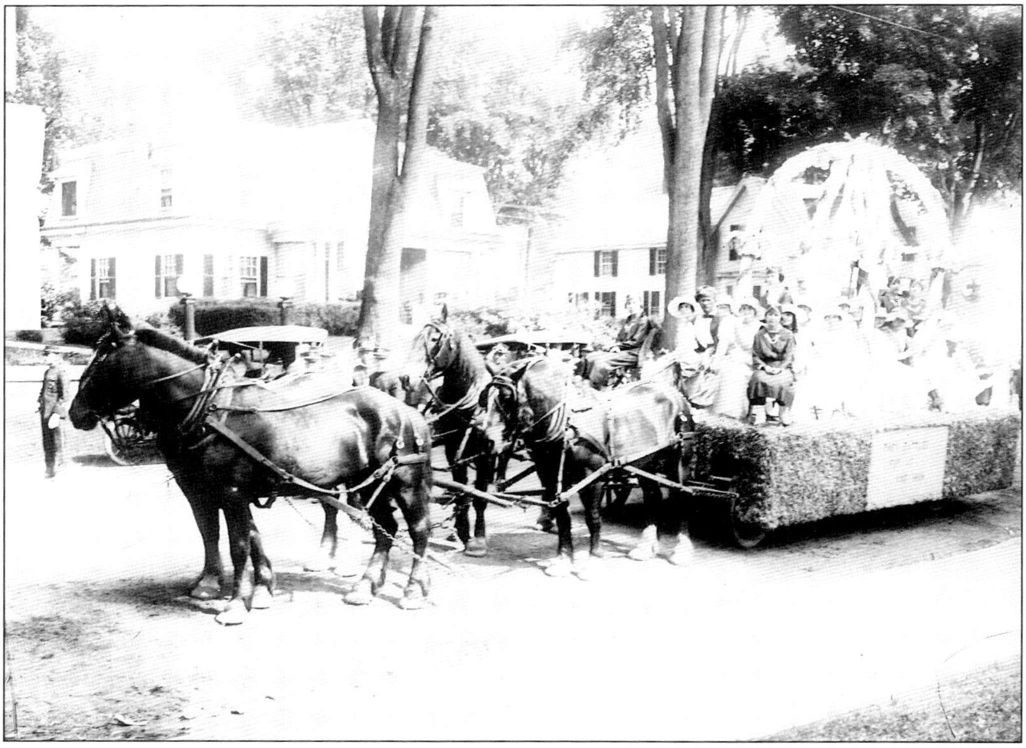

A possible pro-women's suffrage float for a Skowhegan parade in the late 1910s, in front of the Swett House on Water Street. Margaret Chase Smith was later to say that she was feminine but not a feminist.

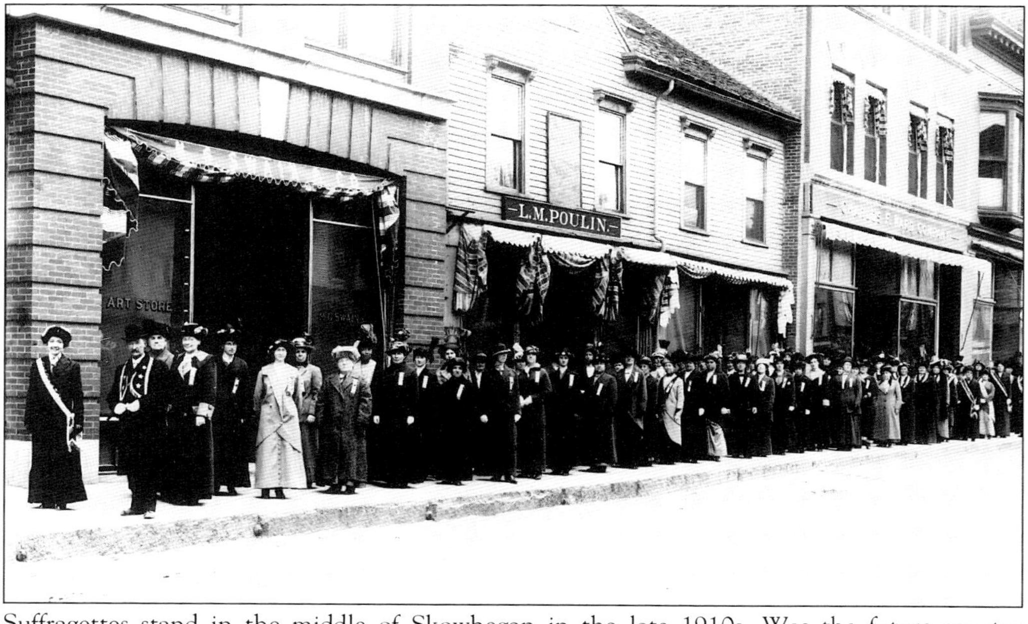


Suffragettes stand in the middle of Skowhegan in the late 1910s. Was the future senator influenced at all by such demonstrations?

*Five*

# People of the Early 1900s

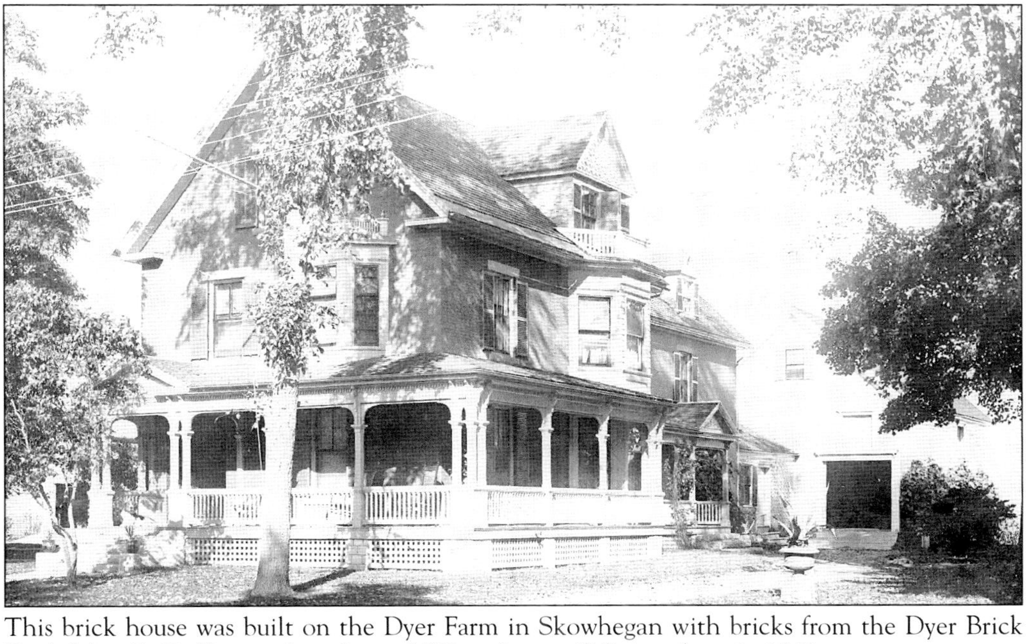

This brick house was built on the Dyer Farm in Skowhegan with bricks from the Dyer Brick Yard. John C. Griffin purchased it in 1891 and was still living there in 1940.

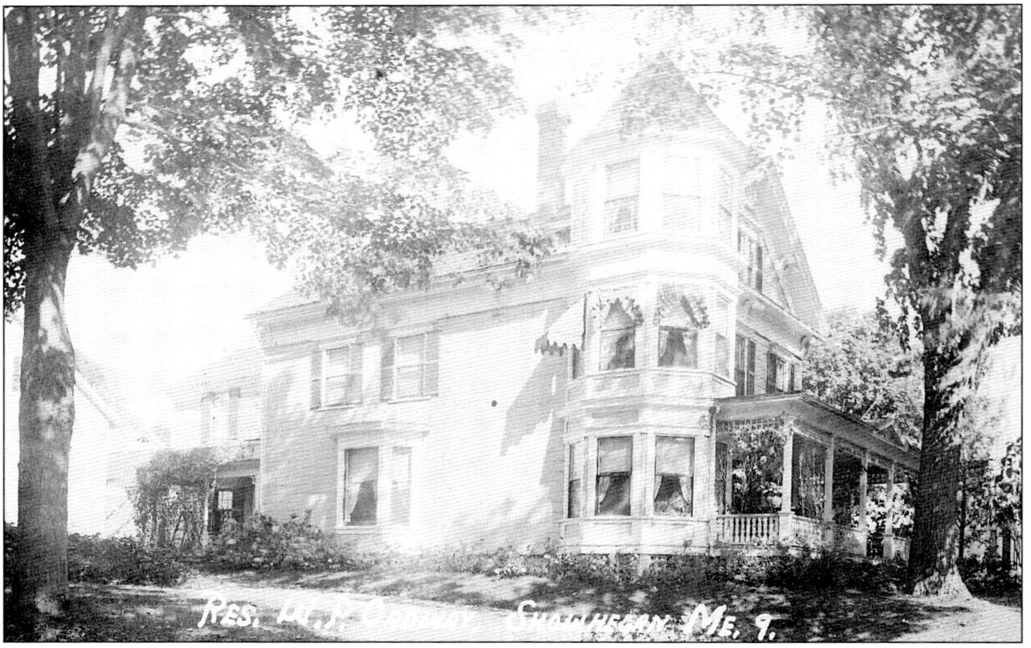

The home of Walter P. Ordway, a Skowhegan businessman for fifty years, in the 1910s.

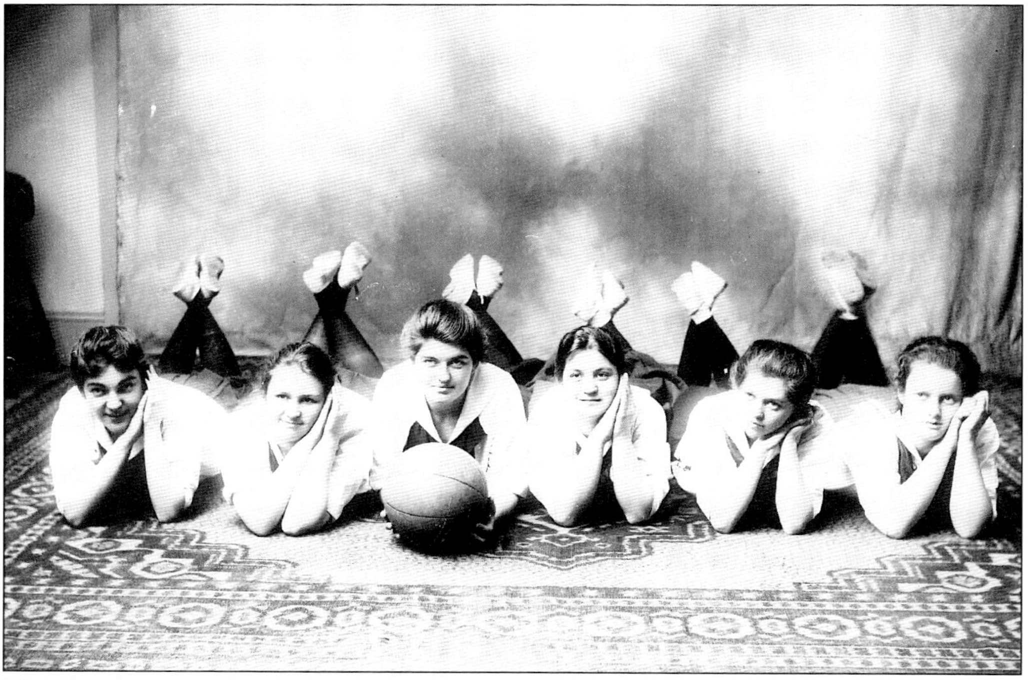

The Skowhegan High girls' basketball team was still posing in 1917, the year after Margaret Chase graduated. From left to right are Fedora Lessard, Martha Steward, Beatrice Smiley, Polly Emery, Doris Wentworth, and Molly Blunt.

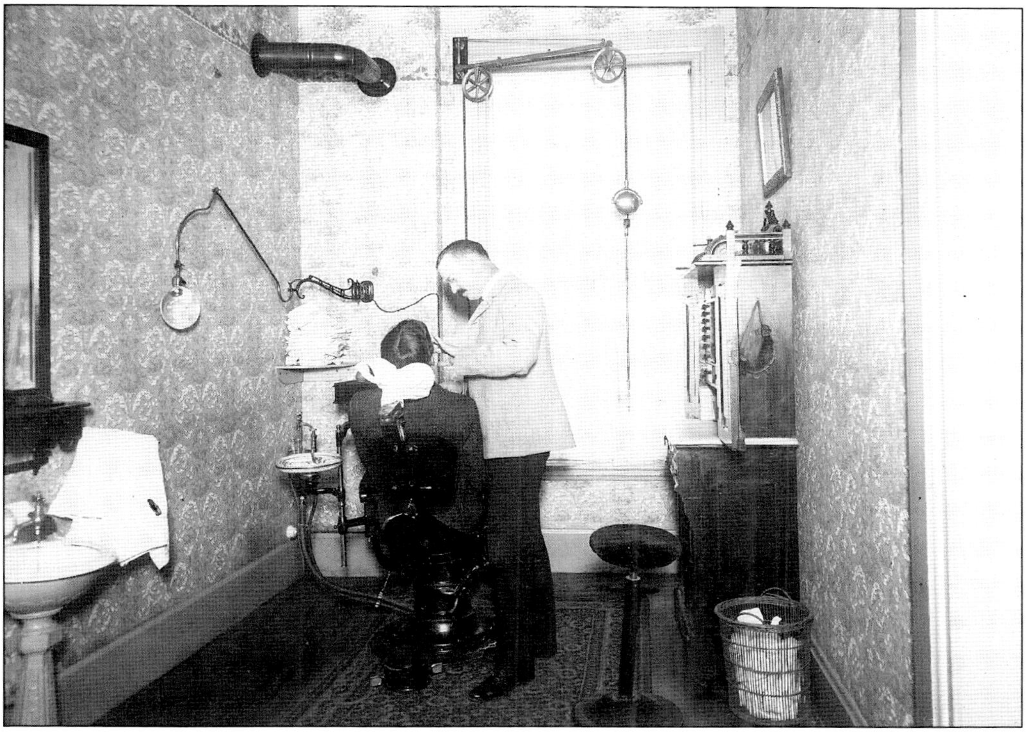

Dr. C.P. Sawyer & Sons, dentists, in 1903. Dr. Sawyer is shown here with an unidentified person in his dentist's chair.

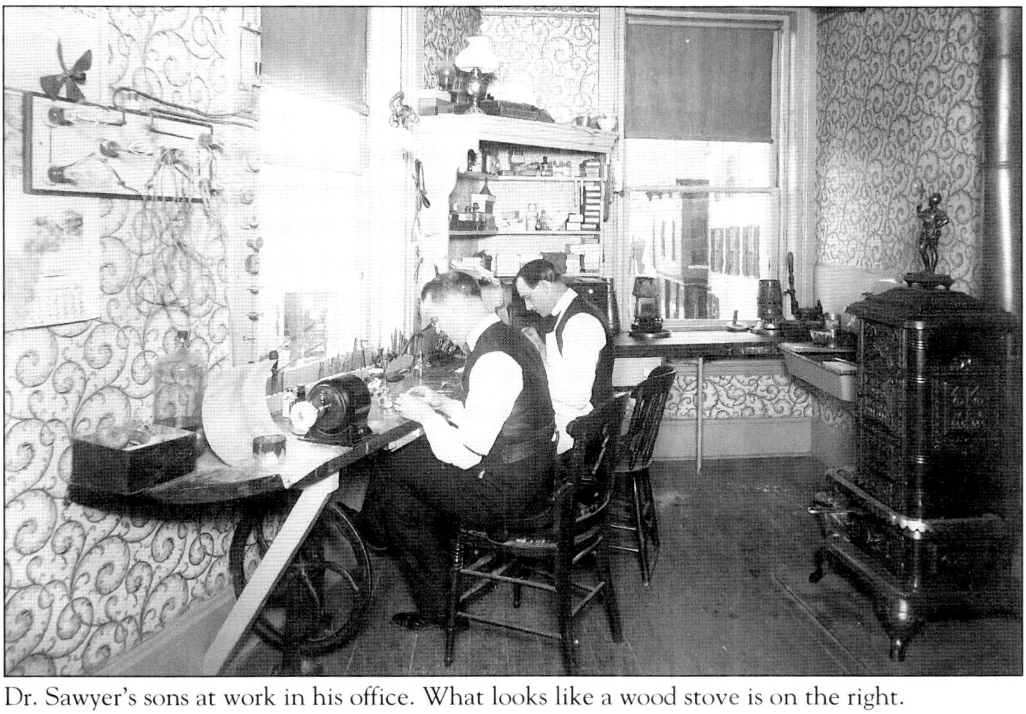

Dr. Sawyer's sons at work in his office. What looks like a wood stove is on the right.

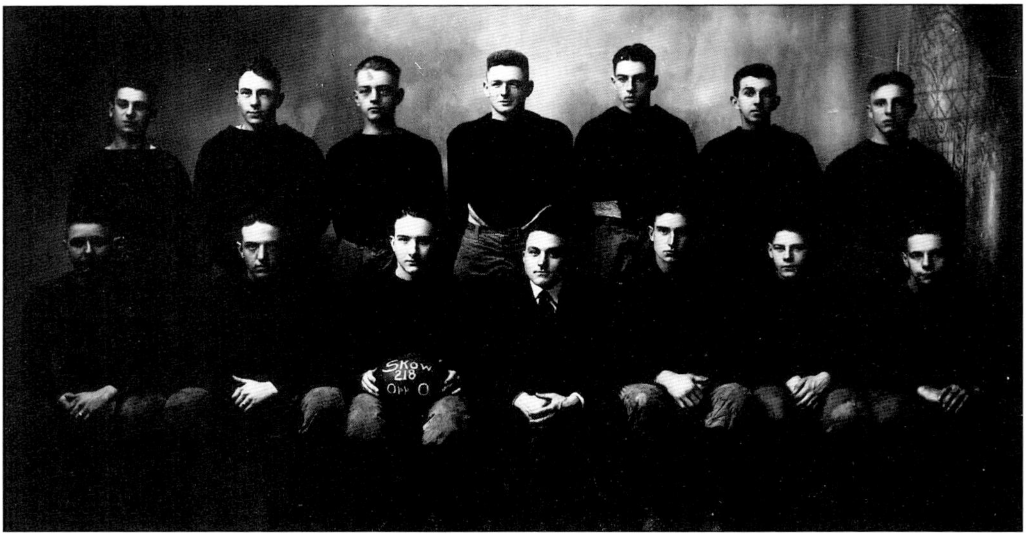


The 1920 Skowhegan High School football team, which outscored its opponents 218–0. From left to right are: (front row) Fay Studley, Bill Philbrick, Lawrence Coleman, unknown, unknown, unknown, and Benny Lewia; (back row) Teddy Beauford, Ivan Cloud, unknown, Ken Smiley, unknown, Ham Murphy, and Emil Dionne.

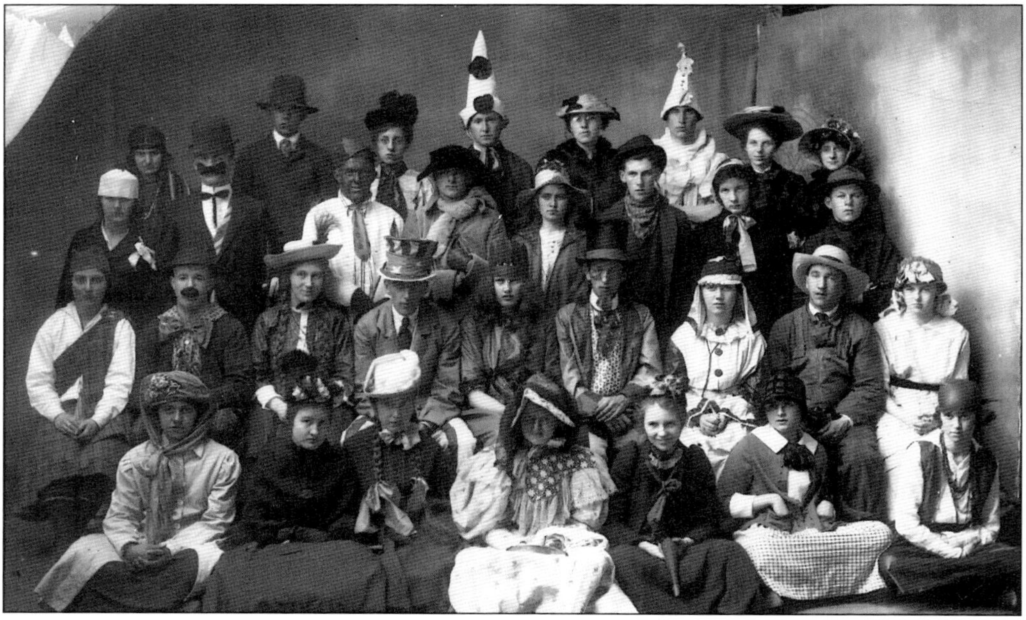

A curling party by the Skowhegan High Class of 1920. From left to right are: (front row) Geneva McLaughlin, Helen Lord, Flora Savage, Helen Day, Ella Flanders, Lovina Murray, and Annie Paradis; (second row) Jean Thomson, Langdon Jewett, Mamir O'Brien, Lawrence Willey, Alta Hoyt, Herman Porter, Julia Cox, unknown, and Marion Merriam; (third row) Arlene Buteau, Mylon Jacobs, unknown, Fred Chase, Flavie Thibault, Earl Hilton, Ruth Homested, and Carl Burkhart: (back row) Katherine McCarthy, unknown, Beatrice McLaughlin, unknown, Mary Friend, unknown, Alta Porter, and Carolyn Gower. Margaret Chase must have known many of these people.

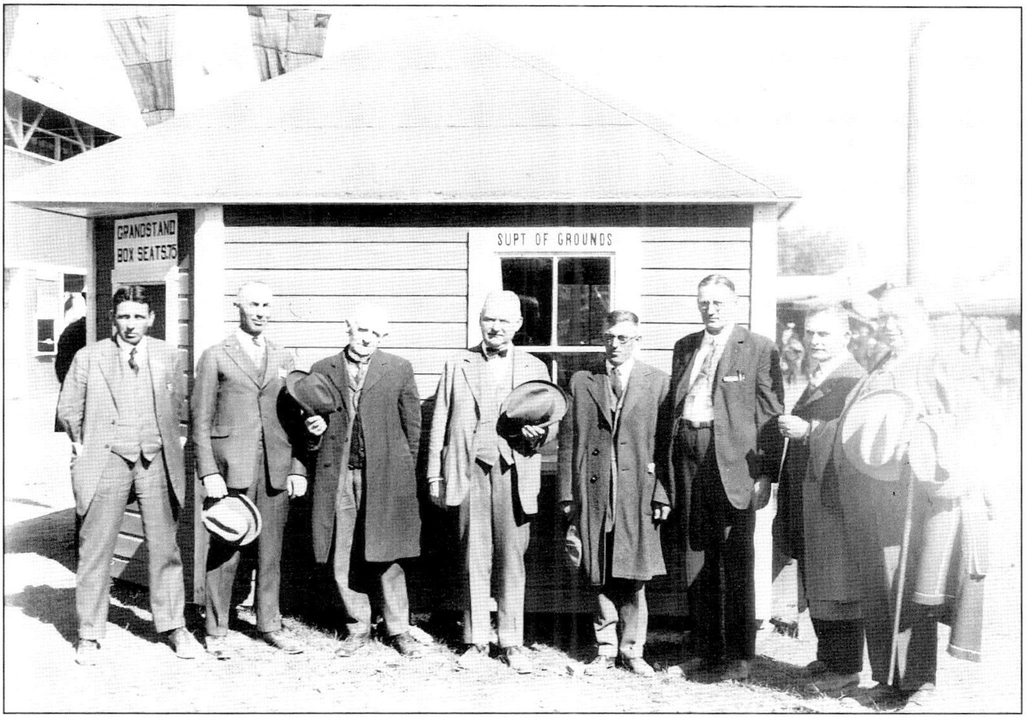


At the Skowhegan Fair Grounds, *c.* 1920s. From left to right are Cecil Tilton, Walter Hight, John Fogler, Walter Ordway, George Plummer, John Lancaster, and two unidentified people. Those named were all prominent businessmen.

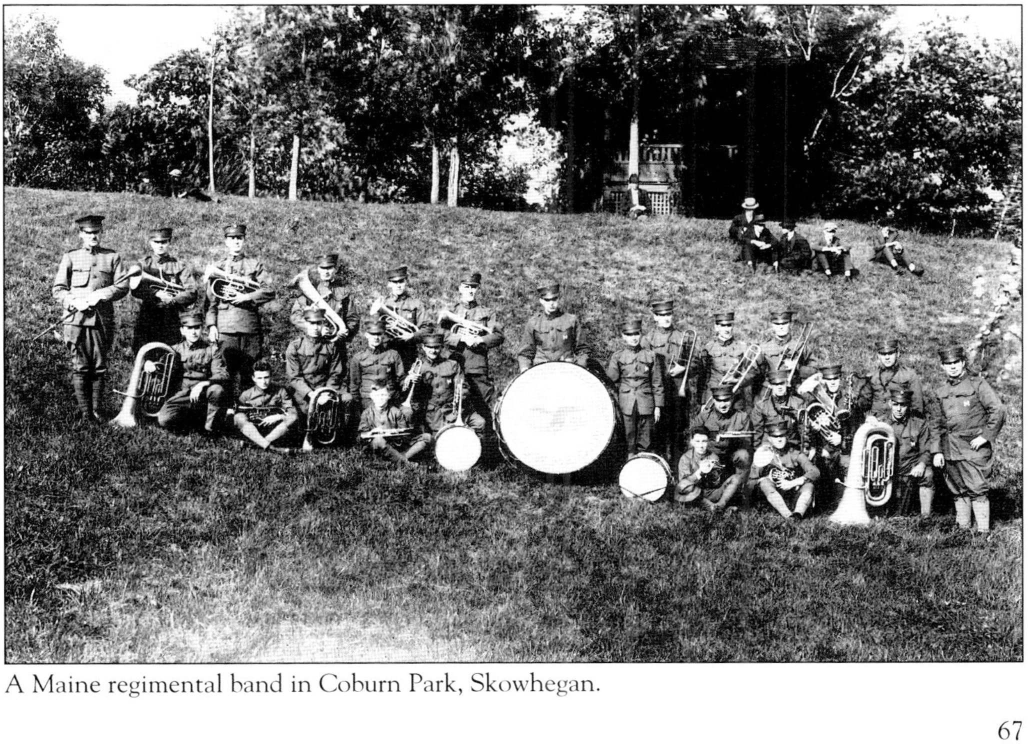

A Maine regimental band in Coburn Park, Skowhegan.

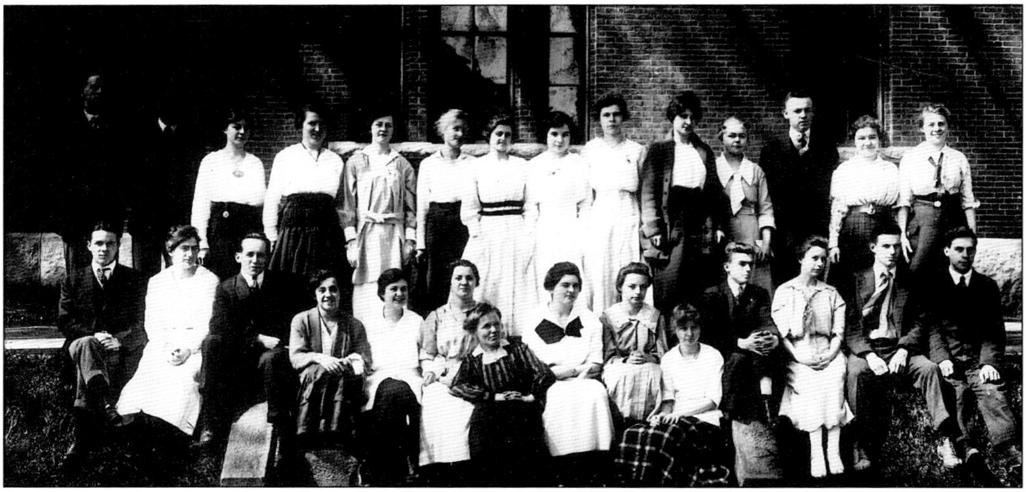

The Skowhegan High Class of 1917, the year after Margaret Chase graduated. From left to right are: (front row) unknown, Beatrice Hodgkins, Libby Pultsiver, Dorothy Potts, Elizabeth Marsh, Polly Emery, Dottie Elliot, Beatrice Smiley, Doris Tobey, Alta Young, Merle Roullaid, Pearl Harville, Alec Thomson, Arthur Lewia, and unknown; (back row) unknown, unknown, Annie Welch, unknown, Doris Gower, Marion Corson, Esther French, Margaret King, Hazel Burkhart, Hazel Russell, Eunice Patten, Joel Taylor, Prudence Wadsworth, and Geneva Smith (or Cora Hopkins).

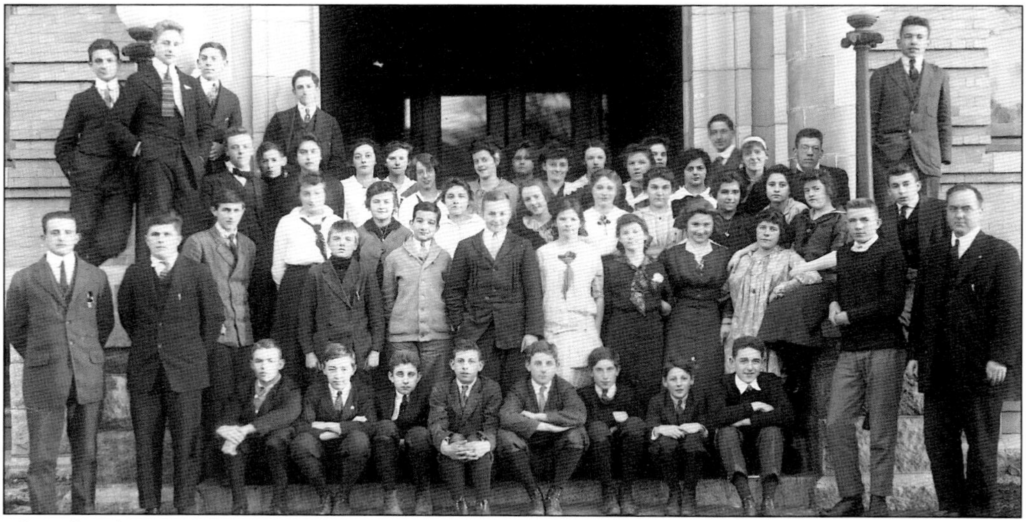

The Skowhegan High Class of 1919. From left to right are: (front row) Earl Grundy, Adolf Giblair, Maurice Ricker, Percy Nutting, Warren Loomis, Harold Pooler, Raymond Fogg, Leland Currier, Karl Roullard, Julian Goodrich, Irving Symonds, and Principal Ralph Leighton; (second row) Richard Turner, Lloyd Holden, Thomas Cockburn, Adolph Bisson, Lena Merrill, Anna Merrill, Eleanor Hawes, and Goldie Keene; (third row) Chantel Bisson, Vida Beauford, Eva Chabot, Alice Comber, Rachel Conant, Fedora Lessard, Grace Paradis, Esther Roderick, Catherine Huchkins, and Elliot Chase; (back row) Theodora Mathieu, David Lyons, Edward Merrill, Willard Paul, Fred Raynor, Ernest Paradis, unknown, Dorothy Pennell, Alice Ricker, Molly Blunt, Martha Steward, Adelaide Lancaster, Maguerite Merriam, Lois Mantor, Elsie Raynor, Letitia Lewia, Karl Philbrick, Pearl Dumont, Roy Keene, and Arthur Corriveau.

Girls knitting socks for servicemen during World War I. They are, from front to back: (front) Albertine Chabot; (second) Thelma Groder; (third) Elizabeth Lewia; (fourth row, from left to right) Catherine Sirois, Blanche Bernier, Gladys Lashon, Evelyn Groder, and Henrietta Poulin; (fifth) unknown; (back) Louise Holt. Everybody did what they could to help the soldiers in the trenches.

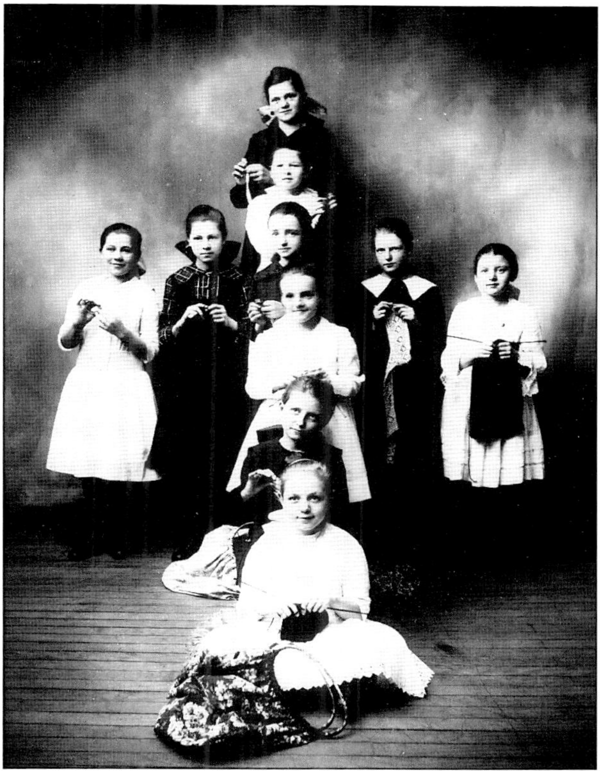

A confirmation class of girls at the Roman Catholic convent, *c.* 1910s.

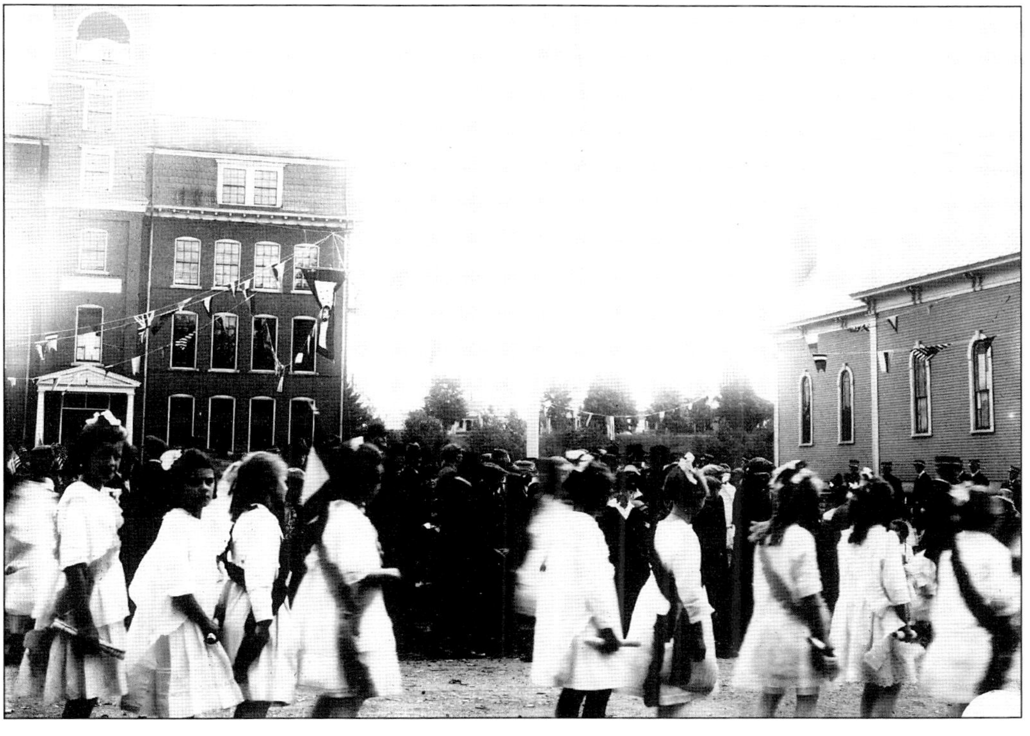

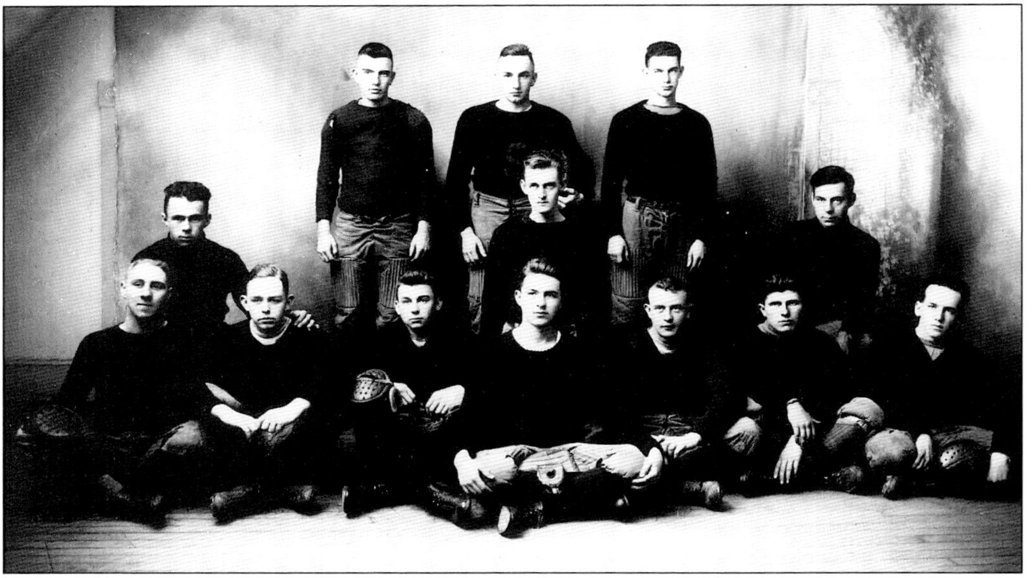

The 1916 Skowhegan High football team. That, of course, was the year Margaret Chase graduated in June. This would have been in the fall of 1916, after her graduation. From left to right are: (front row) Clyde Badger, Alvin Bucknam, Bruce White, unknown, Adolph Gilbair, and Libby Pulsiver; (middle row) Francis Croteau, John French (killed at Pearl Harbor), and Arthur Lewia; (back row) Rex St. Ledger (Senator Smith's brother-in-law), Cas Bisson, and Alex Thomson.

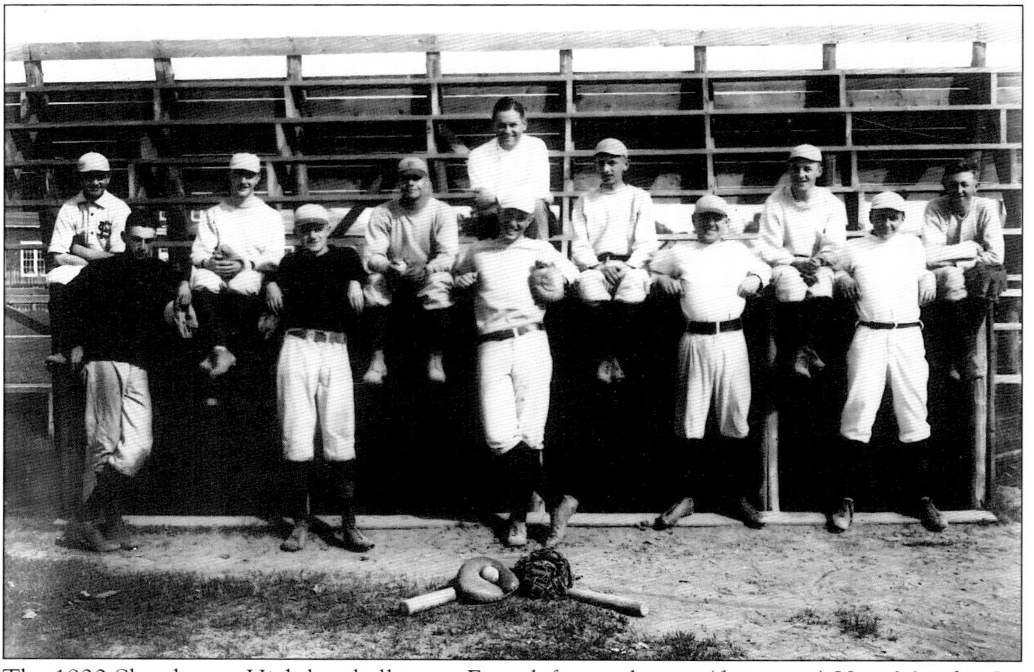

The 1920 Skowhegan High baseball team. From left to right are: (front row) Ham Murphy, Lo Jacobs, Bill Philbrick, Fay Studley, and G. Beals; (back row) Dick Thibeault, Lawrence ?, Benny Lewia, Herman Porter, Ivan Cloud, and Carlton Gamage. John Lewis is the coach.

# *Six*

# The Influential Dead

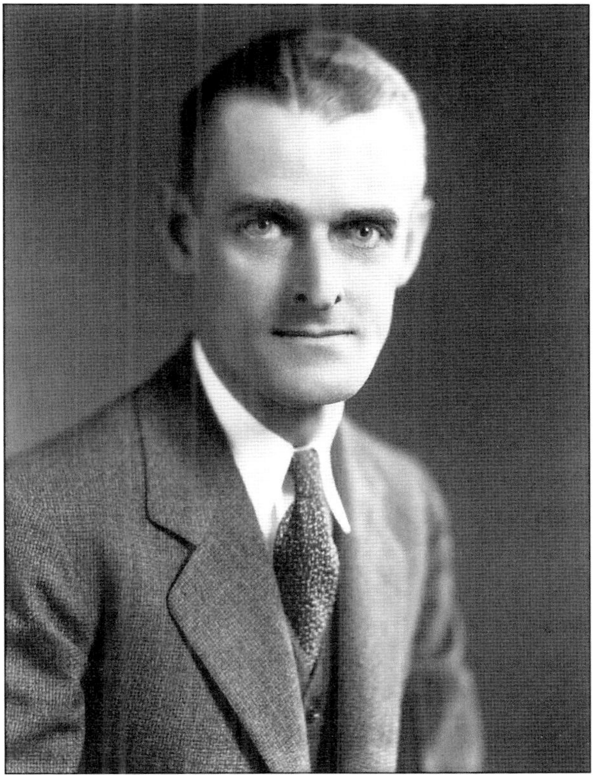

Lieutenant Commander John Edward French, killed at Pearl Harbor on December 7, 1941, when the battleship *Arizona,* on which he was the navigation officer, was destroyed. French graduated from Skowhegan High the year after Margaret Chase did, and his death may have stiffened her attitude regarding matters of defense. Harry St. Ledger, her first date ever, was killed in World War I.

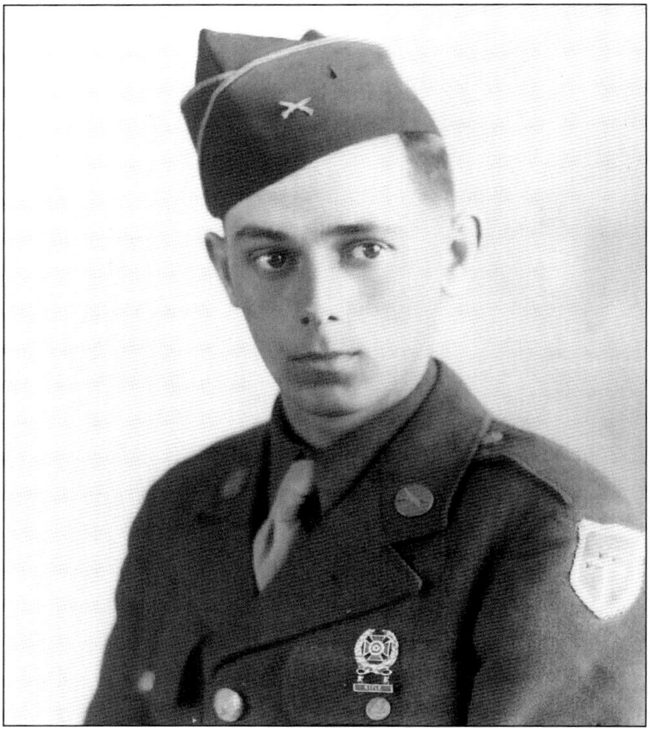

PFC Robert F. Riel, killed July 5, 1944, in Normandy, France. He was twenty, and graduated from Skowhegan High in 1942. Al Skoczenski, a New York City boy, chaperoned Robert's body to his parents. Skoczenski met and later married Shirley Riel, Robert's sister. The couple named their first son Bobby after his dead uncle.

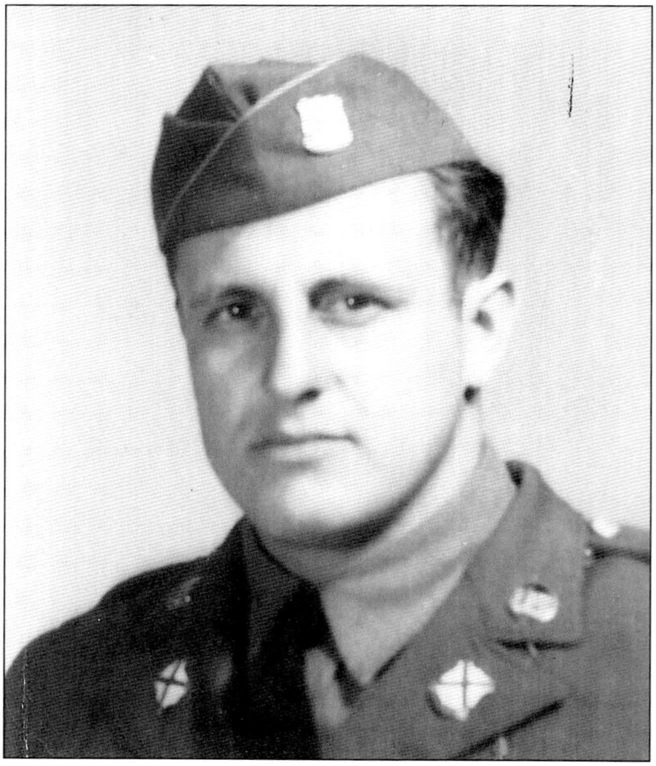

Sergeant Omar T. Pomerleau was killed by a Japanese sniper during the Battle of Munda on July 28, 1943, on New Georgia, Solomon Islands, South Pacific. A 1937 Skowhegan High graduate, he was twice an all-state center in football and went to Hebron Academy for a year.

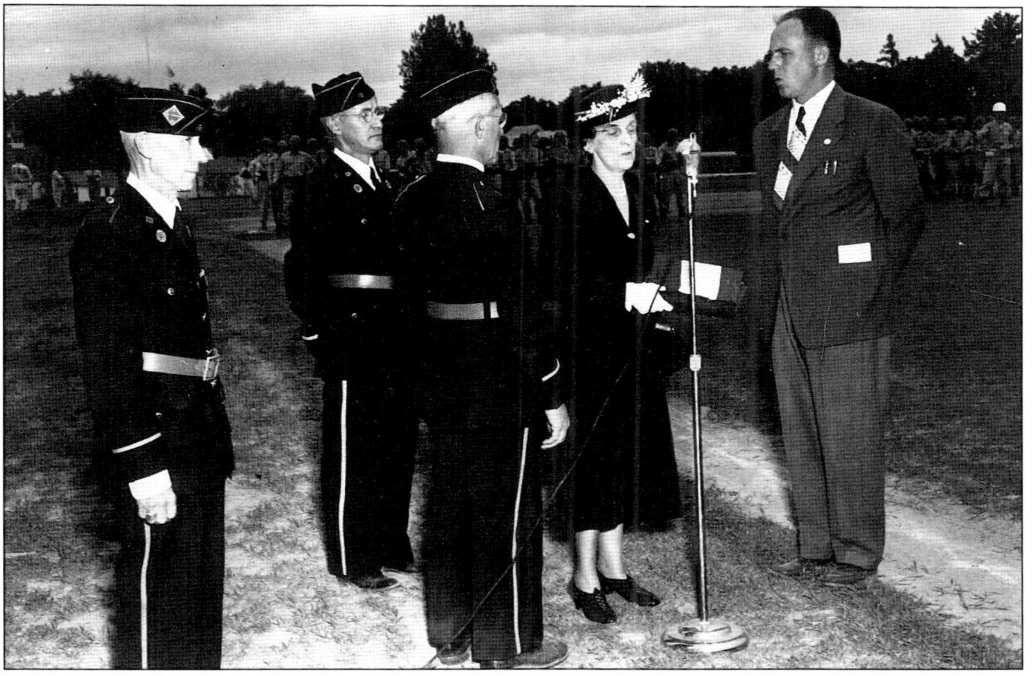

Mrs. Pearl Pomerleau hands over a flag in honor of her son, Omar, at the May 30, 1950 ceremony dedicating Memorial Field to him. It was the same flag that was draped over his coffin.

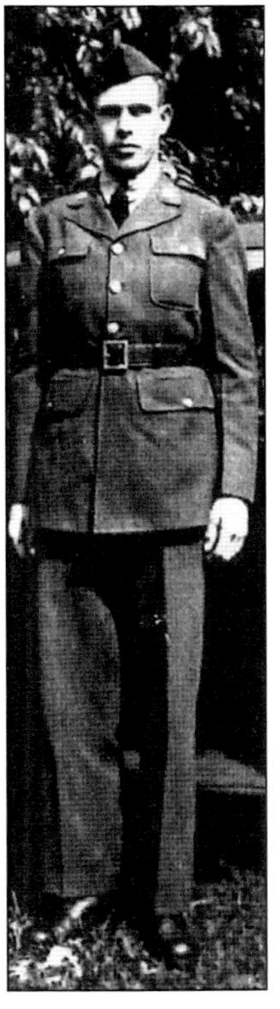

Tech 4 Almon E. Jackson survived the Bataan Death March in the Philippines, only to die of diphtheria four days after his 20th birthday in a Japanese prison camp. He had wanted to be an aviator and, therefore, resigned his post in Skowhegan's Company L, 103rd Infantry Regiment to enlist in the regular Army shortly after his graduation from Skowhegan High in 1940. He died on July 24, 1942, at Camp O'Donnell, 85 miles north of Bataan, a former American training post.

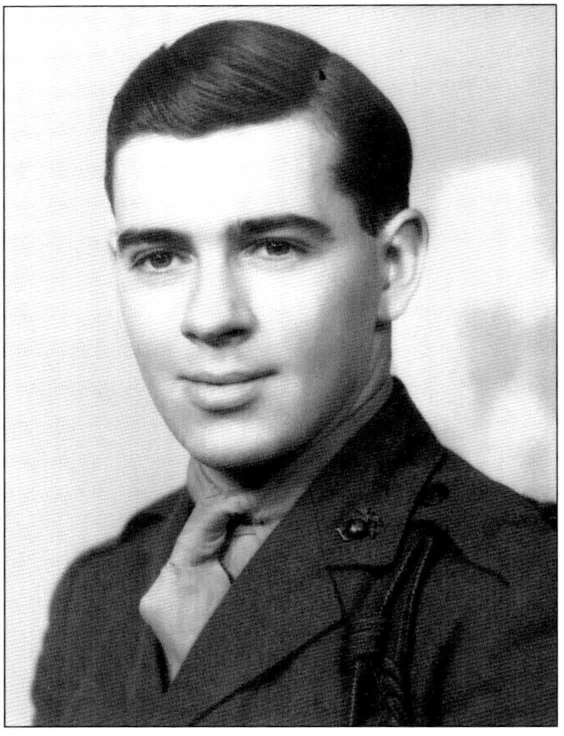

PFC Kenneth C. Cowette was killed on March 15, 1945, on Iwo Jima, one of four Skowhegan boys to die there. He was twenty-three, had enlisted two days after Pearl Harbor, and had been wounded at Guadalcanal.

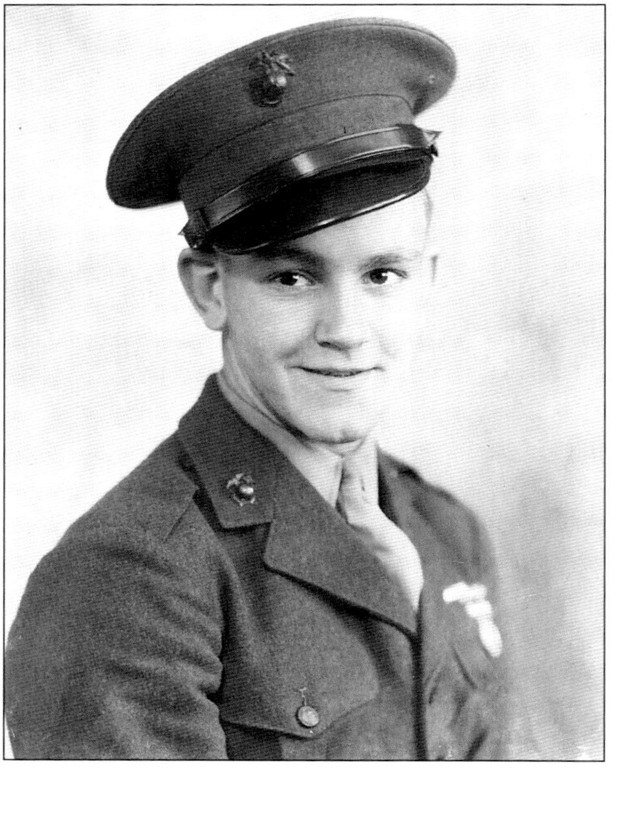

PFC Raymond E. Mercier died on March 2, 1945, on Iwo Jima. He had enlisted in the Marines only a week after his 17th birthday.

Private James A. Stoodley, killed on March 28, 1945, on Iwo Jima. A 1937 Skowhegan High graduate, he was a member of the track and basketball teams. The twenty-five year old enlisted in April 1944, and was married.

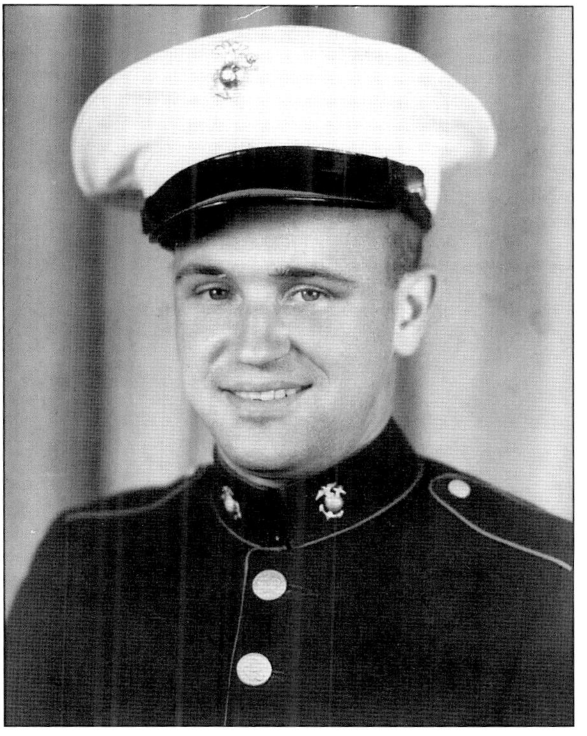

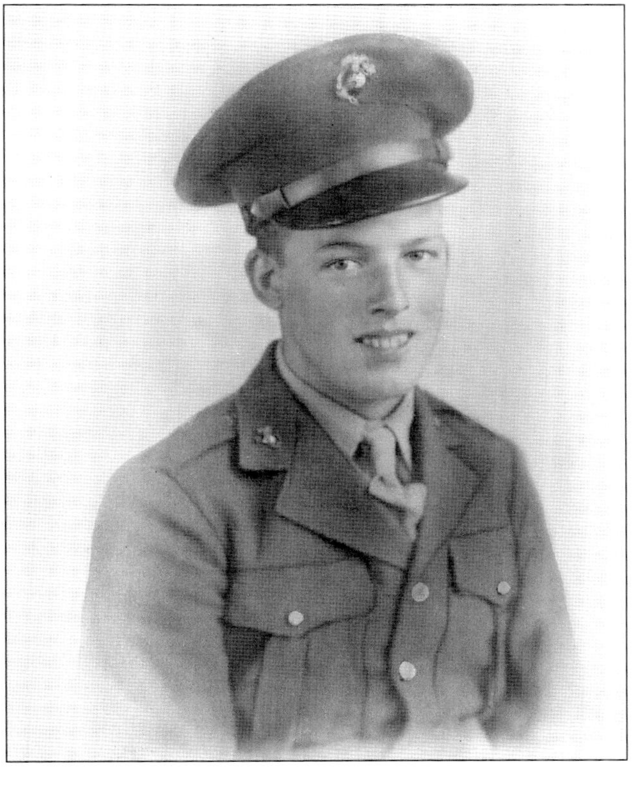

PFC Howard L. Lombard Jr., killed February 25, 1945, on Iwo Jima.

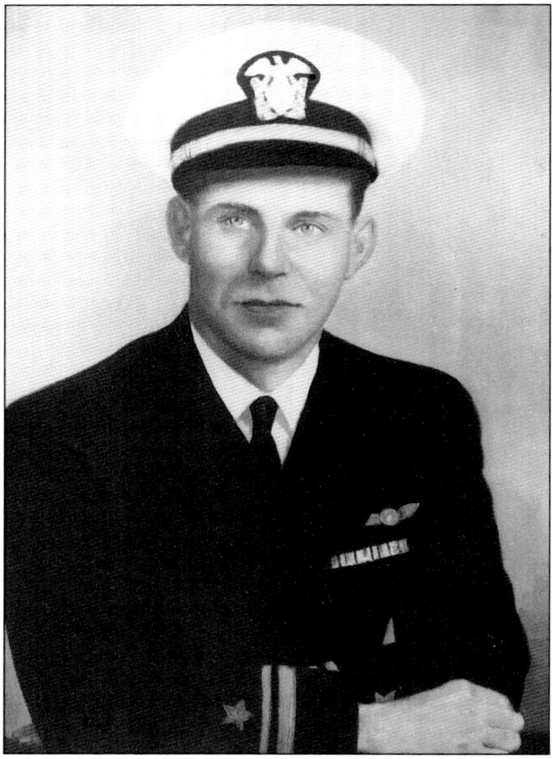

Lieutenant (JG) Norman A. Taylor died on October 22, 1944, when the PBY on which he was a crew member crashed into the Pacific. The salutatorian of the Skowhegan High Class of 1929, he was a 1934 Colby College graduate, and earned a master's degree from Columbia University in 1941. He taught four years at North Yarmouth Academy and at the Higgins Classical Institute as well as in New Hampshire and Michigan.

The telegram on the death of Lieutenant (JG) Taylor, dated January 18, 1945, almost three months after he died.

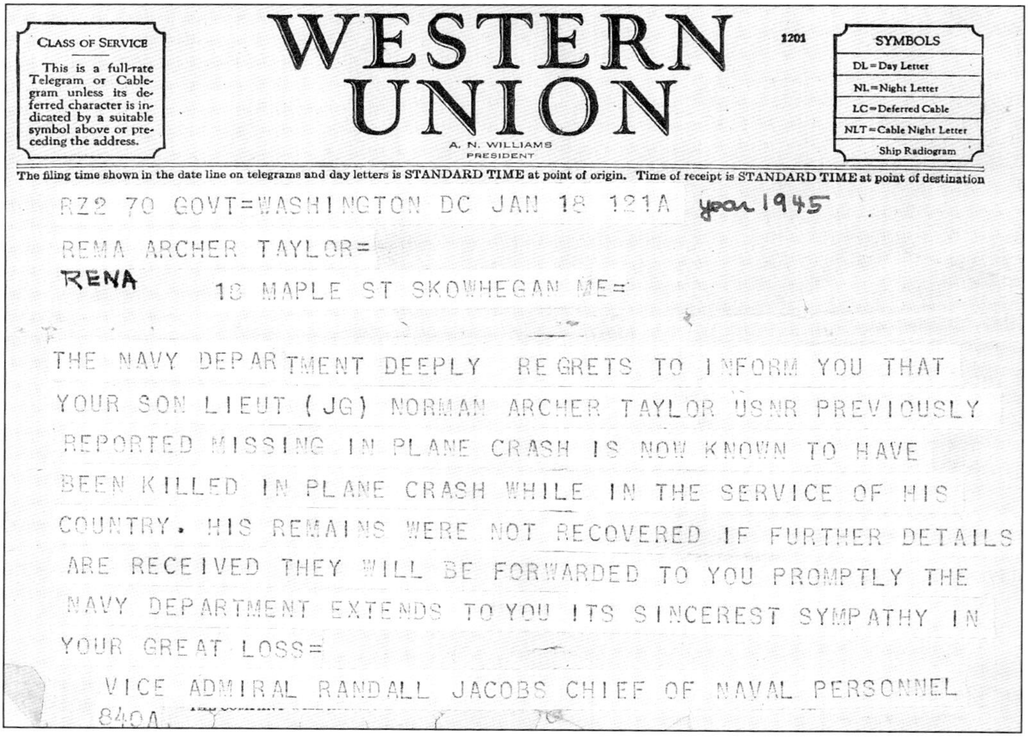

CLASS OF SERVICE

This is a full-rate Telegram or Cablegram unless its deferred character is indicated by a suitable symbol above or preceding the address.

# WESTERN UNION

A. N. WILLIAMS
PRESIDENT

1201

SYMBOLS

DL=Day Letter
NL=Night Letter
LC=Deferred Cable
NLT=Cable Night Letter
Ship Radiogram

The filing time shown in the date line on telegrams and day letters is STANDARD TIME at point of origin. Time of receipt is STANDARD TIME at point of destination

RZ2 70 GOVT=WASHINGTON DC JAN 18 121A year 1945

REMA ARCHER TAYLOR=

RENA 18 MAPLE ST SKOWHEGAN ME=

THE NAVY DEPARTMENT DEEPLY REGRETS TO INFORM YOU THAT YOUR SON LIEUT (JG) NORMAN ARCHER TAYLOR USNR PREVIOUSLY REPORTED MISSING IN PLANE CRASH IS NOW KNOWN TO HAVE BEEN KILLED IN PLANE CRASH WHILE IN THE SERVICE OF HIS COUNTRY. HIS REMAINS WERE NOT RECOVERED IF FURTHER DETAILS ARE RECEIVED THEY WILL BE FORWARDED TO YOU PROMPTLY THE NAVY DEPARTMENT EXTENDS TO YOU ITS SINCEREST SYMPATHY IN YOUR GREAT LOSS=

VICE ADMIRAL RANDALL JACOBS CHIEF OF NAVAL PERSONNEL

840A.

PFC Wendal F. Nightingale, killed June 18, 1944, on Saipan. He died three days after 21,618 Marines landed on the island. PFC Nightingale was a Maine farm boy who enlisted in the Marines in November 1942. He was twenty-one years old when he died. His parents had to wait until June 1964 before they received his Purple Heart and meritorious conduct citation.

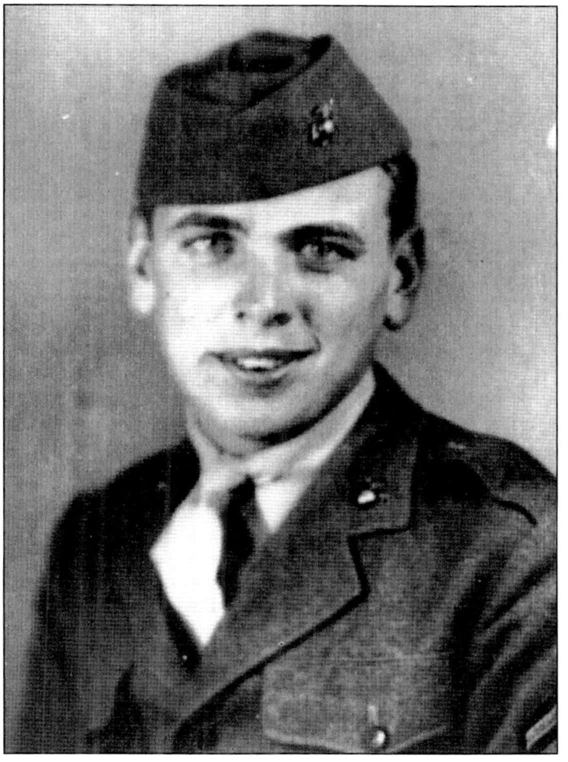

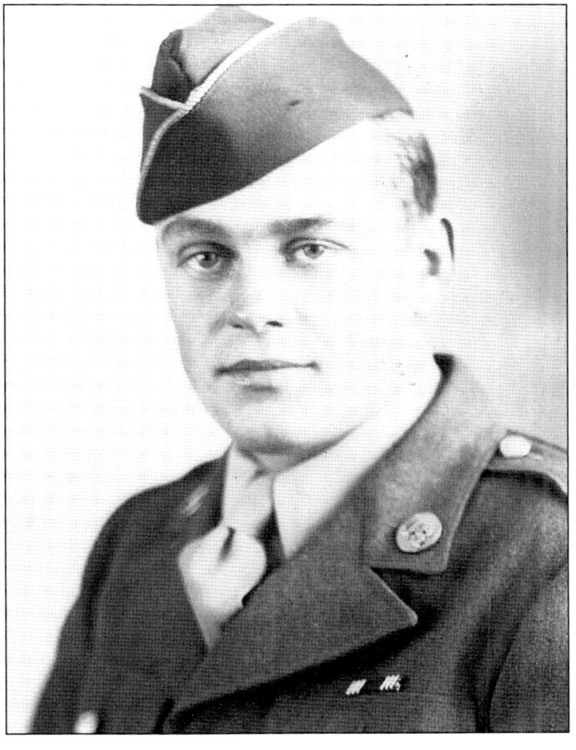

PFC Robert Arsenault, killed July 2, 1944, in Burma. Four Skowhegan boys were killed in that month. Arsenault was twenty-two when he was killed on combat duty. On furlough, he told several in Skowhegan that he feared being killed if transferred to the China-Burma-India Theater. Three of his brothers were in the service.

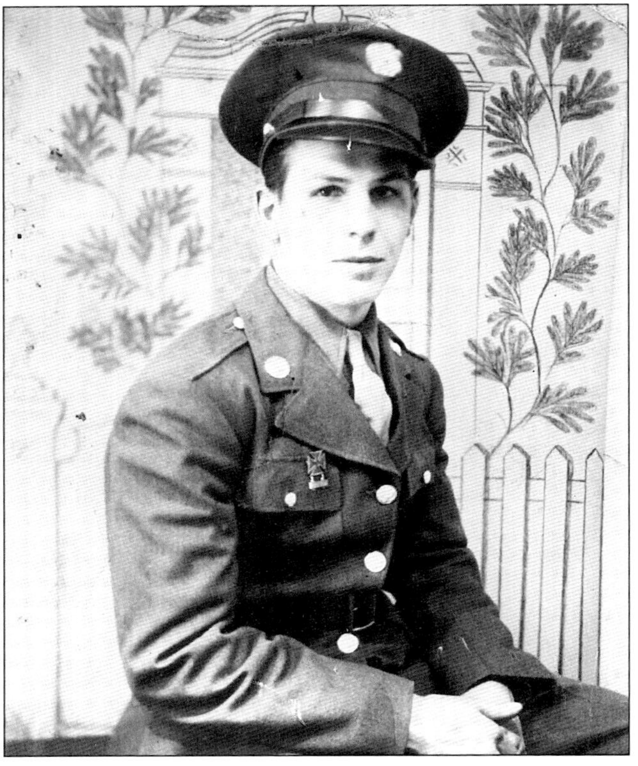

PFC Roland Jarvais, killed August 9, 1944, in Northern France. He entered the service on December 9, 1943, at the age of eighteen.

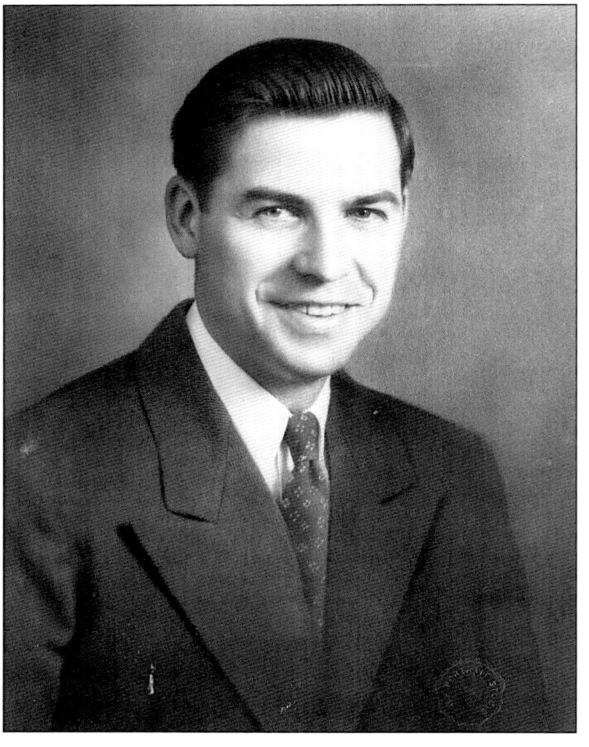

PFC Neil U. Flemming, killed April 5, 1945, in Germany.

PFC Donald A. Perry, killed May 10, 1945, on Okinawa.

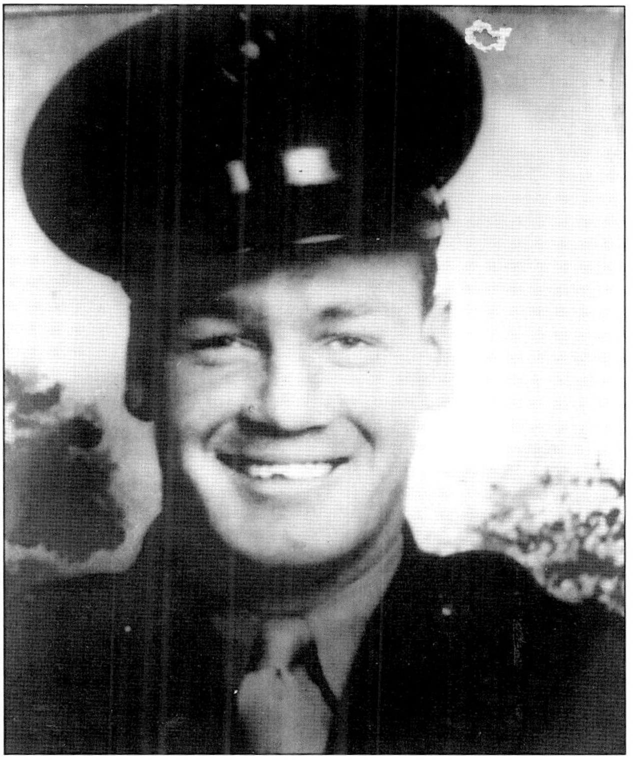

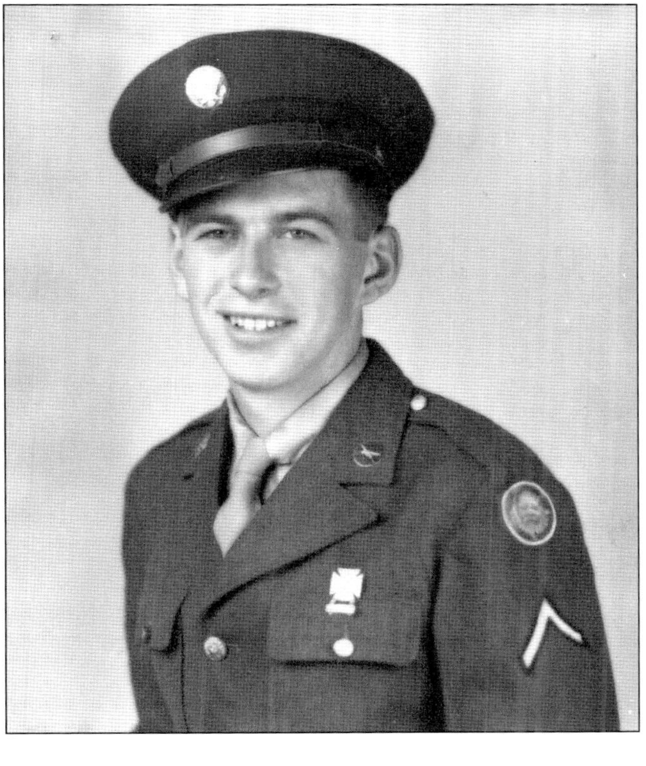

PFC Thomas J. Shortier died on November 25, 1944, in Germany. He was twenty and was killed near the Saar River. On July 23, 1944, Shortier had been seriously wounded in France, but he later rejoined his company and moved with it into Germany. He is the Shortier for whom the Peters-Shortier Post 16, American Legion, in Skowhegan is named.

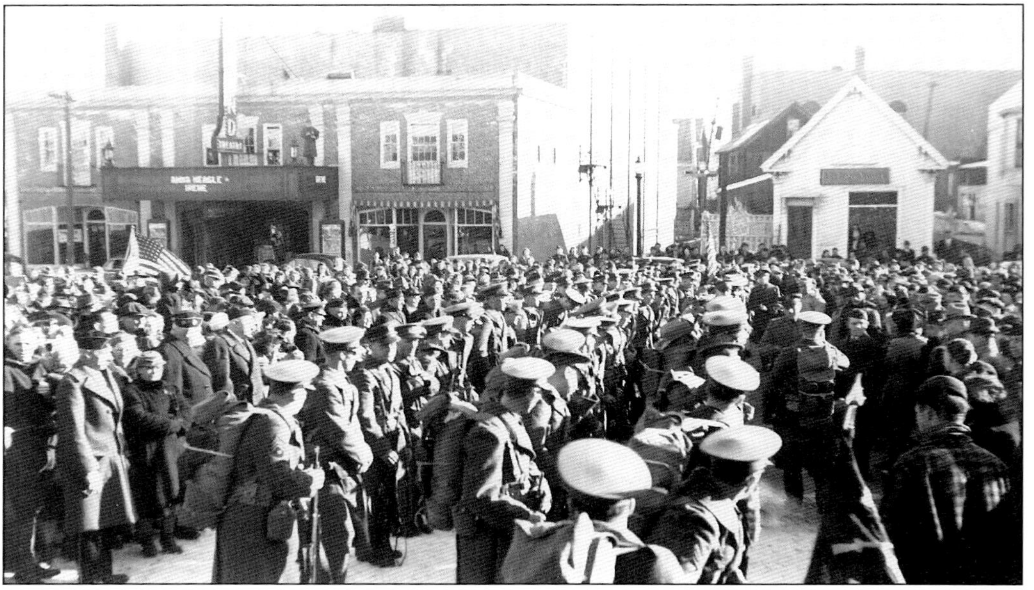

Members of Company L, 103rd Regiment, line up in the center of Skowhegan on February 24, 1941, after being called up for active duty ten months before Pearl Harbor. The Strand Theater can be seen in the left background with Alan's Cut Above Barber Shop on the right. The company was called into federal service by presidential order. Skowhegan children were let out of school to view the scene. It was a very cold day.

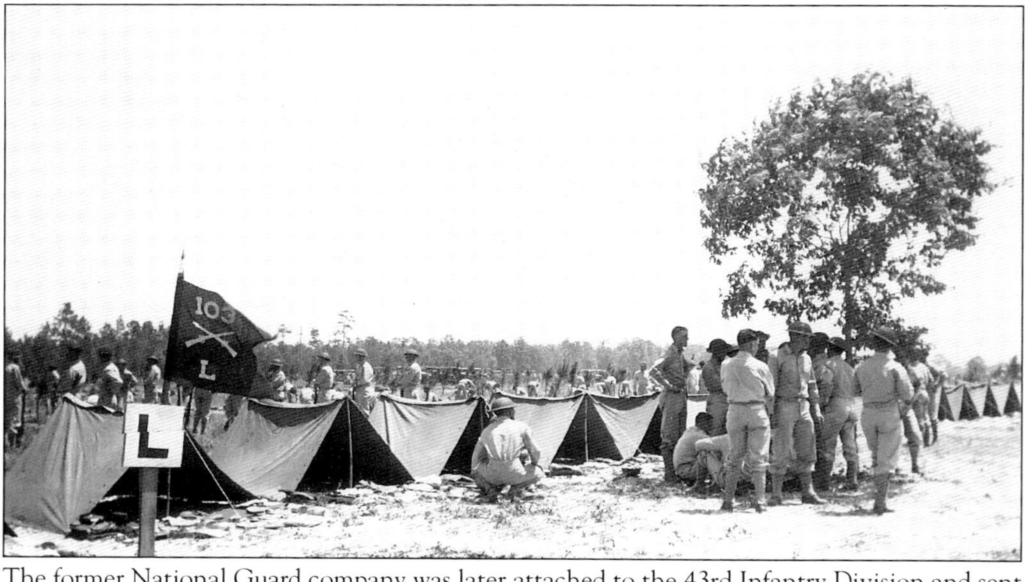


The former National Guard company was later attached to the 43rd Infantry Division and sent to the South Pacific after training. Among other places, it trained at Camp Blanding in Florida, living at first in tents. In it were individuals like Omar Pomerleau, Romeo Gallant, Leonard Pooler, Ed Tessier, Donald Bisson, Louis Boulette, and Wilbur Whitney.

# *Seven*

# Doers and Shakers

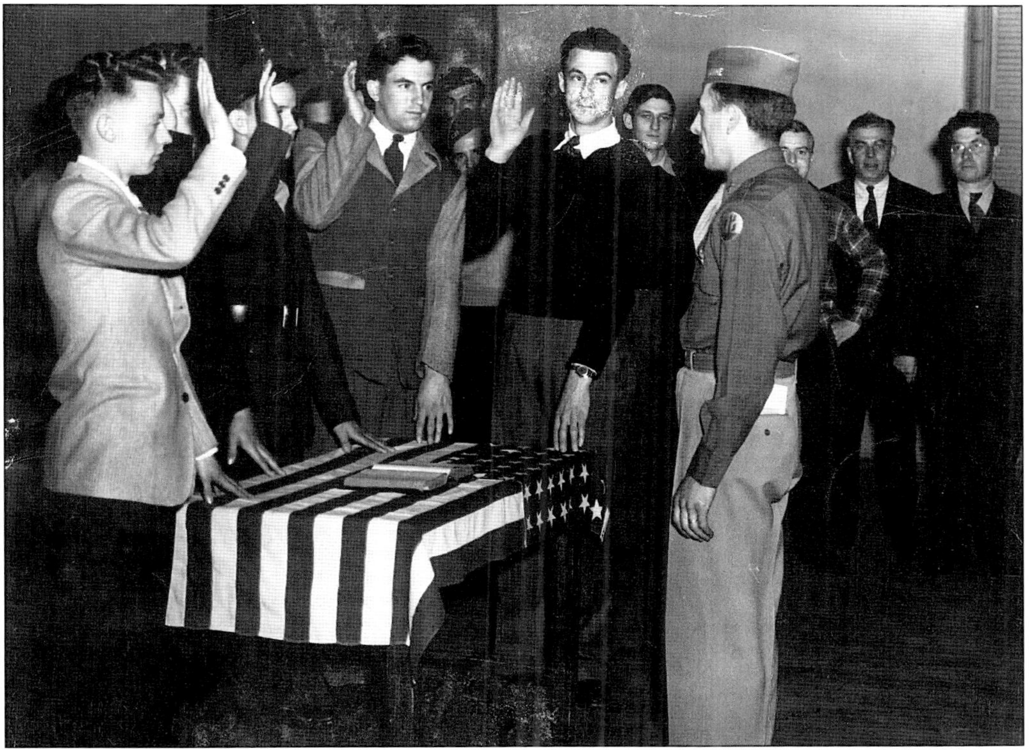

The Whittemore brothers of Skowhegan are sworn into service in World War II. From left to right are Carlton, Alton, Kendall (Joe), Warren, and Henry. All were successful businessmen.

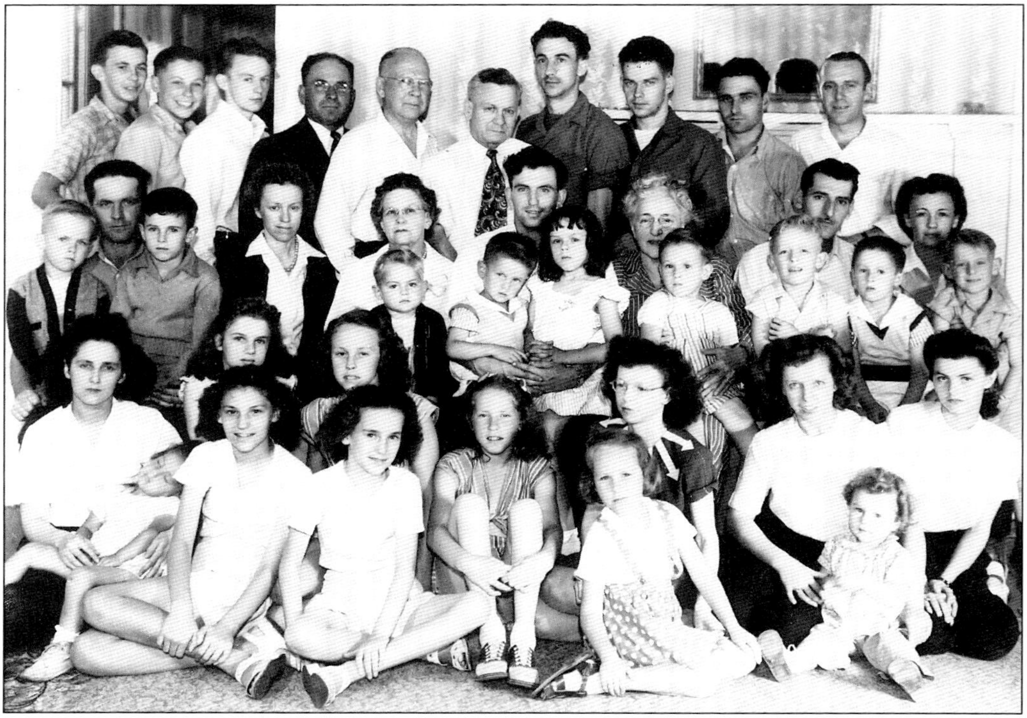

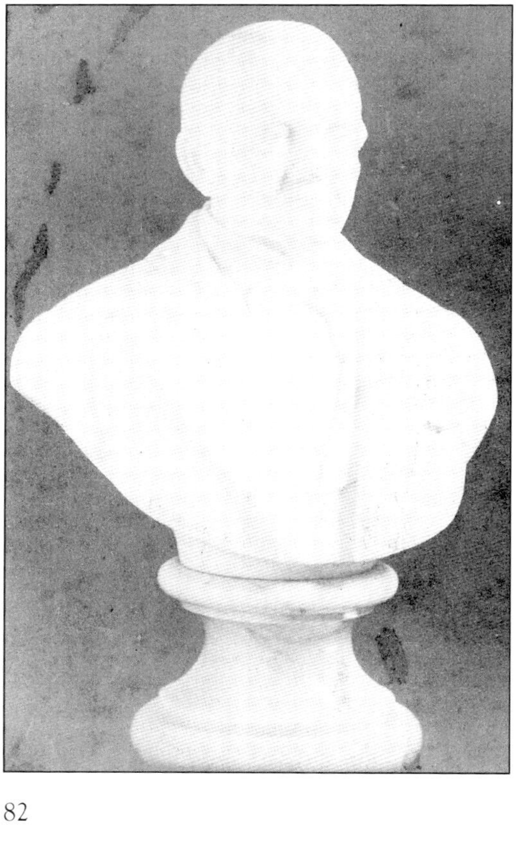

A Whittemore family reunion in the summer of 1946. From left to right are: (front row) Paula Henderson, Connie Cornell, Diane Byron, Frances Greenlaw, Nancy Clement, and Linda Whittemore; (second row) Virginia Whittemore, Mary Davies, Alice Thibeault, Marguerite Richardson, Lauretta Whittemore, and Lucille Whittemore; (third row) James Cahill holding Doug Cahill and Wardell Whittemore, Altena Cahill, Gertrude Cates holding Carlton Whittemore Jr., Henry Whittemore holding John Whittemore and Caroline Henderson, Marguerite Whittemore holding Terry Whittemore, Edward Giroux holding Gary Richardson and David Whittemore, and Katherine Giroux holding Kendall Richardson; (back row) Wallace Giroux, James Cahill Jr., Carlton Whittemore Sr., Carroll Whittemore, William Whittemore, Alton Whittemore, Kendall Whittemore, Alton Whittemore Jr., Warren Whittemore, and Clayton Richardson.

Former Governor Abner Coburn of Skowhegan.

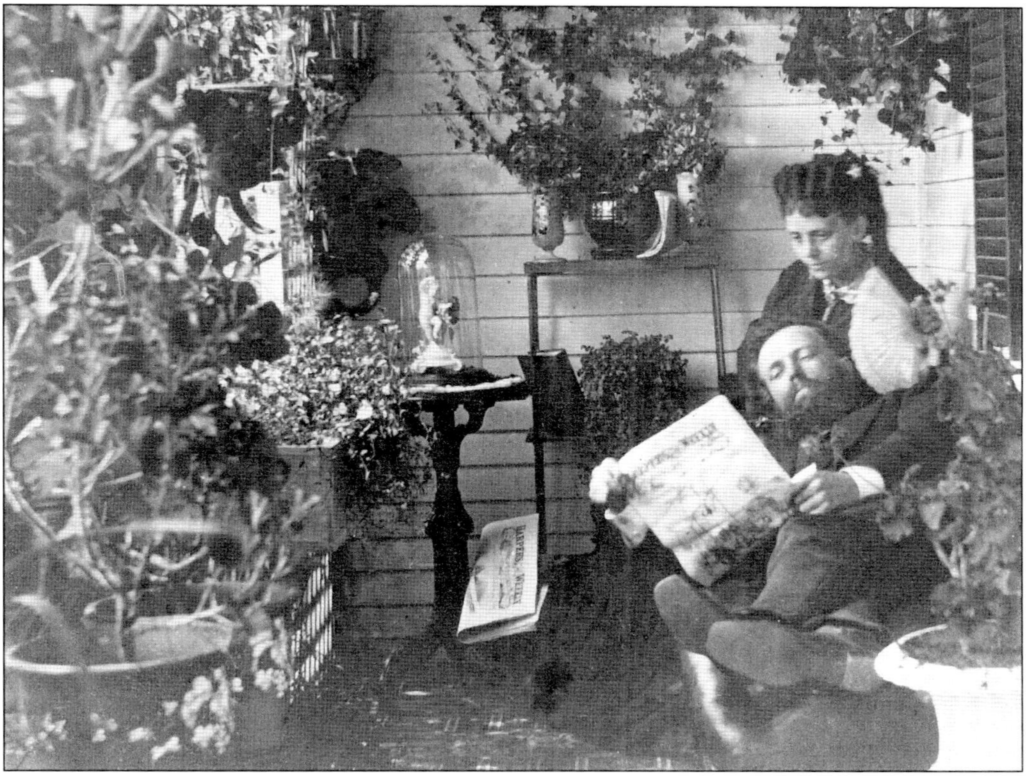

A self-portrait of S.S. Vose, Skowhegan photographer, and his wife.

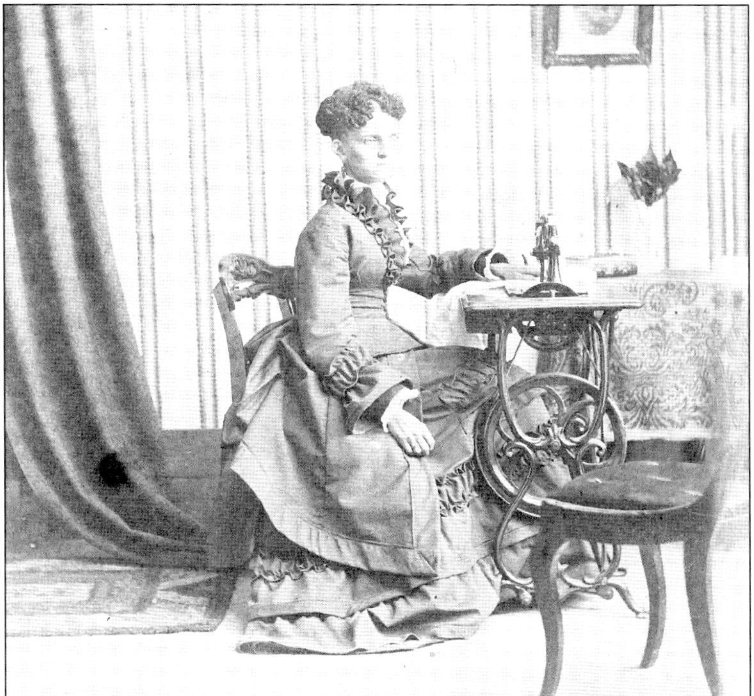

Mrs. S.S. Vose sits and sews.

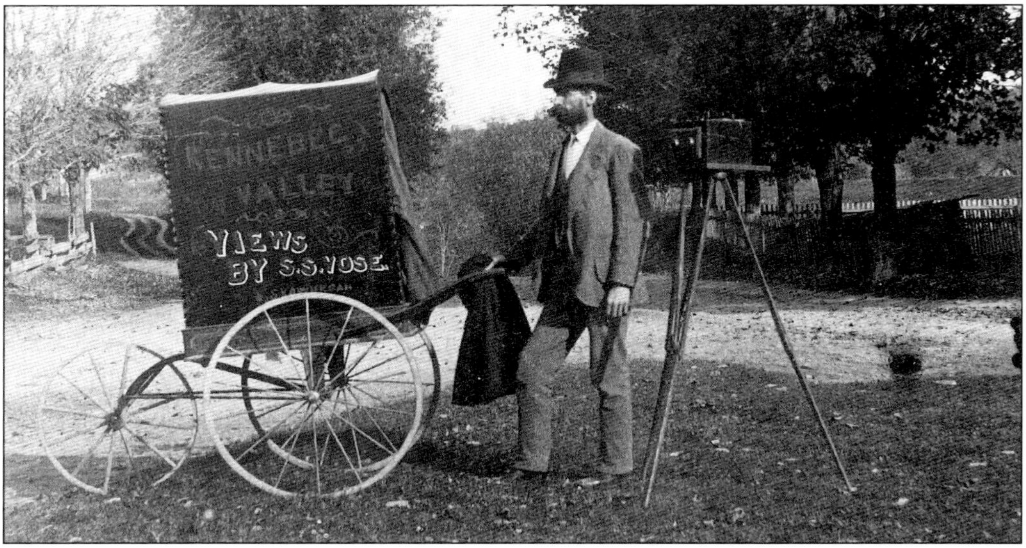


S.S. Vose standing by his little photo wagon.

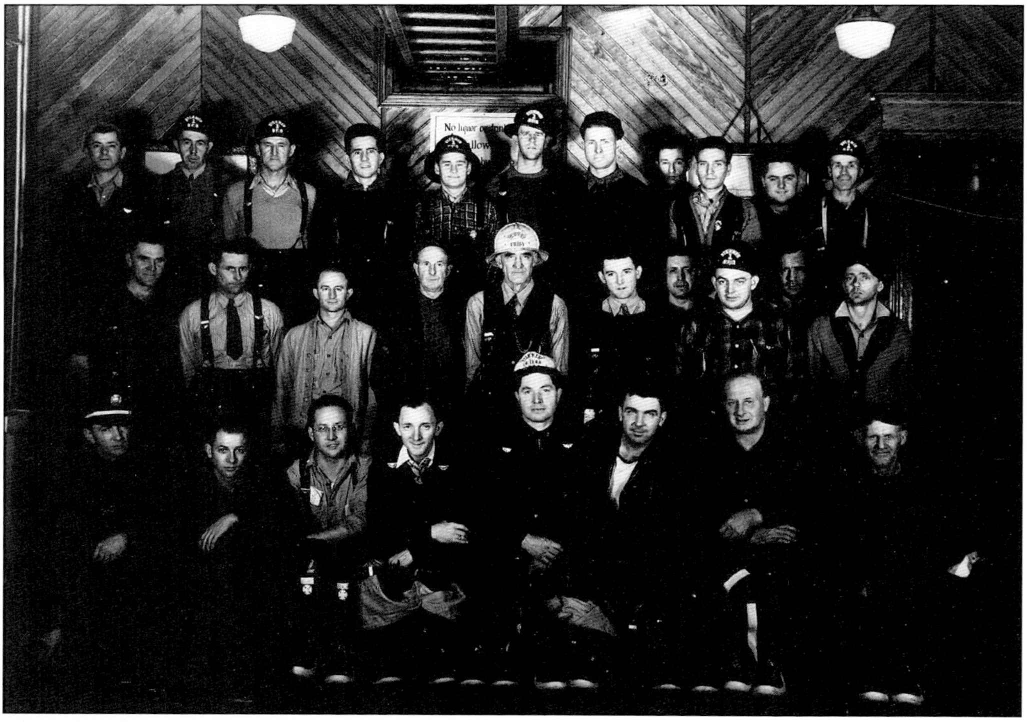

The Skowhegan Fire Department, *c.* 1935. From left to right are: (front row) Linwood Meader, Donald Dugas, Sebastian Roderick, Frank Fortier, Walter Thornhill, Harold Brown, John Dugas, and Arthur Gibbs; (middle row) Lee Savage, Louis Paradis, Henry Valliere, Olin Valliere, Charles Griffin, Herbert Paradis, Erland Mullen, Winthrop Morrell, Curlie Kew, and Orville Butler; (back row) Raymond Pooler, William Lebroke, Walter Ames, Wilfred Paradis, Andrew Mack, Arnold Libby, Lester Kyes, Kenneth Dore, Henry Ricker, Francis Roderick, and ? Fish.

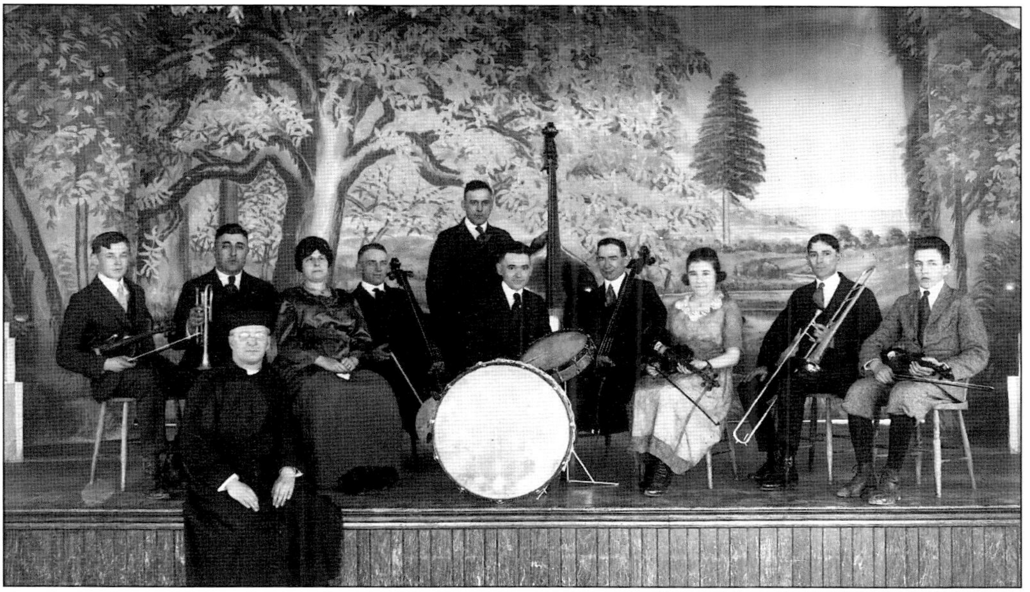

The St. Cecilia Orchestra, Notre Dame de Lourdes Church, Water Street, Skowhegan. Father Renaud is in front, and from left to right are Willard Dunbar, Andrew Lessard, Mrs. Rose Borden, Roy Pooler, Alton Roderick, Walter Murray, Cecile Lessard, Harry Murray, and Hector Chabot. This is a *c.* 1920s photograph.

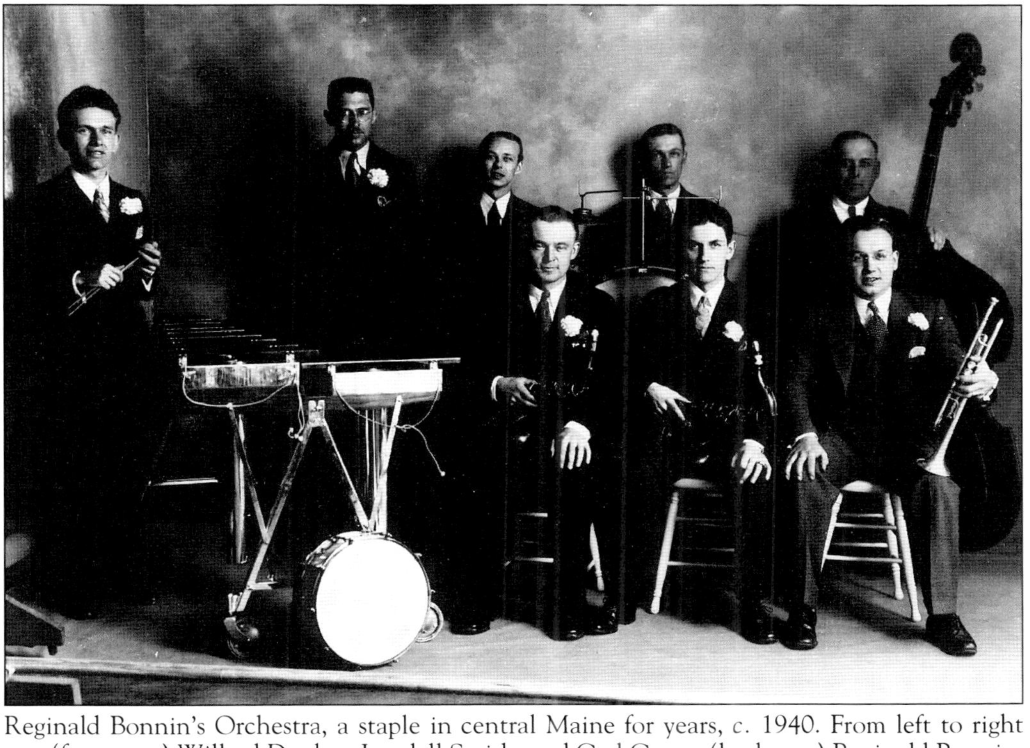

Reginald Bonnin's Orchestra, a staple in central Maine for years, *c.* 1940. From left to right are: (front row) Willard Dunbar, Lyndall Smith, and Carl Croce; (back row) Reginald Bonnin, Claude Bouchard, Gordon Chipman, Charley Moore, Carl Russell, and Alton Roderick.

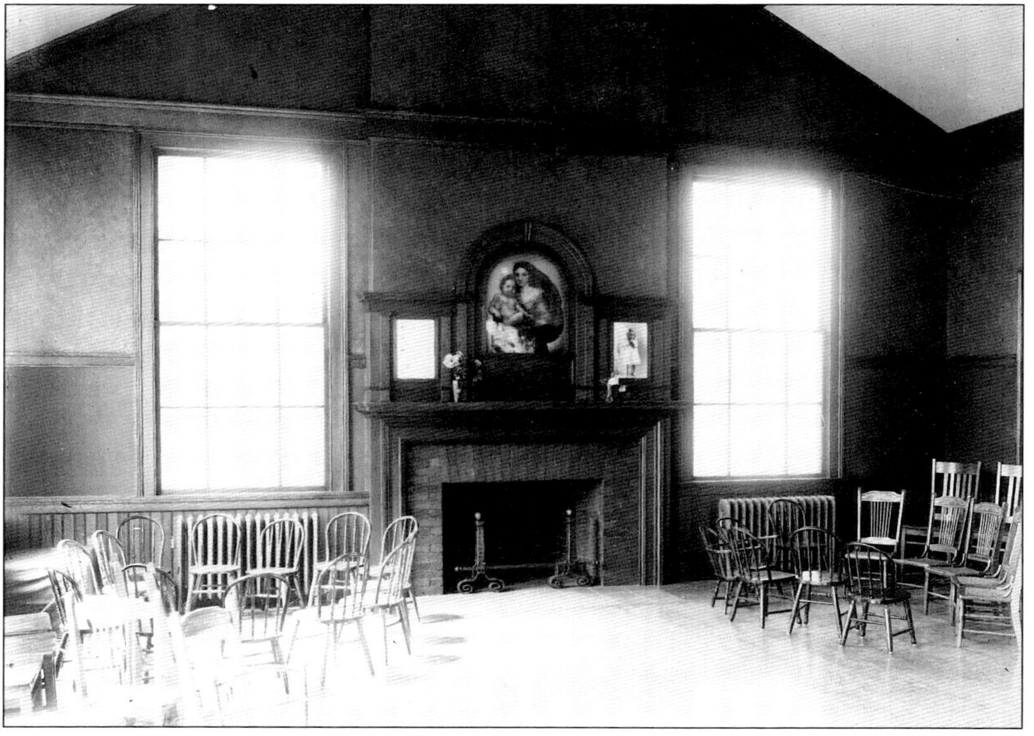

The Primary Room was built on the rear of Bethany Church by Dr. and Mrs. George Otis Smith in memory of their daughter, Elizabeth Coburn Smith, who died at the age of six from rheumatism that had derived from tonsillitis.

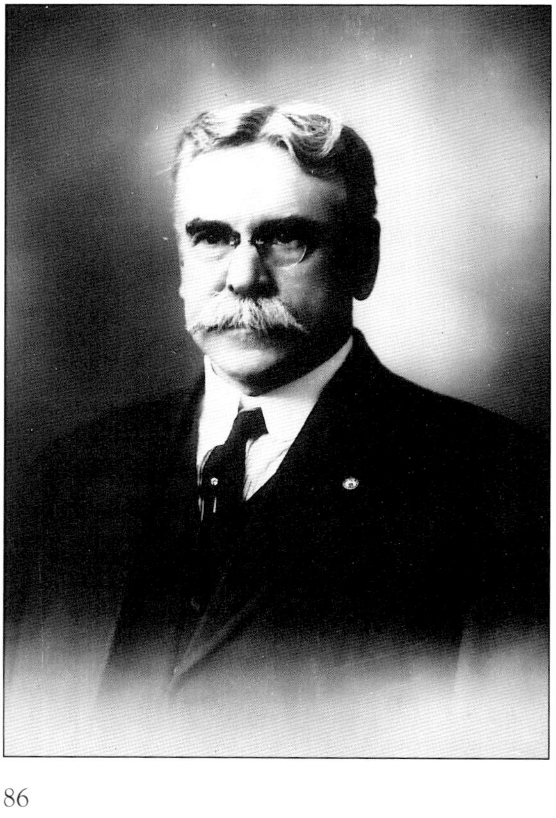

Dr. Leander Almarin Dascombe, who practiced in Skowhegan from 1884 to 1931.

# *Eight*

# Sports

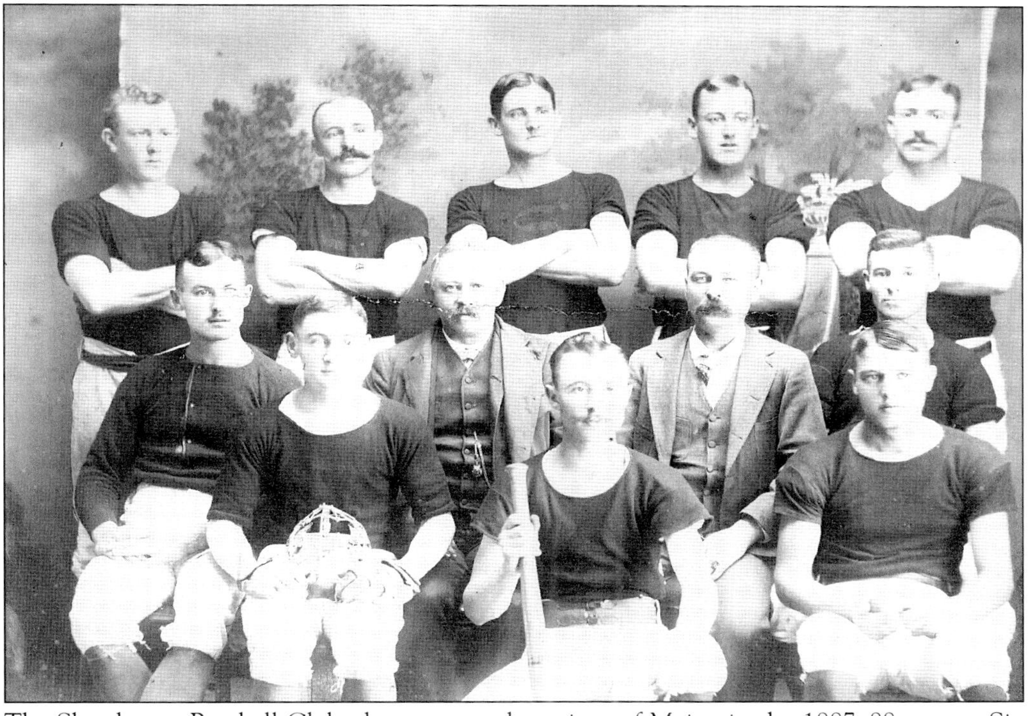

The Skowhegan Baseball Club, the amateur champions of Maine in the 1887–88 season. Six state championships were held in Skowhegan that year: the rifle team, half-mile bicycle, mile bicycle, three-mile bicycle, and bicycle team championships were the other five. From left to right are: (front row) Ned Matthews, right field and sub; W.L. Pushor, catcher; Ed Leach, president of the Skowhegan Baseball Association; W.P. Goodwin, infield; George W. Hawes, manager; George Simpson, left field; and John Russell, pitcher; (back row) E.F. Goodwin, third base; E.P. King, shortstop; Fred Hobbs, first base; Will Tufts, center field; and A. Lumsden, second base.

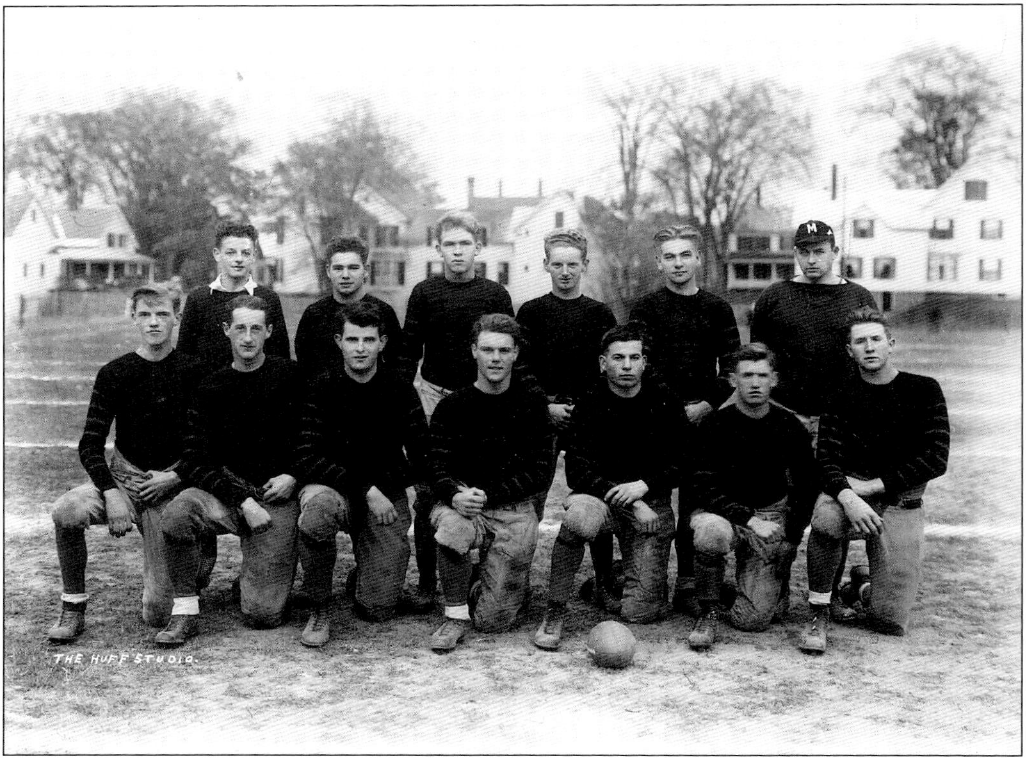


The Skowhegan High football team was once coached by Bernard "Mose" Johnston, who later became chief executive of the Maine Publicity Bureau. He is on the right in back. From left to right are: (front row) Ray Blethen, Phillip Tozier, Clifton Sargent, Linwood Nutting, Dean Flemming, Harland "Toad" McGowan, and Bernard Foster; (back row) Wallace Bilodeau, Oran Atkinson, Rabbit Oddy, Bucky ?, Hector Thibeault, and Johnston.

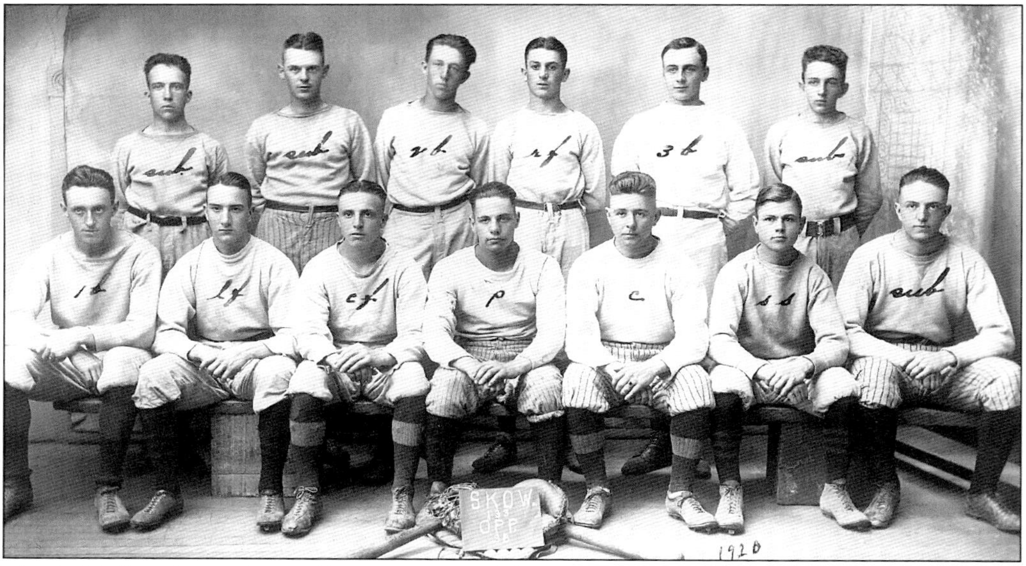


The 1920 Skowhegan baseball team outscored the opposition 133–38.

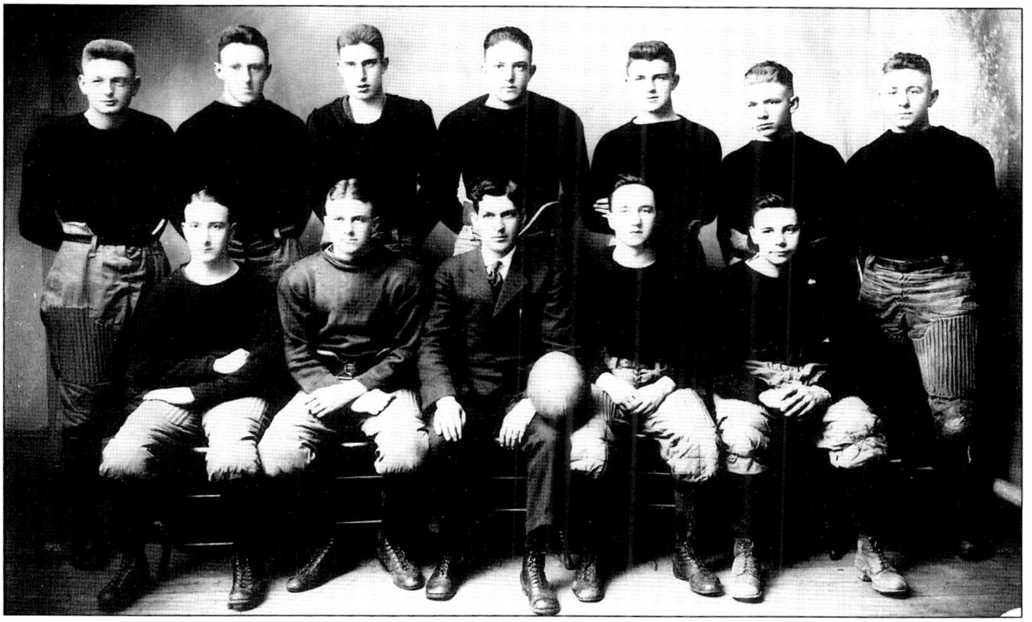

The 1919 Skowhegan High football team, three years after Margaret Chase graduated and a year after she coached the girls' basketball team. From left to right are: (front row) Lawrence Cockburn, Fred Chase, Frank Madden, Roy McDonald, and Ben Lewia; (back row) Kenneth Smiley, Errol Buker, Leland Currier, William Philbrick, Mylon Jacobs, Cecil Briggs, and Fay Studley.

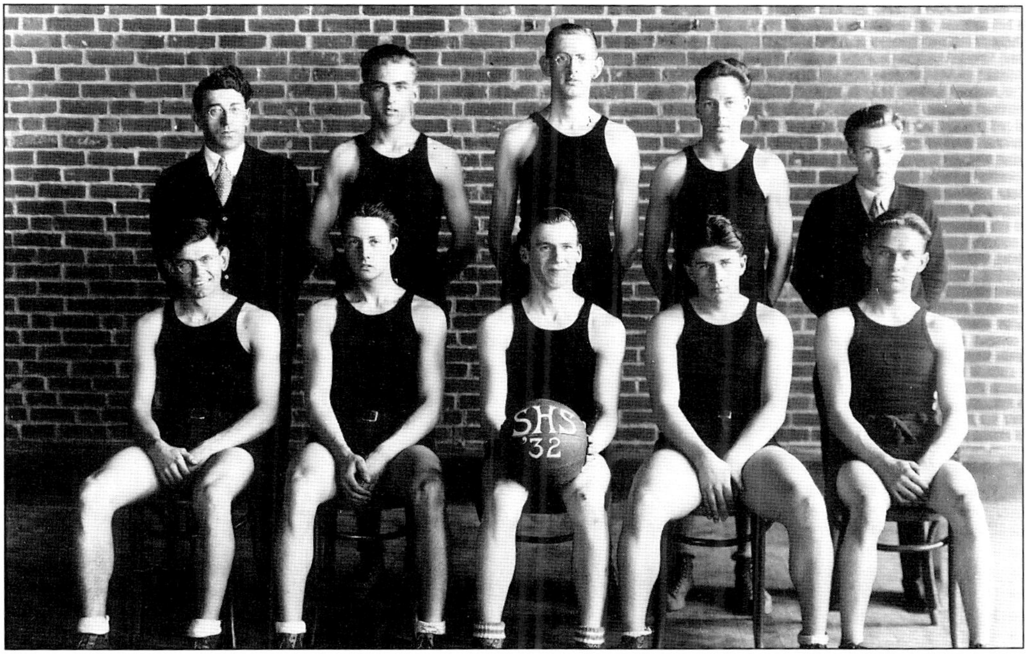


The 1932 Skowhegan High boys' basketball team consisted of: (front row) Lionel Hallee, Joe Viles, unknown, unknown, and Harold Boardman; (back row) coach Archie Dostie, Carmen Gardiner, unknown, Phil Hoyt, and Bob Pratt.

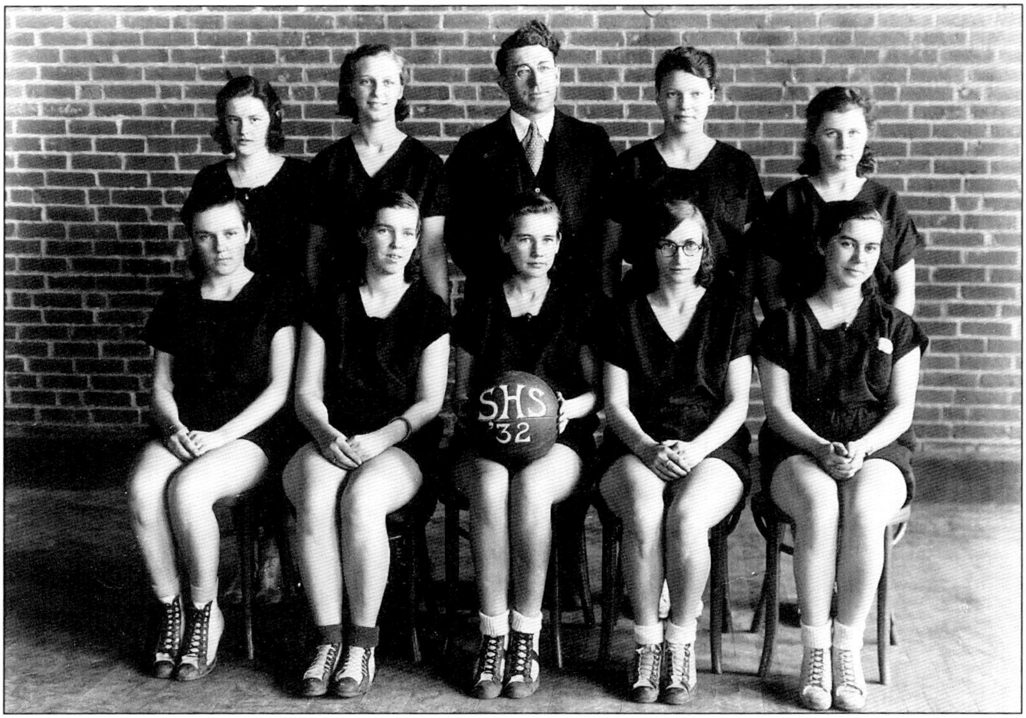


The 1932 Skowhegan High girls' basketball team, with Archie Dostie as coach. A legend, Dostie coached both boys' and girls' teams.

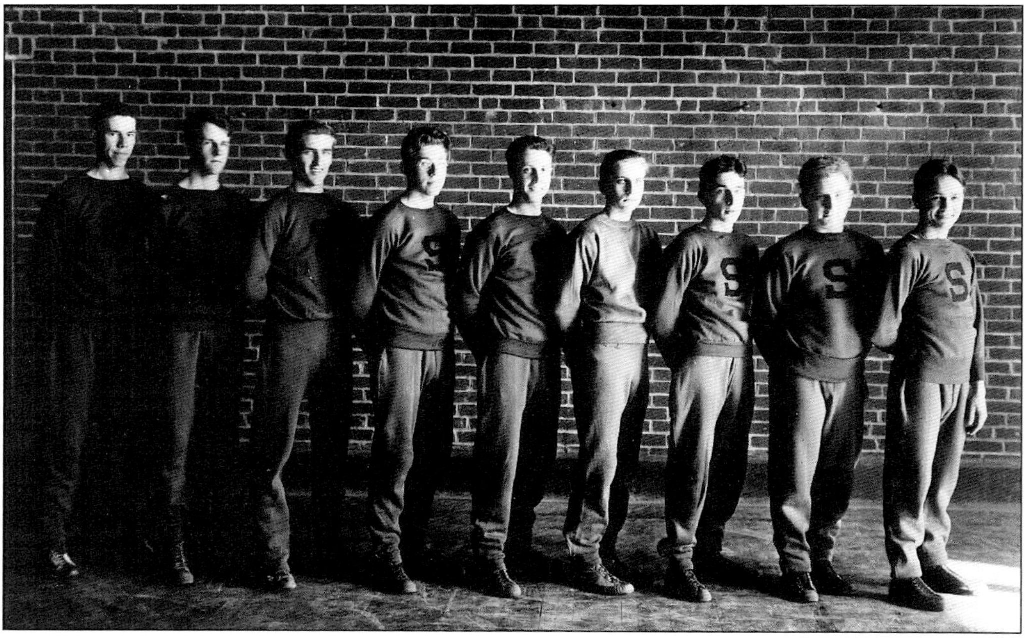

The 1933 Skowhegan High boys' basketball team. There was no posing here. From left to right are Lloyd Edwards, Arnold Libby, Carmen Gardiner, Blynn Packard, John Plummer, Elwood Gordon, William "Torchy" Lessard, Frank Lipman, and Jim Stinchfield.

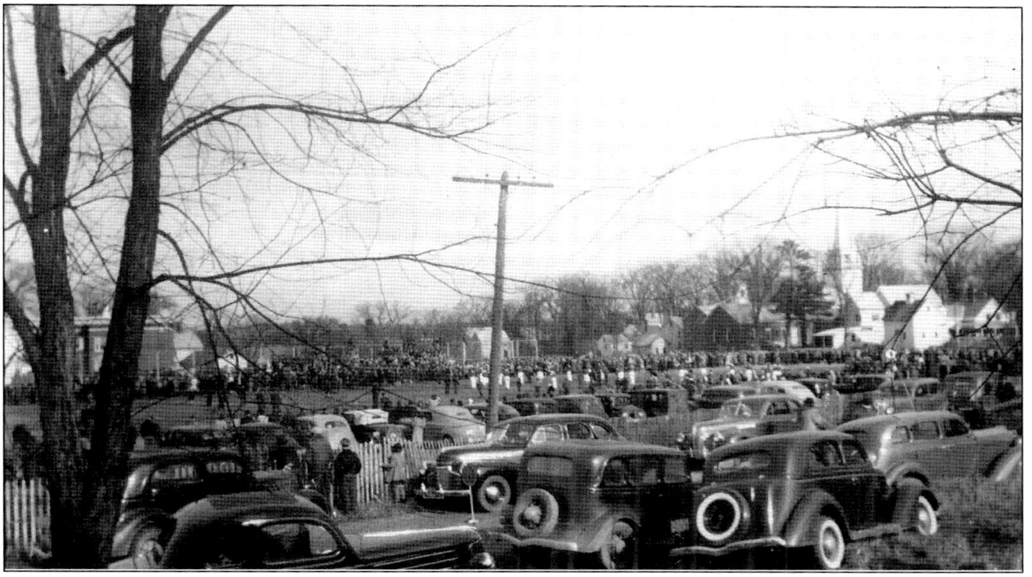

A football game in 1941 at the Skowhegan High School field. The field is no longer used by the school.

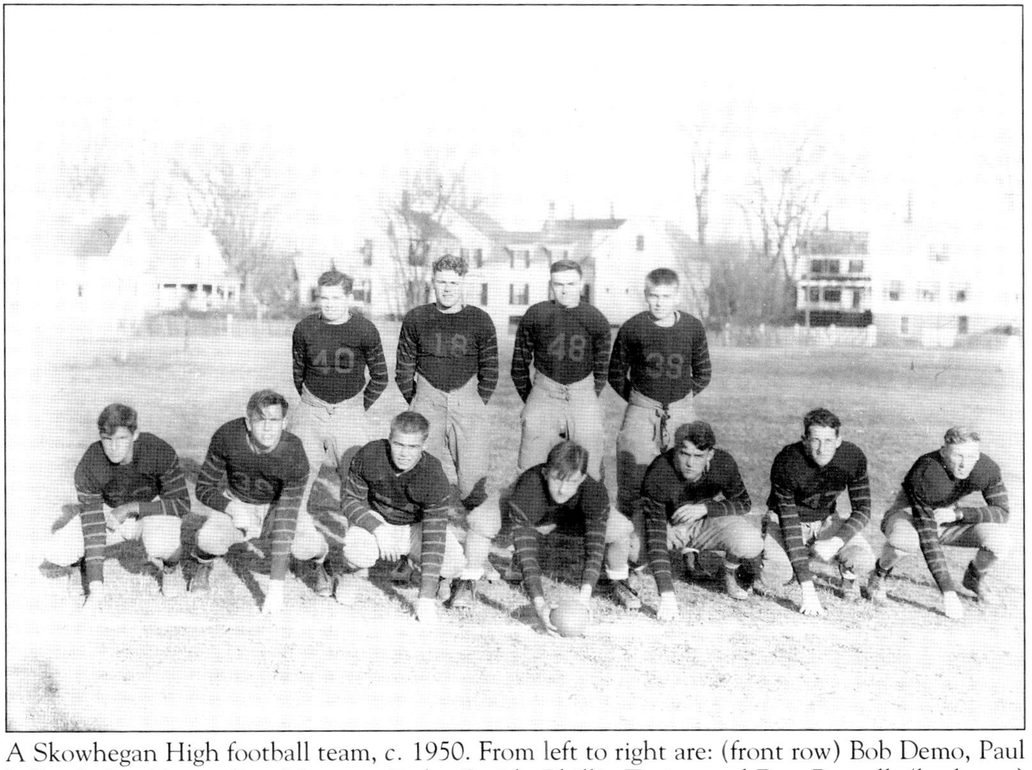

A Skowhegan High football team, *c.* 1950. From left to right are: (front row) Bob Demo, Paul LaFond, Ray Demo, Roy Marston, Perley Smith, Phillip Tozier, and Don Brunell; (back row) Oran Atkinson, Linwood Nutting, James Perkins, and Hector Thibeault.

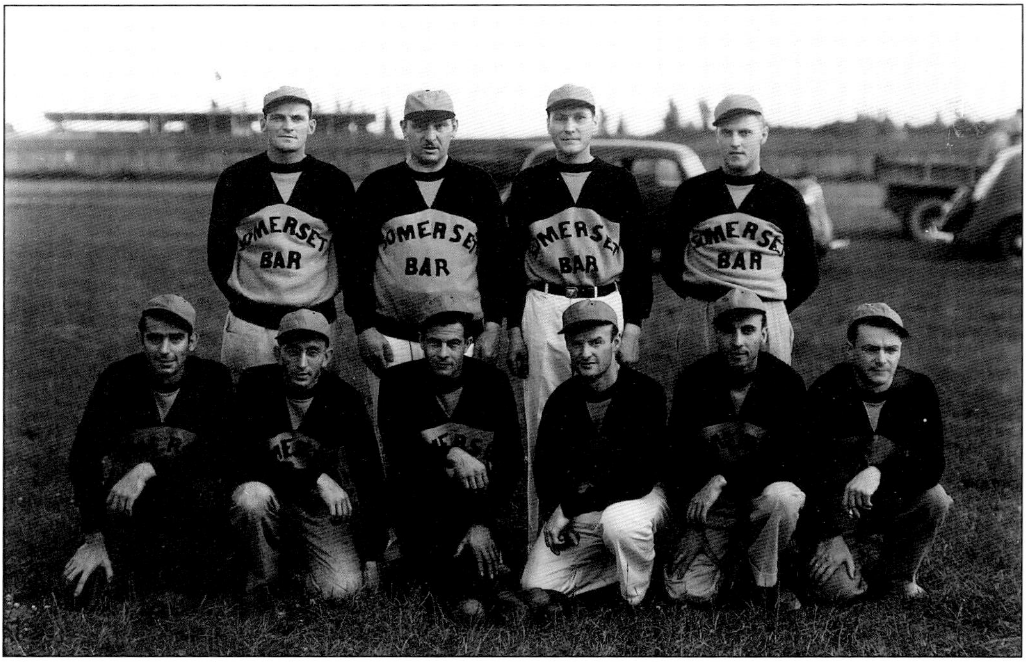


The Somerset Bar baseball team, *c.* 1940s. From left to right are: (front row) Darky Lachon, Alonzo Bilodeau, ? Oliver, Leon Plourde, Froggy Dionne, and Pete Lewia: (back row) Louie Ratheal, Al Dansereau, Paul Sirois, and Fred Violette.

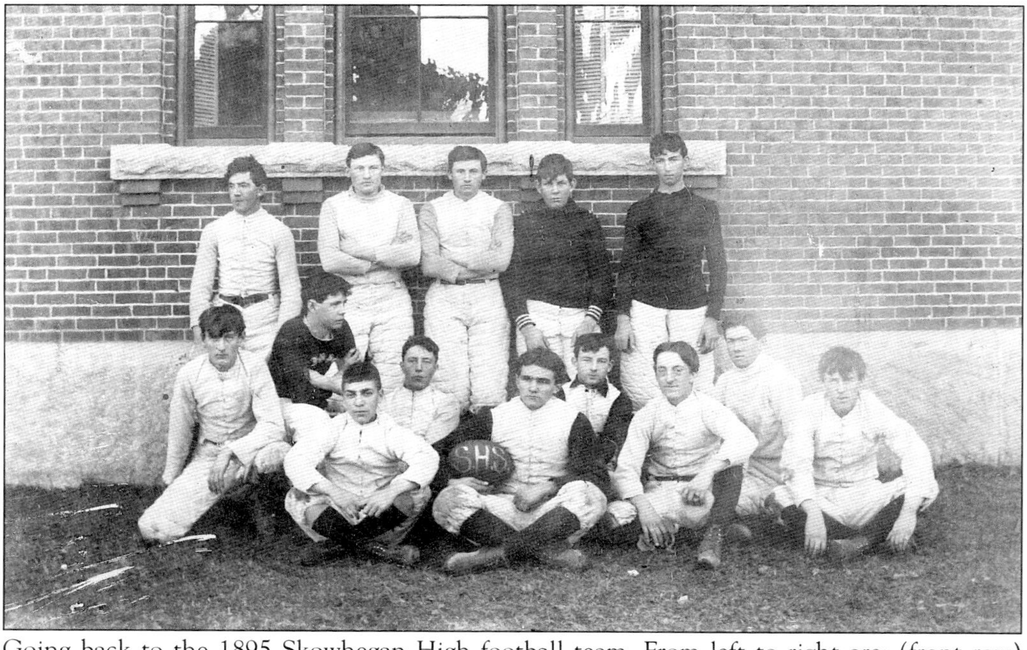


Going back to the 1895 Skowhegan High football team. From left to right are: (front row) Harold C. Woodbury, J. Wallace Blunt, Tom Lyons, John Swain, Charles Whittier, Harold Hanson, Roy L. Marston, Edward P. Barry, and Joe Lawley; (back row) C. Wesley Grover, Charles R. Viles, Marshall Viles, Norris Trafton, and Bert Avare.

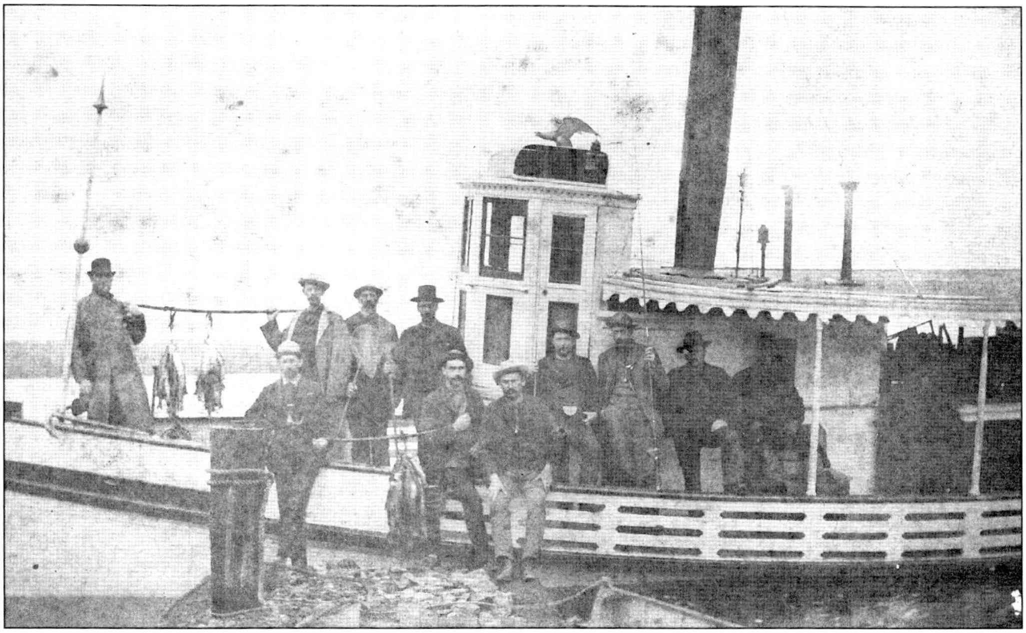

Fishing on the Kennebec River from a small steamer in the 1880s or 1890s.

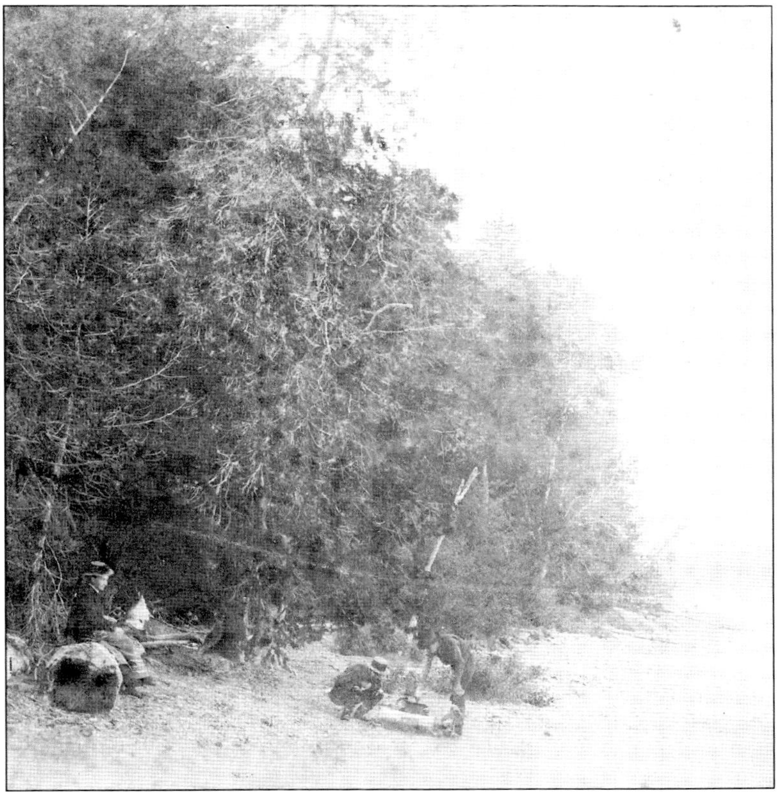

A canoe landing on the Kennebec. Two men are making coffee while another apparently rests on a log. It was all part of leisure activity.

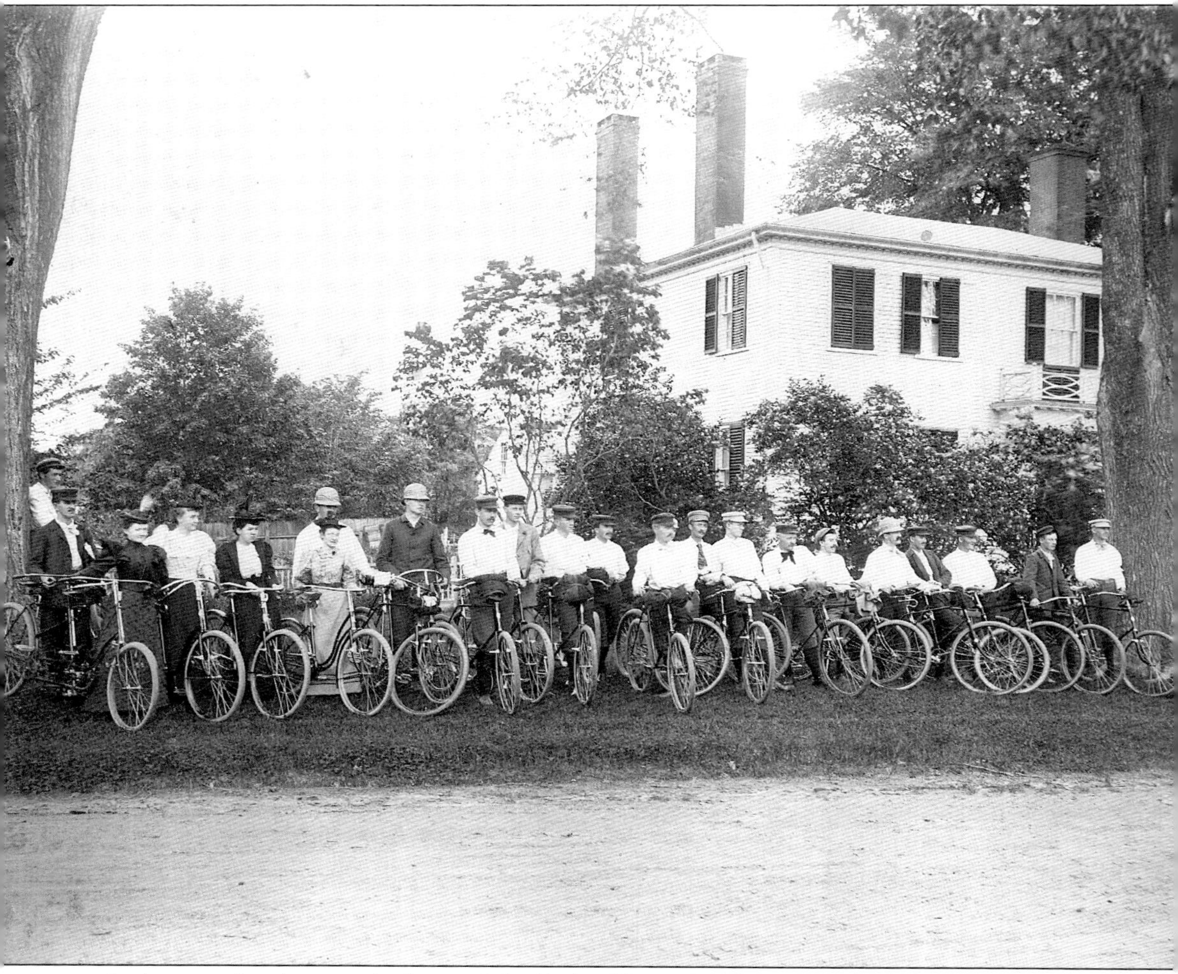

A photograph taken on the lawn of the Parlin House on Elm Street about 1892. The property was later owned by the American Woolen Company. There are nineteen bicycles and riders. From left to right are: Fred C. Dow, Ed and Grace Wentworth Durrell, Gertrude Goodwin (Owen), Elizabeth Williams (Dyer), Eolia Bray (Holmes), Roland T. Patten, Tom Farrand, unknown, Harry Cushing, Horace Bickford, James Lumsden, Ned Lambert, Charles Ward, Ernest Avare, Nay Varney, Harold C. Woodbury, and Linwood Day.

# *Nine*

# Before Margaret

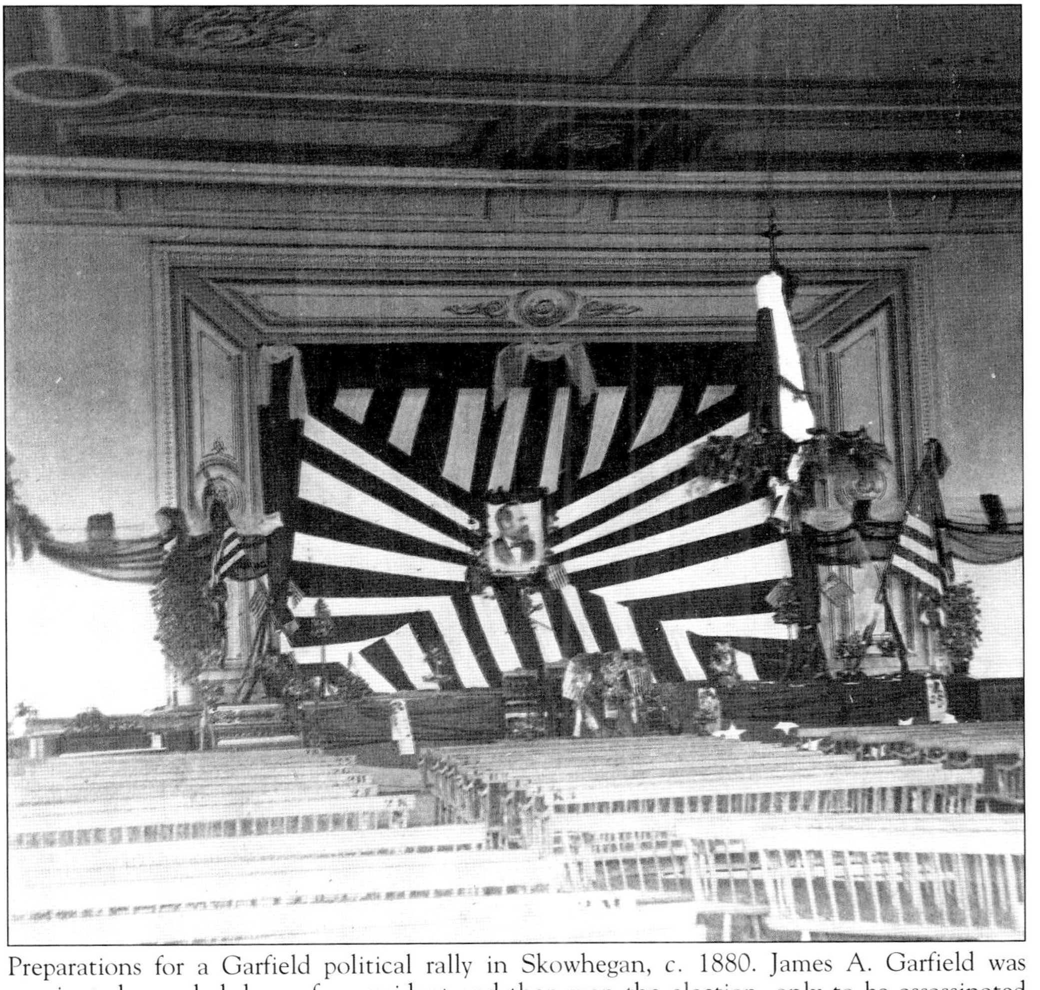

Preparations for a Garfield political rally in Skowhegan, c. 1880. James A. Garfield was nominated as a dark horse for president and then won the election, only to be assassinated in 1881.

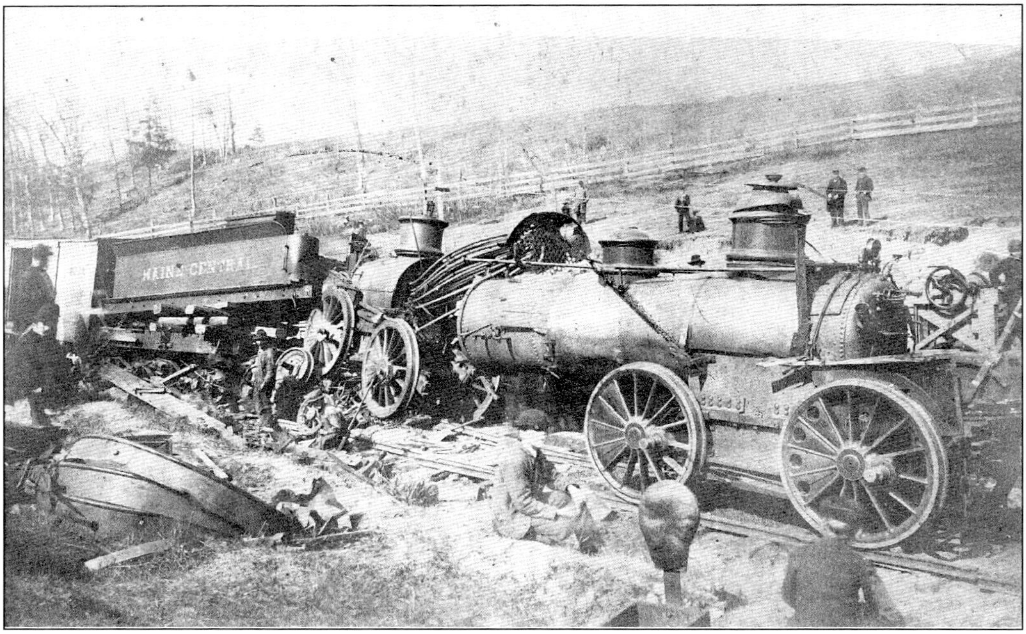


A Maine Central train wreck in Skowhegan, *c.* 1890s.

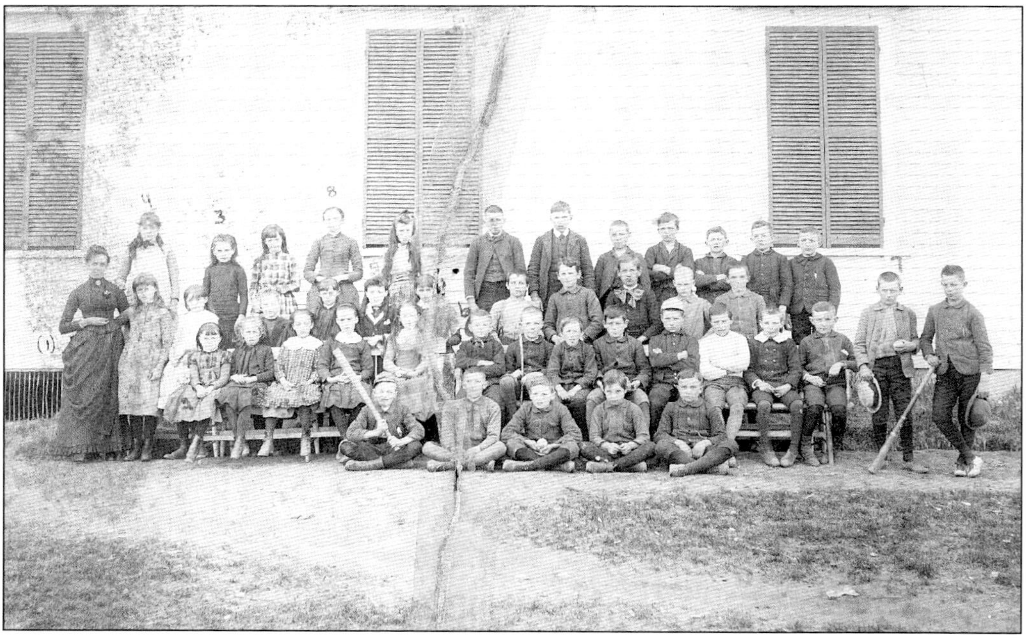

The Leavitt Street School in 1886. Number "one" is May Pollard, the teacher. The others are Vivian Graves (Woodbury), two; May Dascombe (Bowman), three; Belle Estes, four; Mamie Clough, five; Harry Graves, six; Harold Woodbury, seven; and Grace Ford, eight.

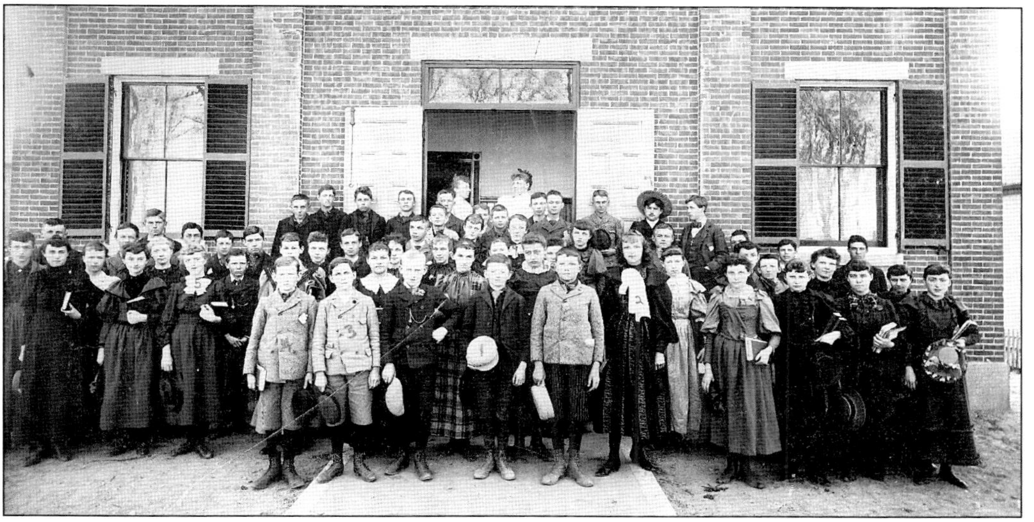

Bloomfield Academy on Baptist Hill, Skowhegan, *c.* 1890s. Teachers Mary Ward and Ruth Cushing are at the rear. In the first row, the boy with the cap in his hand is Harry Graves. Leva Copeland is the girl with the white tie, while Carl Curtis is the boy with his hat in his hand. In the second row, Hattie Marble is the girl with the big white bow, and Gertrude Carter is diagonally behind Harry Graves. Seymour Rawles is the boy with the sombrero-like hat in the back row.

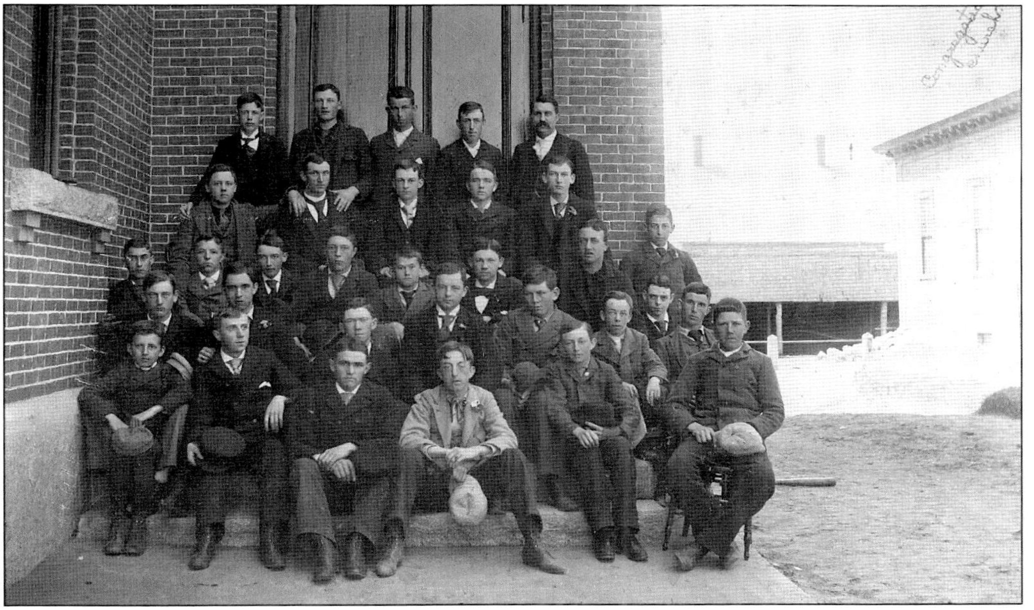

Skowhegan High on the Island in 1894. From left to right are: (front row) Fred F. Lawrence, Walter Harding, Charles Whittier, Roy Marston, Basil Jordan, and Wilbur Palmer; (second row) Harold Woodbury, unknown, Ed Barry, Harold Hanson, Norris Trafton, and Lorenzo Thompson; (third row) Harold Phillips, Chester Mills, Maurice Pratt, John Swain, Howard Wyman, Will Whittemore, Dana Lawrence, and Charles Allen; (fourth row) Will Clough, Richard Sprague, Leon Gage, unknown, and unknown; (back row) Wallace Blunt, Charles Viles, Bert Avare, unknown, and Dana W. Hall (principal).

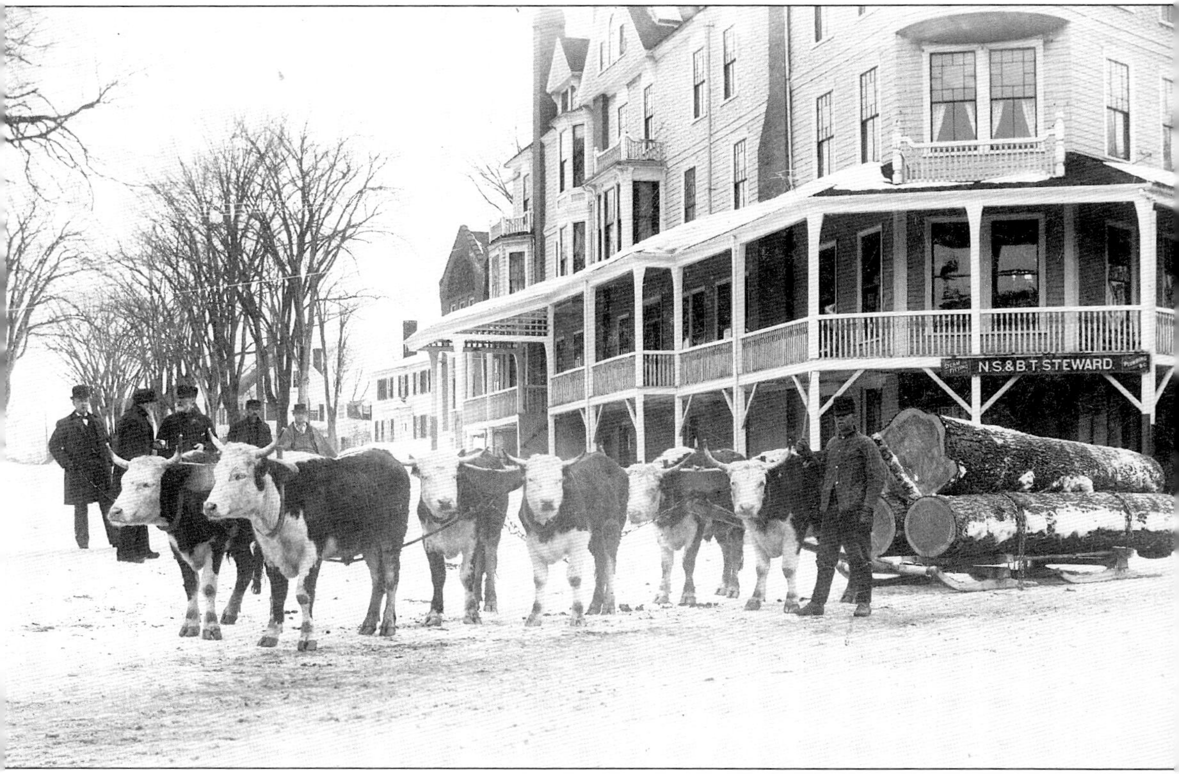


A six-ox team hauling logs in front of N.S. and B.T. Steward in downtown Skowhegan.

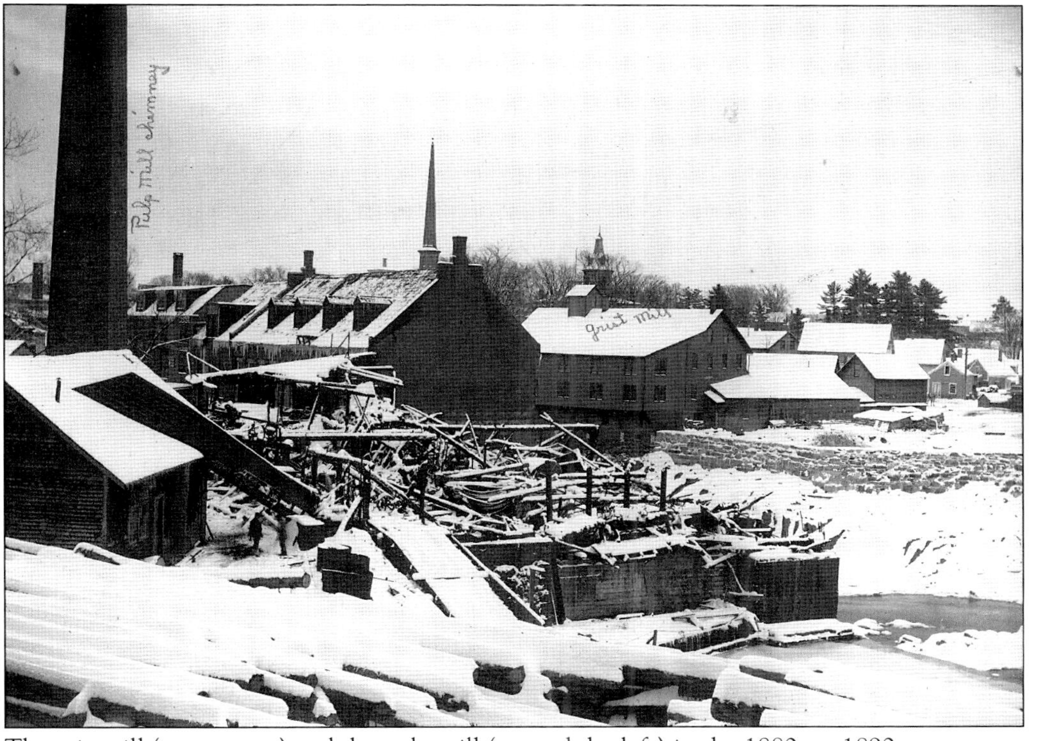


The gristmill (rear center) and the pulp mill (toward the left) in the 1880s or 1890s.

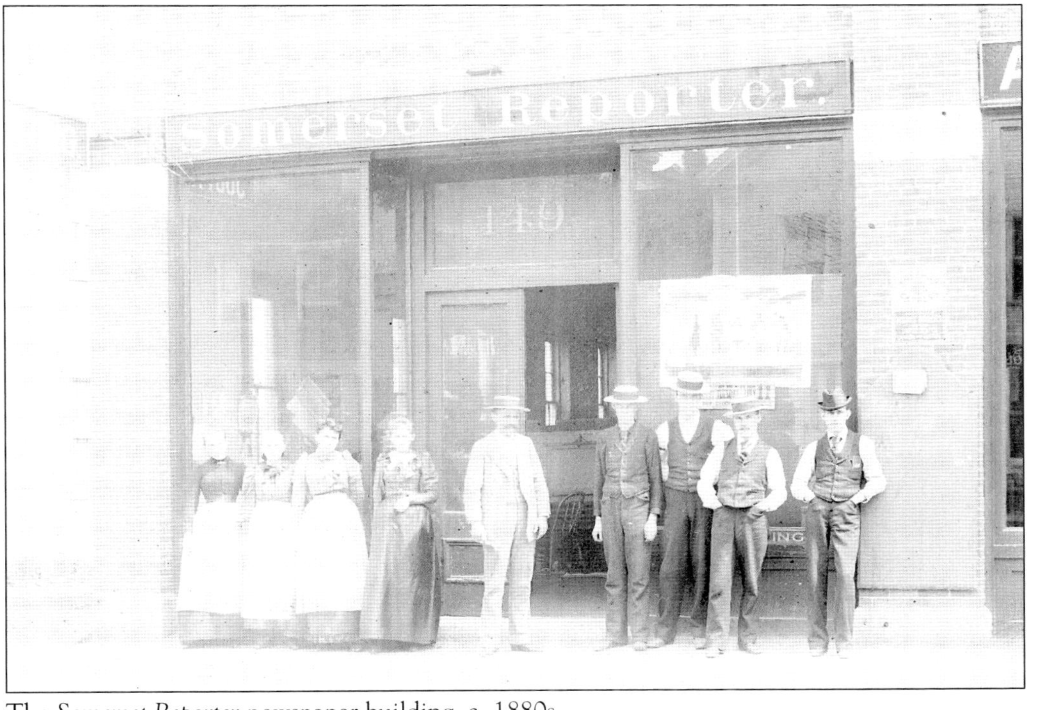


The *Somerset Reporter* newspaper building, *c.* 1880s.

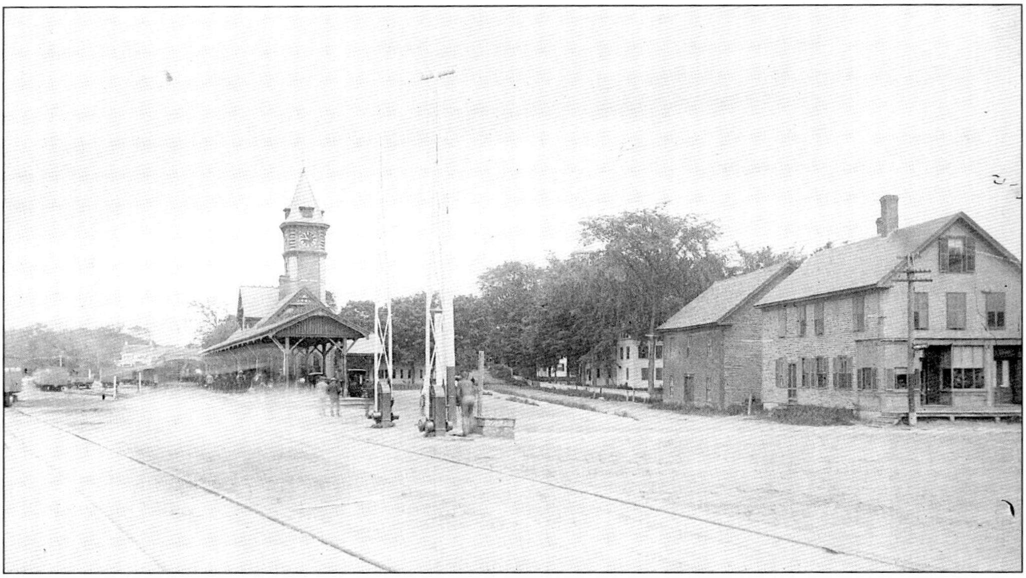

Skowhegan's railroad station. It was 10:45 am when this photograph was taken; the year, however, remains difficult to pinpoint. It was probably taken *c.* 1890s.

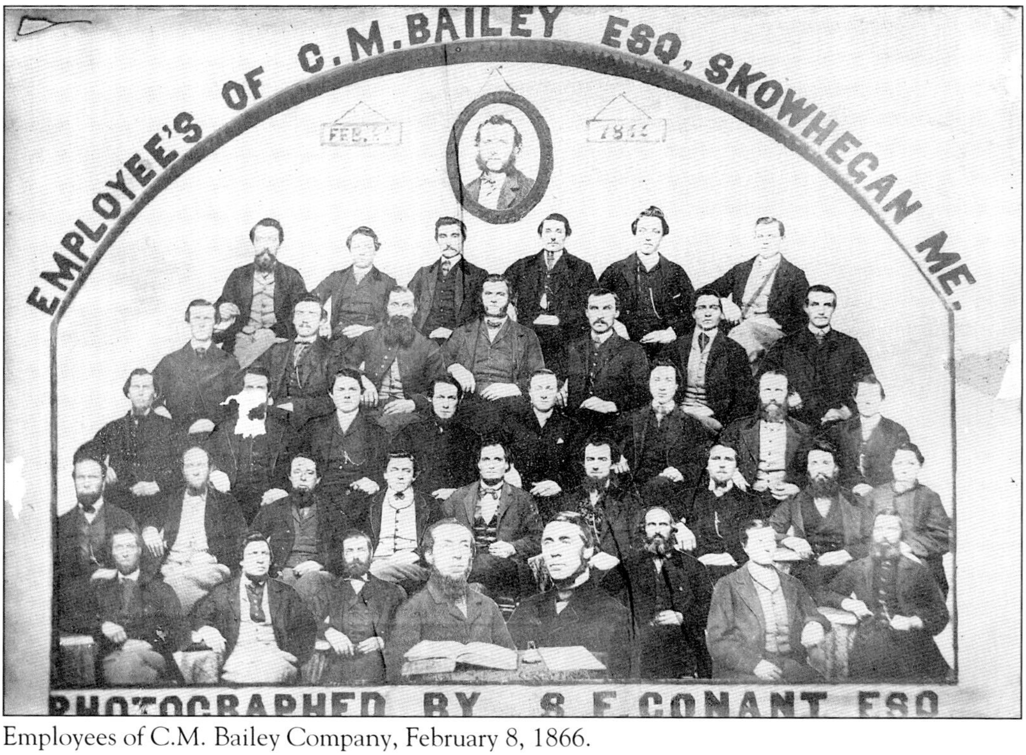


Employees of C.M. Bailey Company, February 8, 1866.

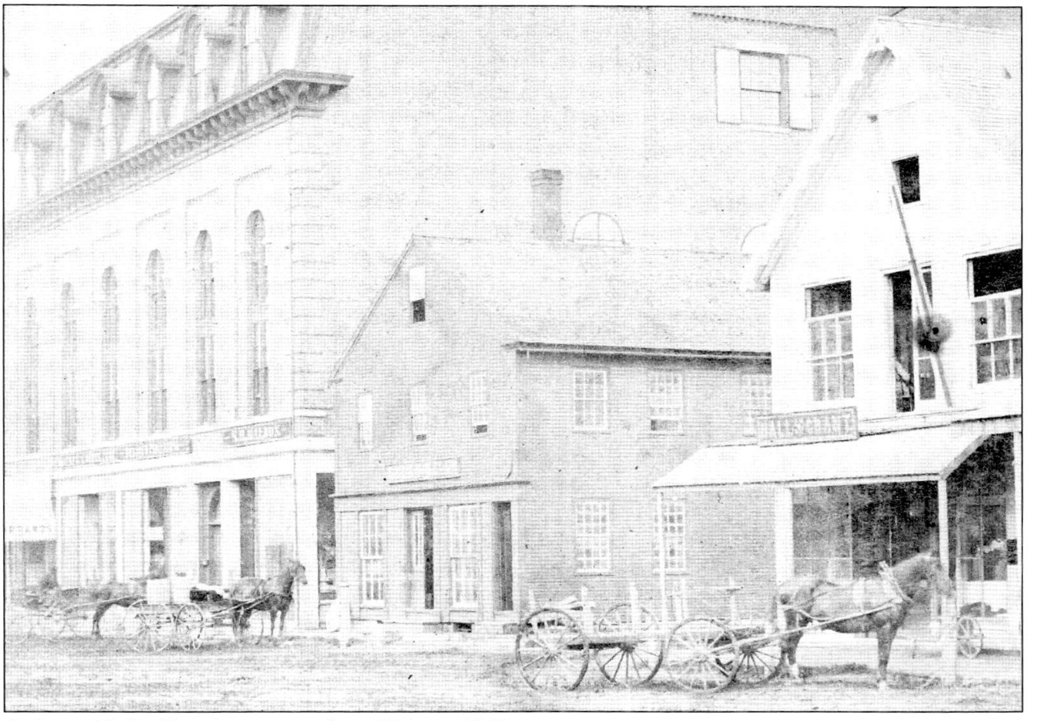

Coburn Hall, Skowhegan, in the 1870s or 1880s.

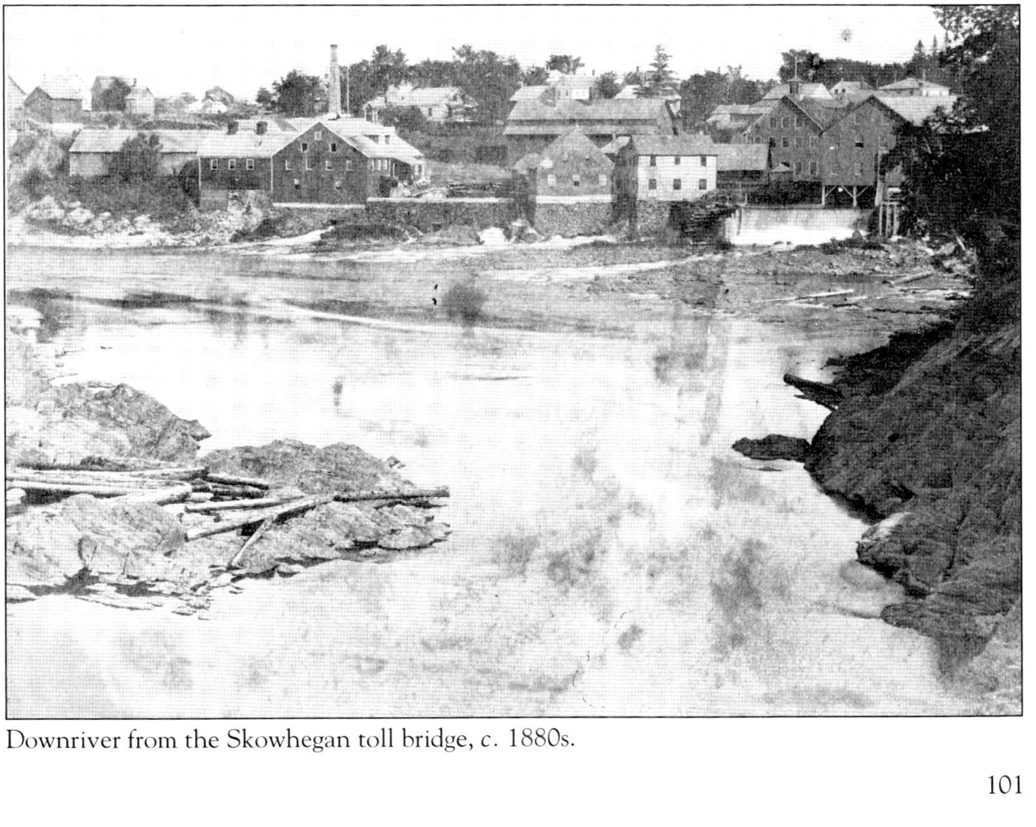

Downriver from the Skowhegan toll bridge, *c.* 1880s.

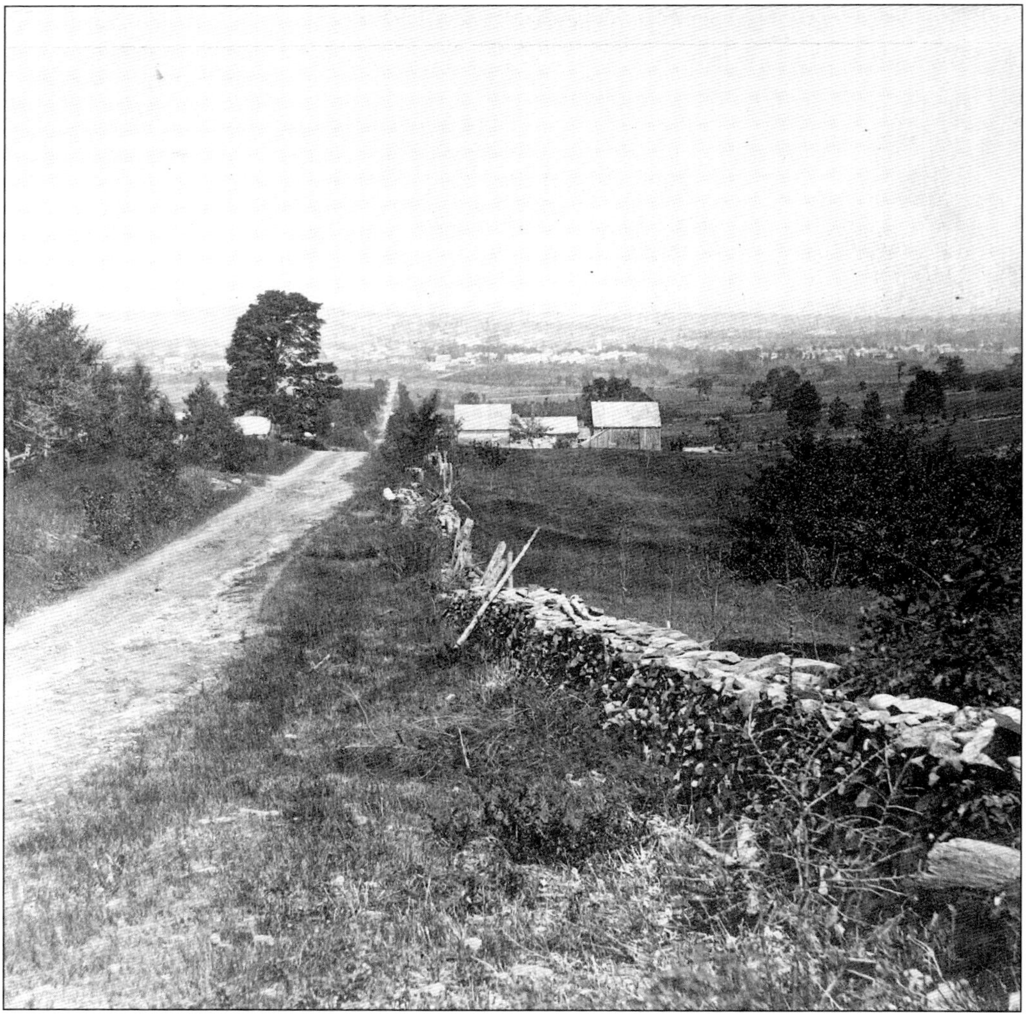
A panoramic view of the area around Bigelow Hill.

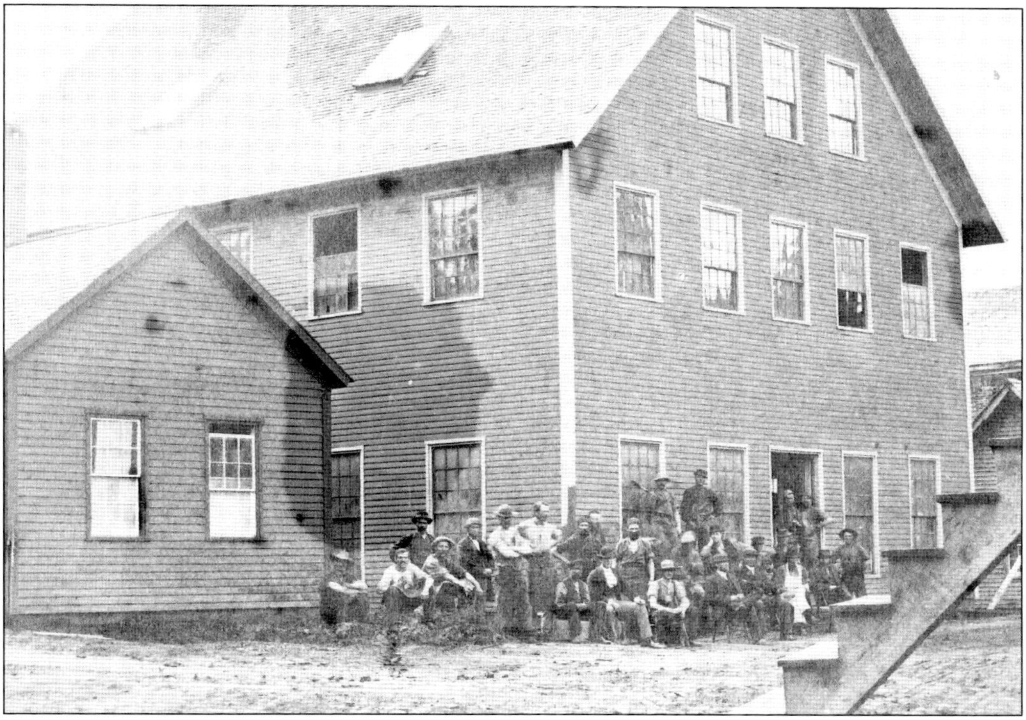

The Steward Williams & Company's axe factory in Skowhegan in the 1880s or 1890s.

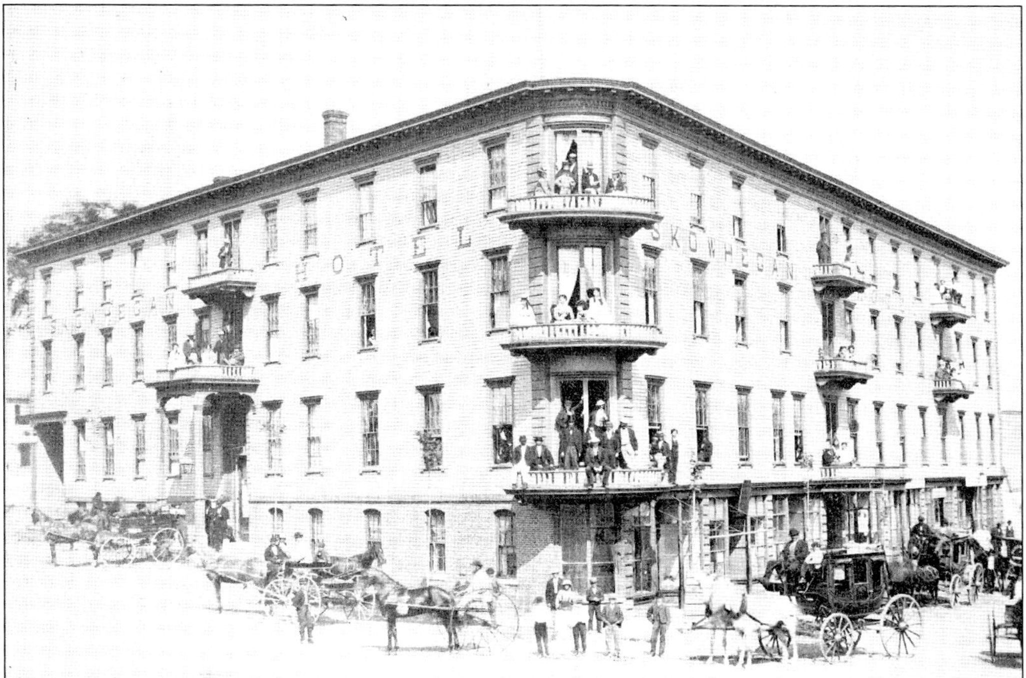


The Skowhegan Hotel at the corner of Elm Street and Madison Avenue. E.B. Mayberry is listed as proprietor.

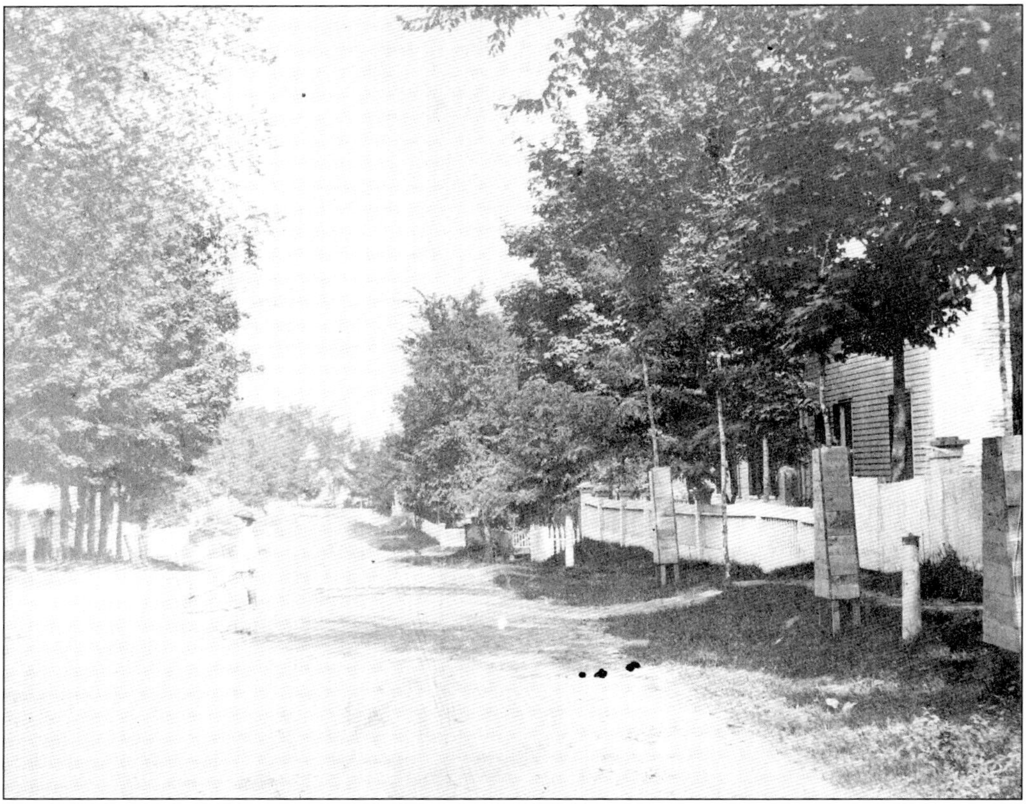

An image of High Street, *c.* 1890s, that brings the word "tranquility" to mind.

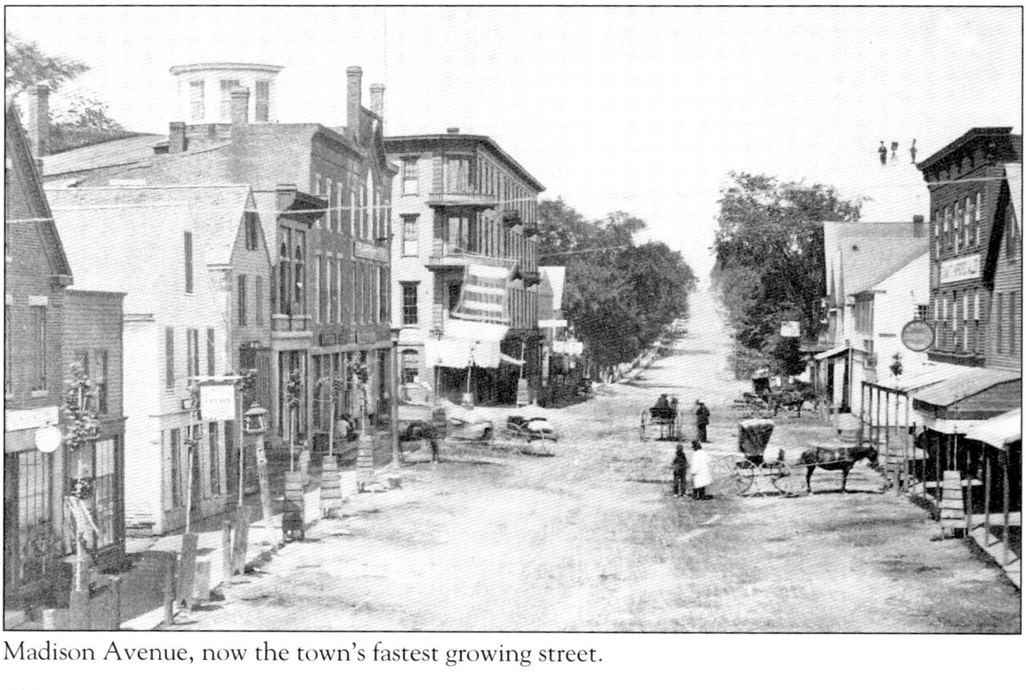

Madison Avenue, now the town's fastest growing street.

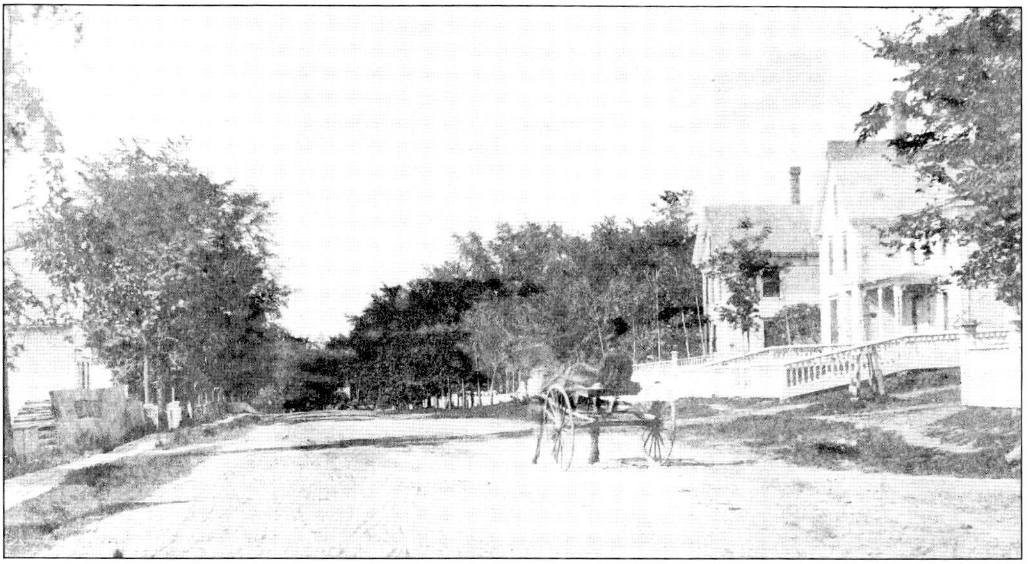

Water Street, looking west. This was, for many years, Skowhegan's busiest (or certainly one of the busiest) streets.

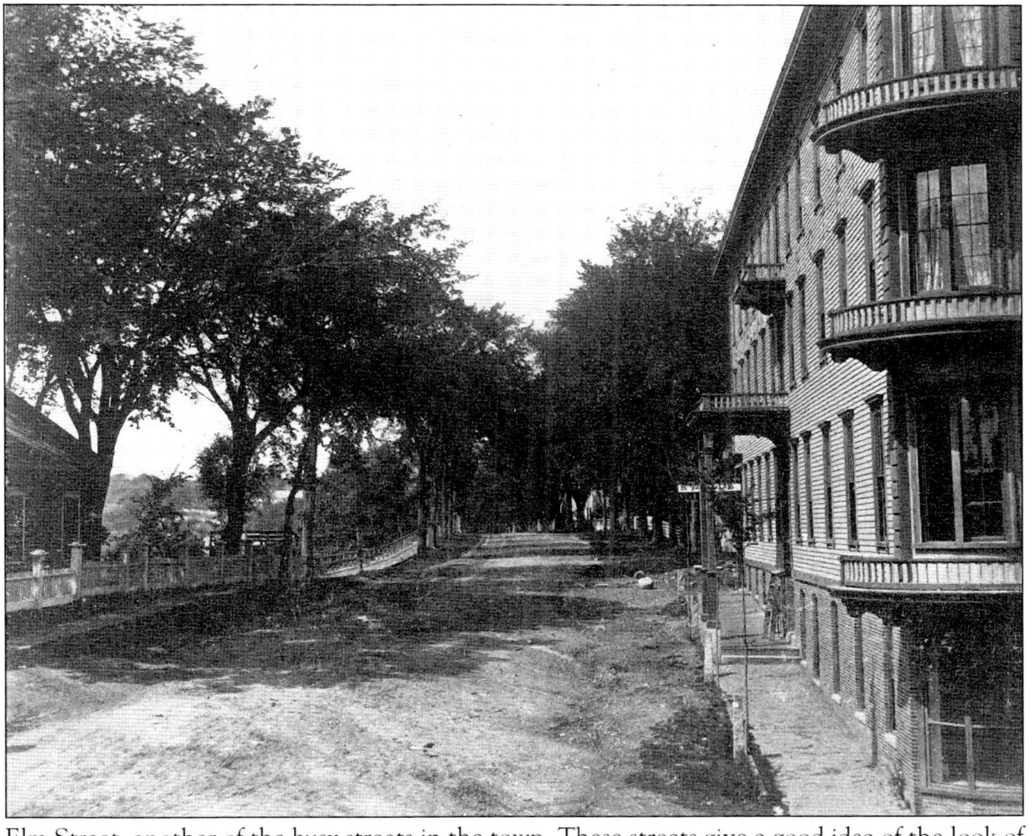

Elm Street, another of the busy streets in the town. These streets give a good idea of the look of Skowhegan before the turn of the century.

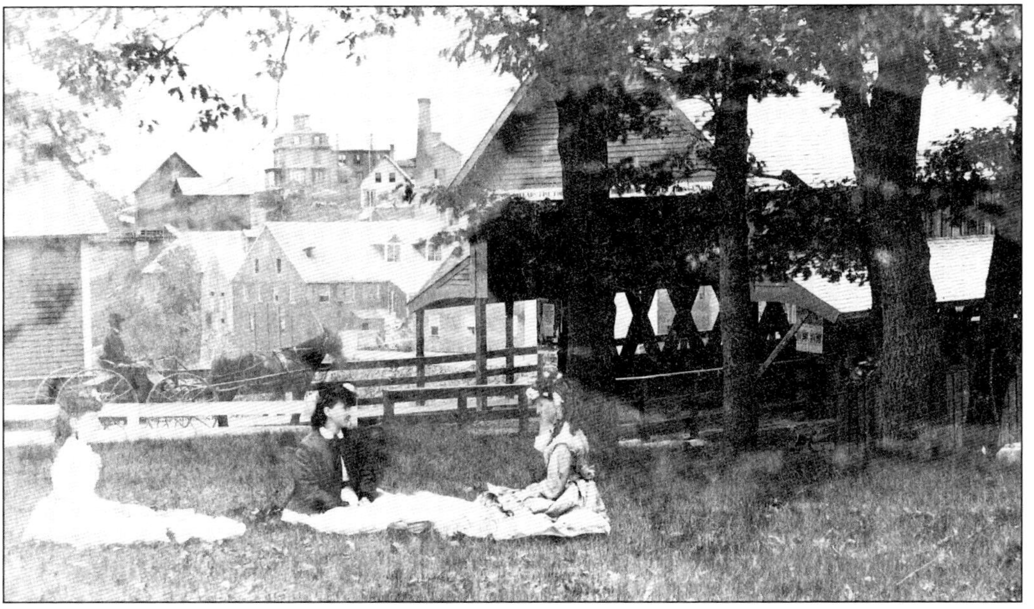

A view southeast from Bloomfield Academy. The three girls in the photograph are enjoying themselves sitting on the grass.

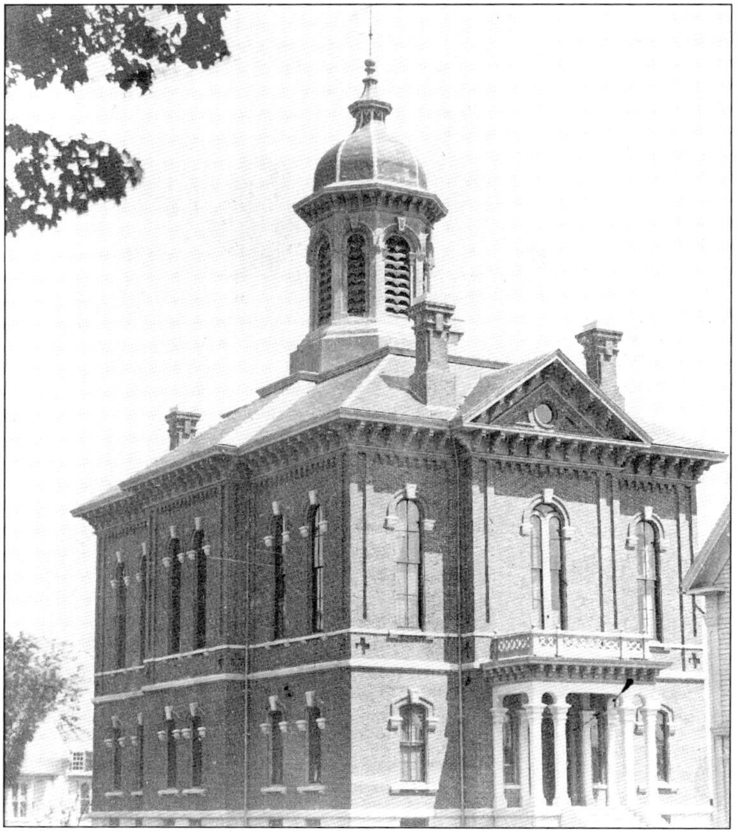

The Somerset County Court House, erected and presented to the county by Abner Coburn, once Maine's governor, in 1873.

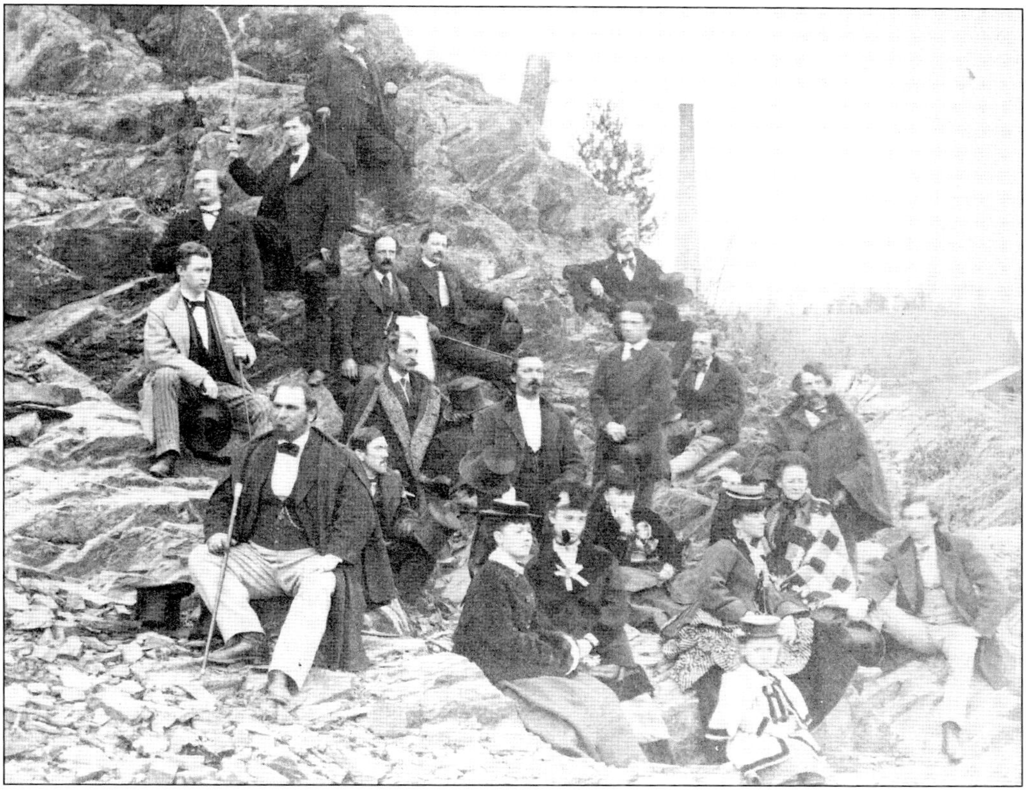

Fannie Herrin, entertainer, and her troupe.

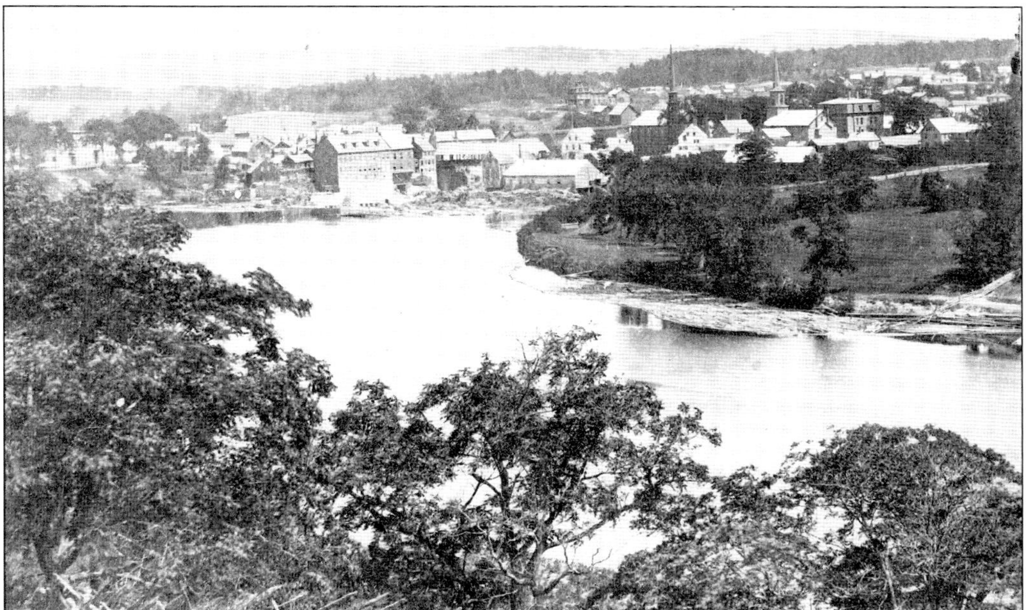

A view from Neil Hill showing a bend in the Kennebec River, with mill buildings on the right in the rear.

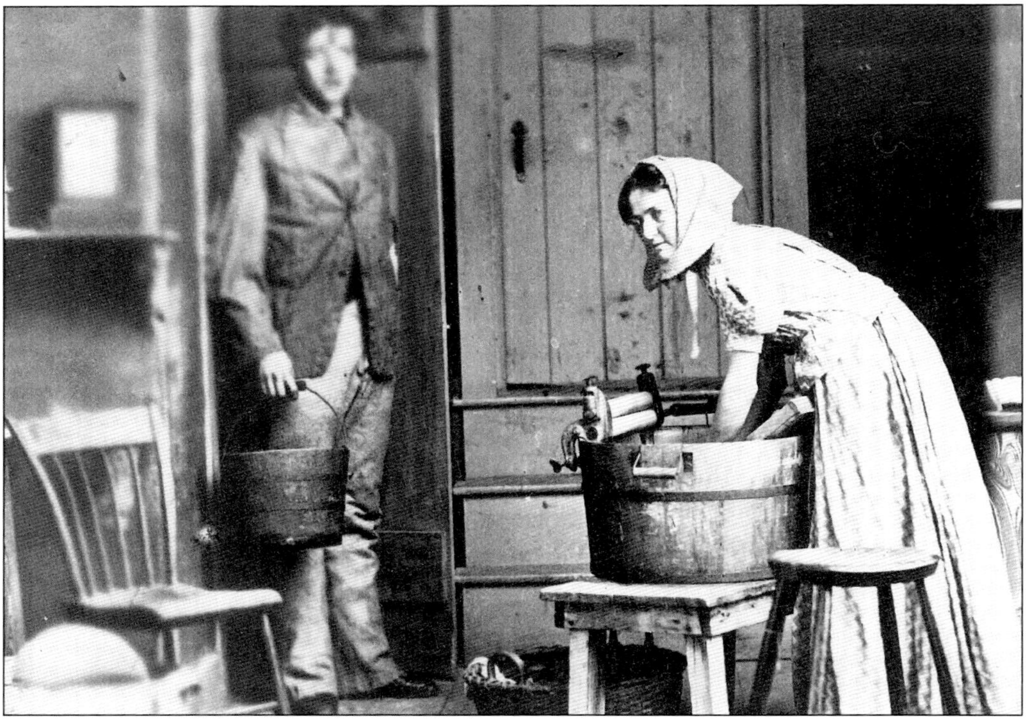

Washing day in the area, in the *c.* 1880s.

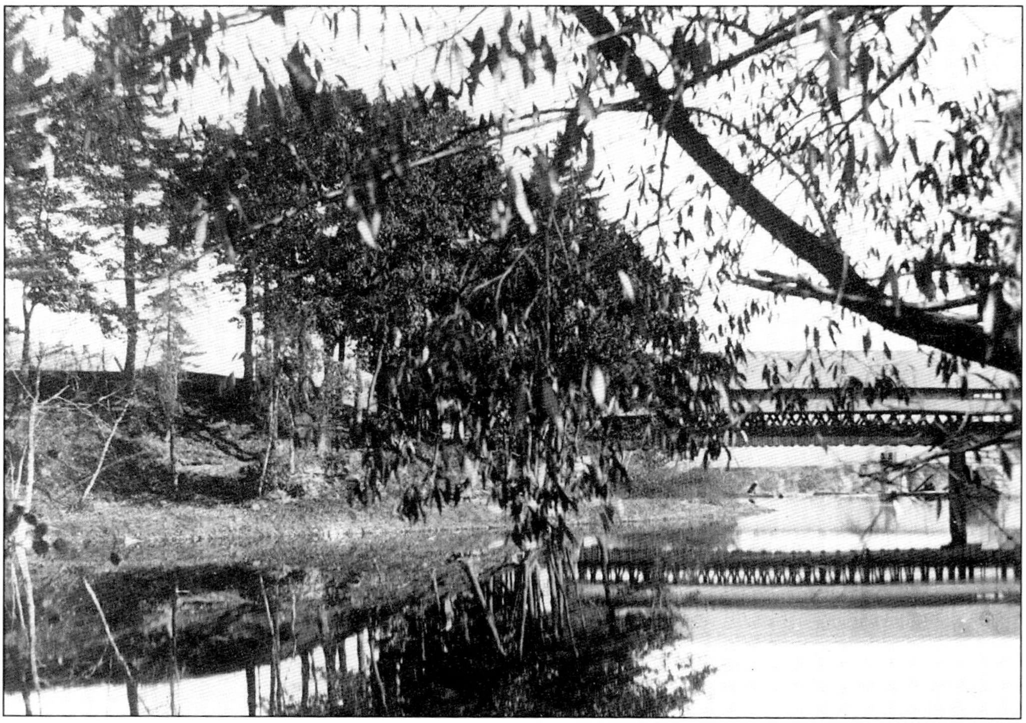

Scenery on the Kennebec in the days when there was still a covered bridge at Skowhegan.

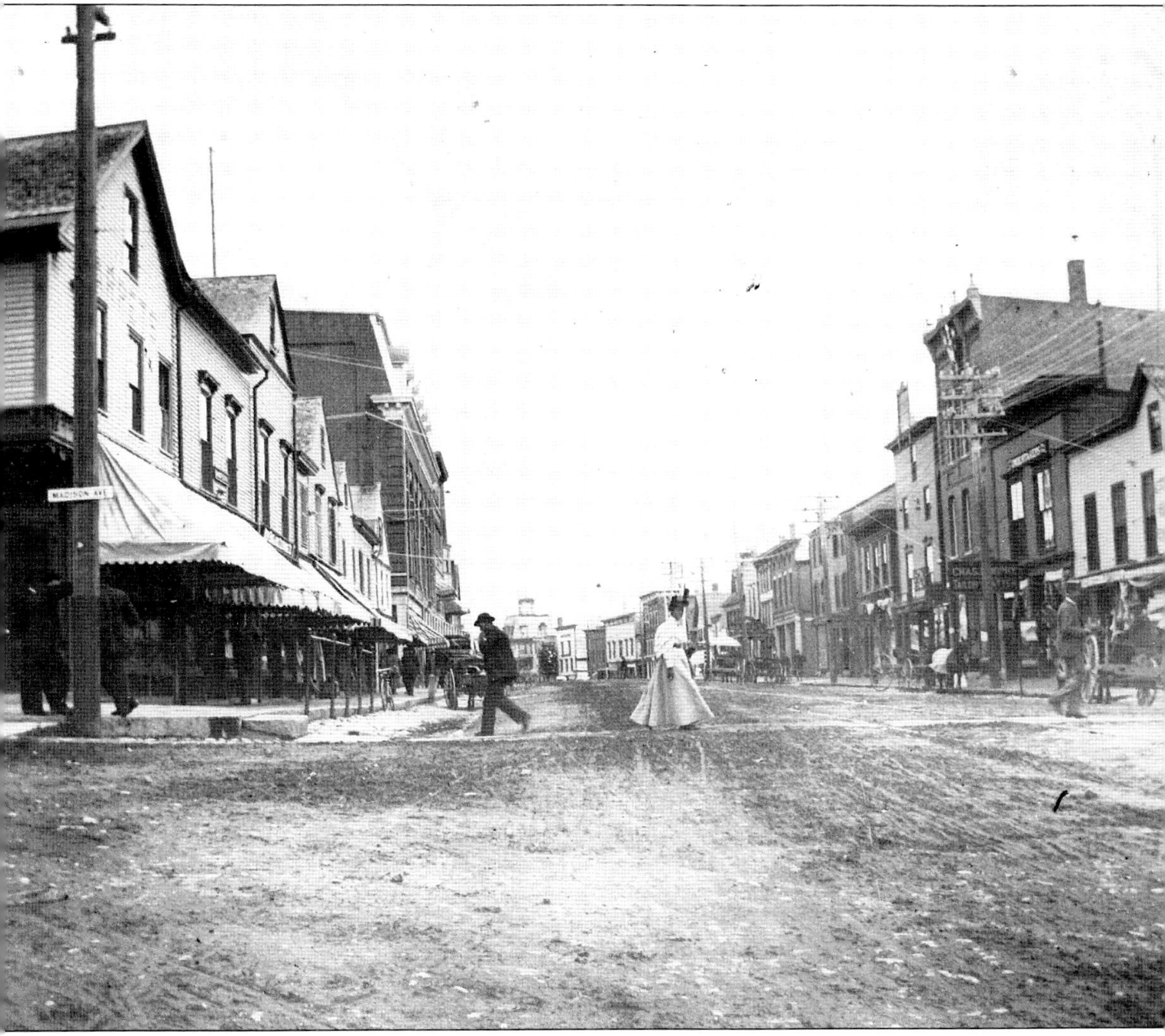


Main Street in Skowhegan in the 1880s. This was generally a busy place.

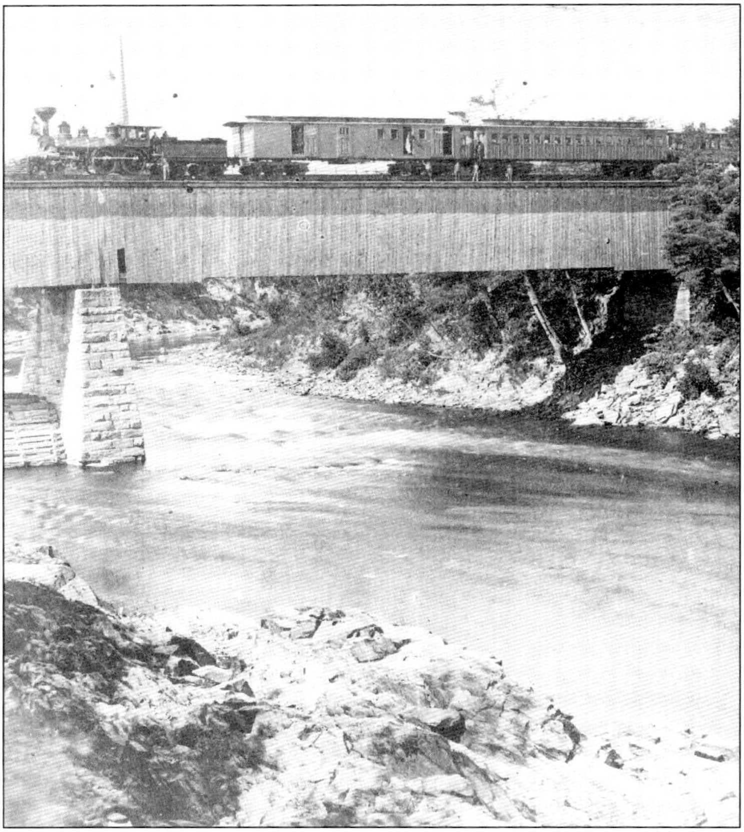

Skowhegan's railroad bridge, complete with a train, in the 1880s.

An *c.* 1880s view from the Osgood Sawyer residence of the island on which part of Skowhegan stands.

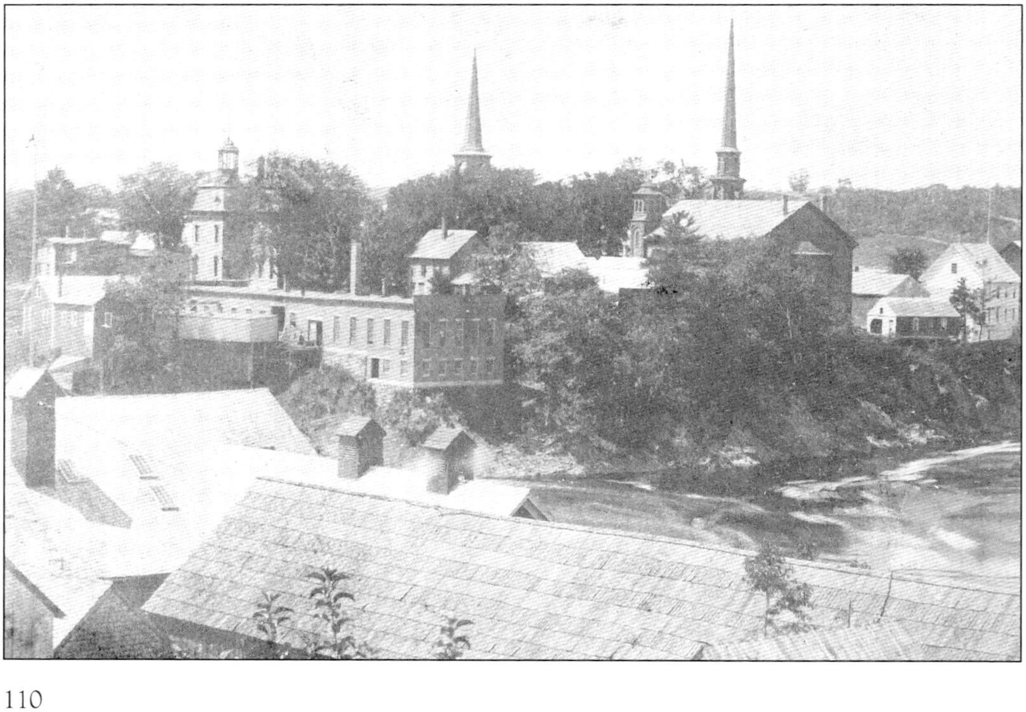

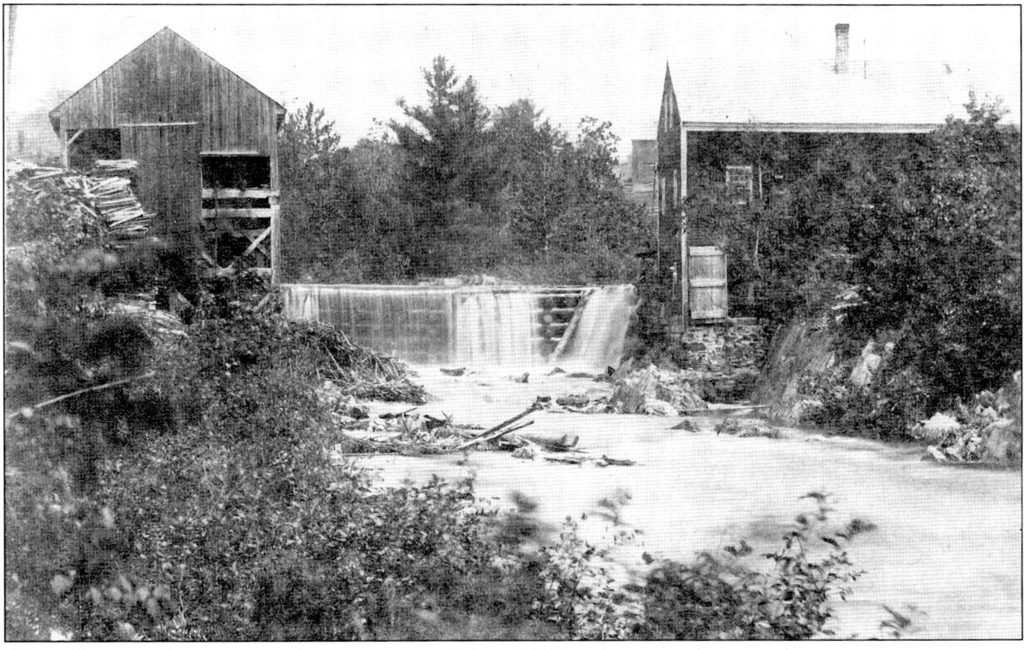

The village mill was very old even when this *c.* 1880s photograph was taken.

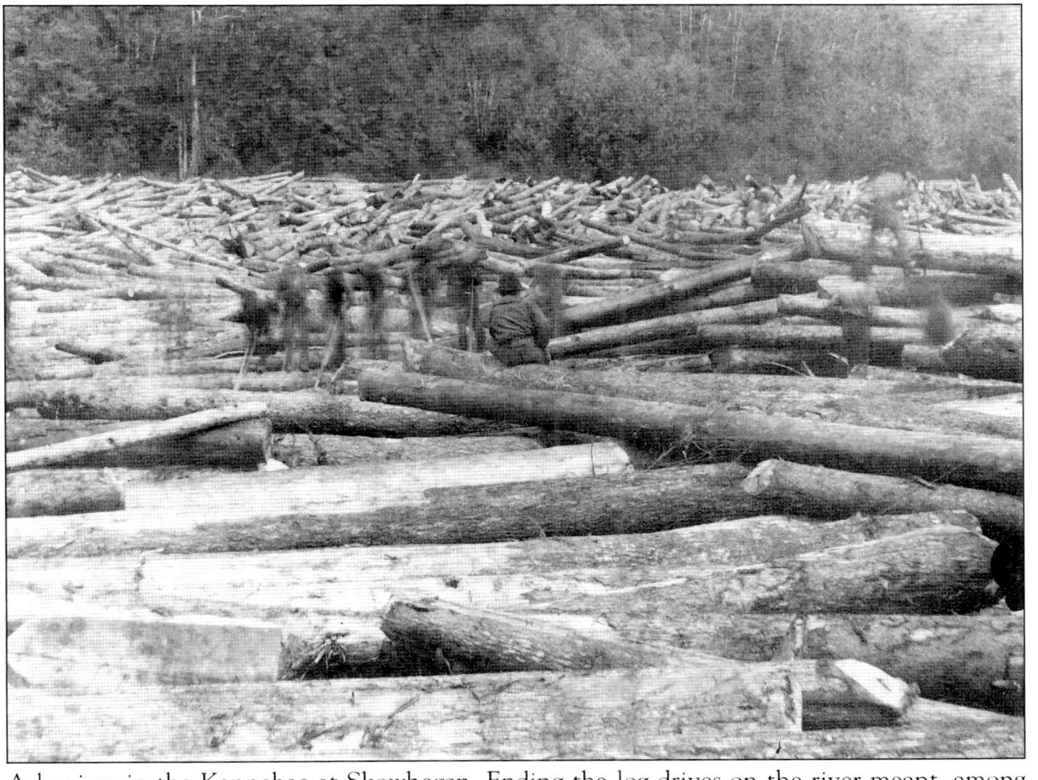

A log jam in the Kennebec at Skowhegan. Ending the log drives on the river meant, among other things, that jams in the river are usually only caused by ice.

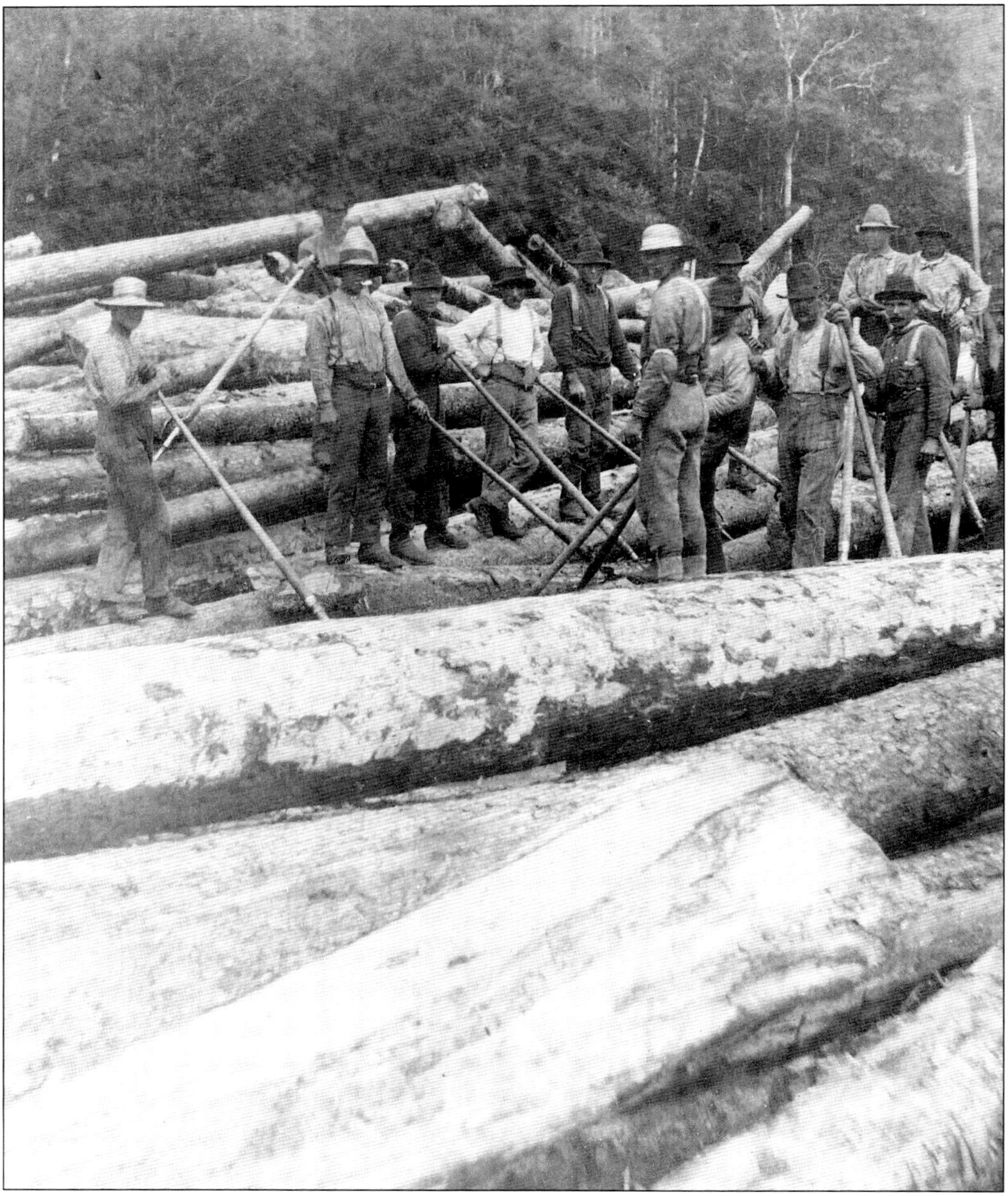

Men work away during the log drives. This group, in Skowhegan before the turn of the century, show off their tools, especially the peaveys for grabbing those logs.

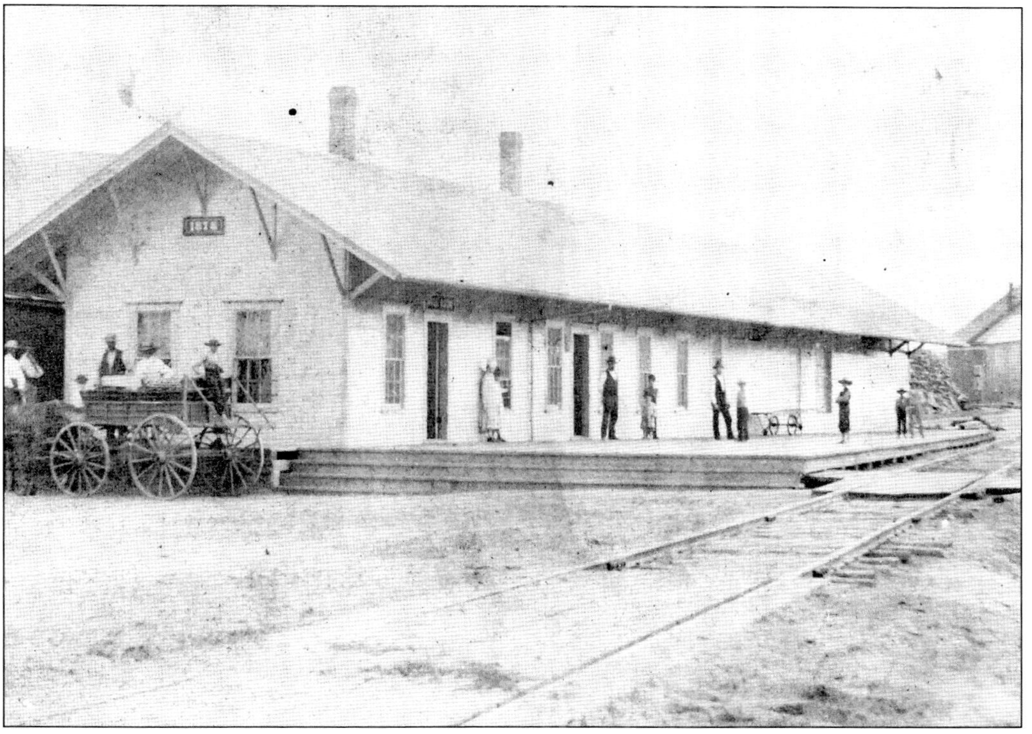

The railroad came to Skowhegan in 1857, and varied facilities were built in connection with it. The building here was either a station or a warehouse.

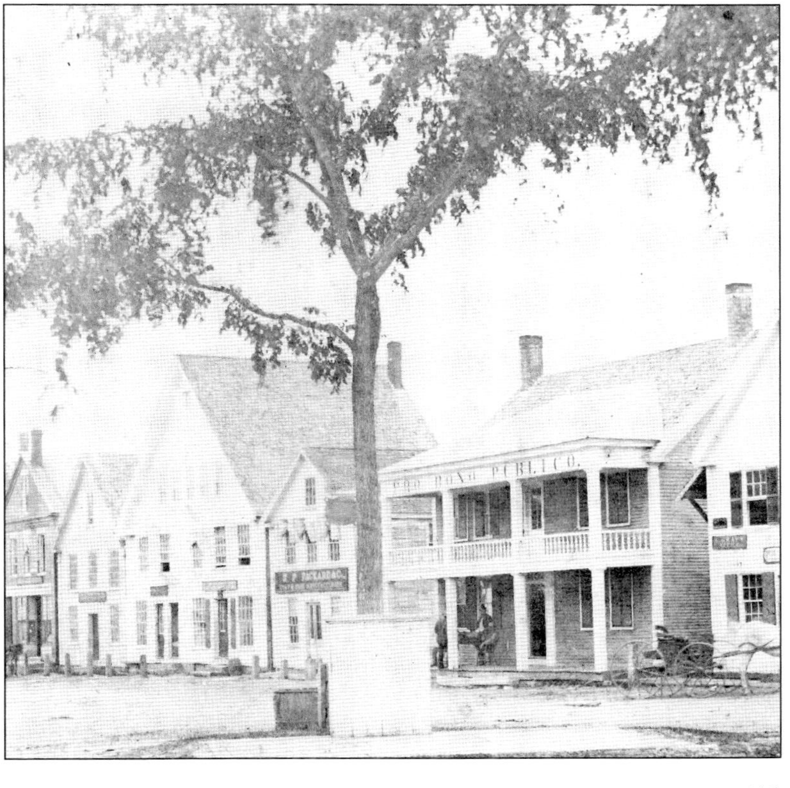

There has always been business in Skowhegan. Here we see J.F.W. Gould groceries, lawyer Gray, and the E.T. Packard Company, which sold shoes.

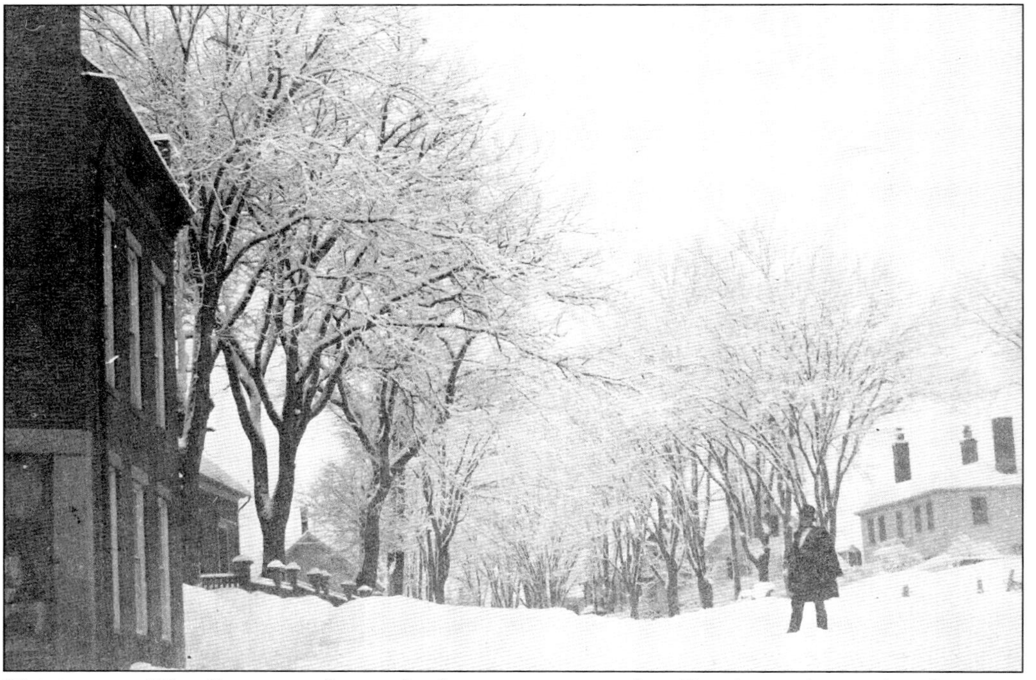

This image of Elm Street testifies to the ferocious winters that Skowhegan has endured.

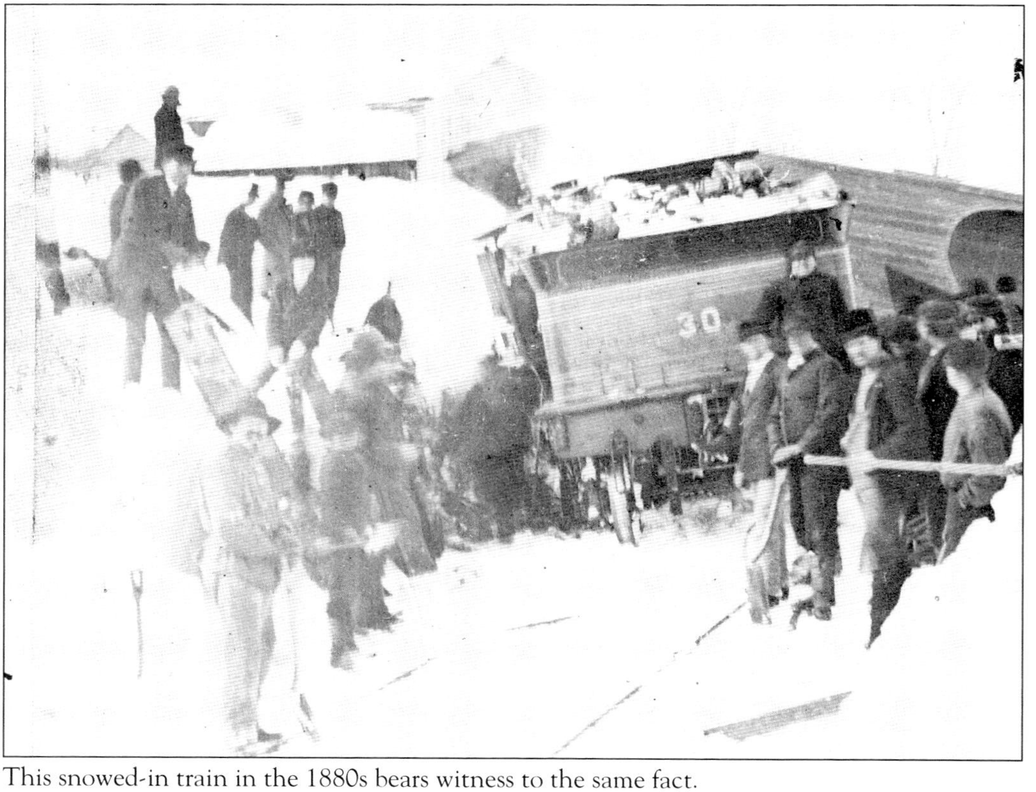

This snowed-in train in the 1880s bears witness to the same fact.

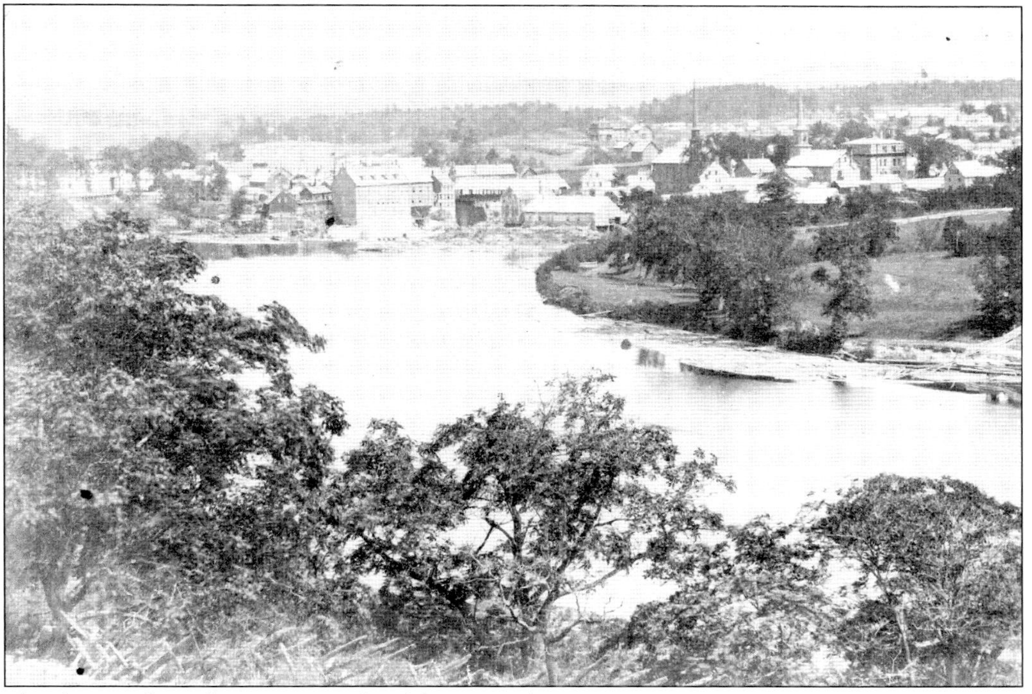
Skowhegan, from the opposite side of the Kennebec River.

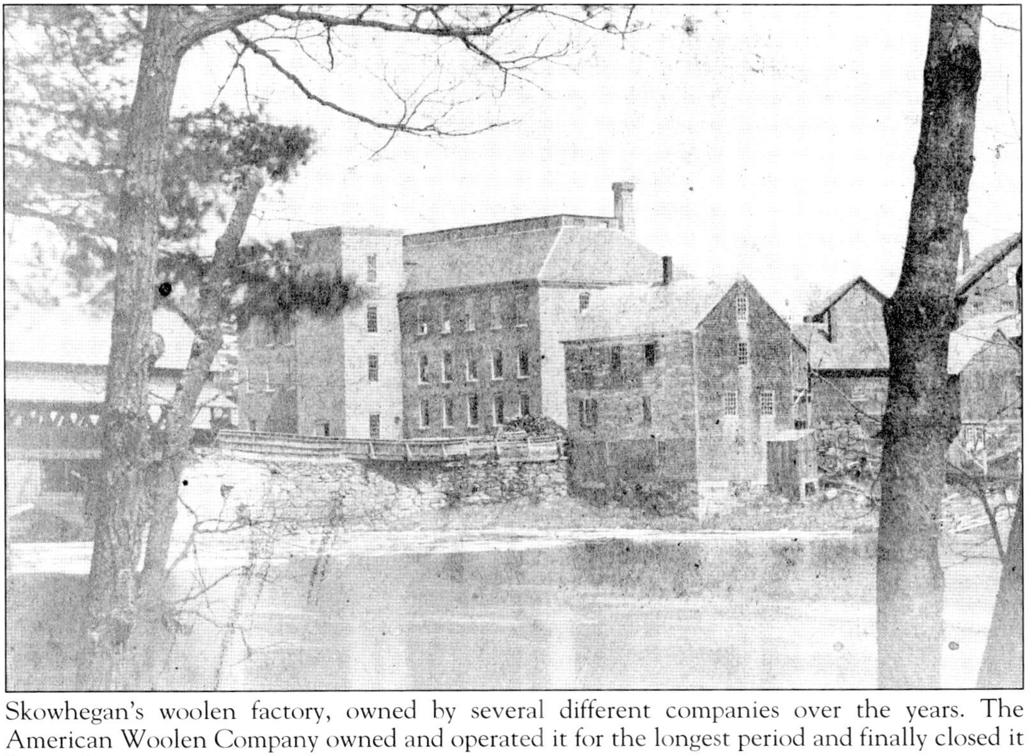
Skowhegan's woolen factory, owned by several different companies over the years. The American Woolen Company owned and operated it for the longest period and finally closed it for good.

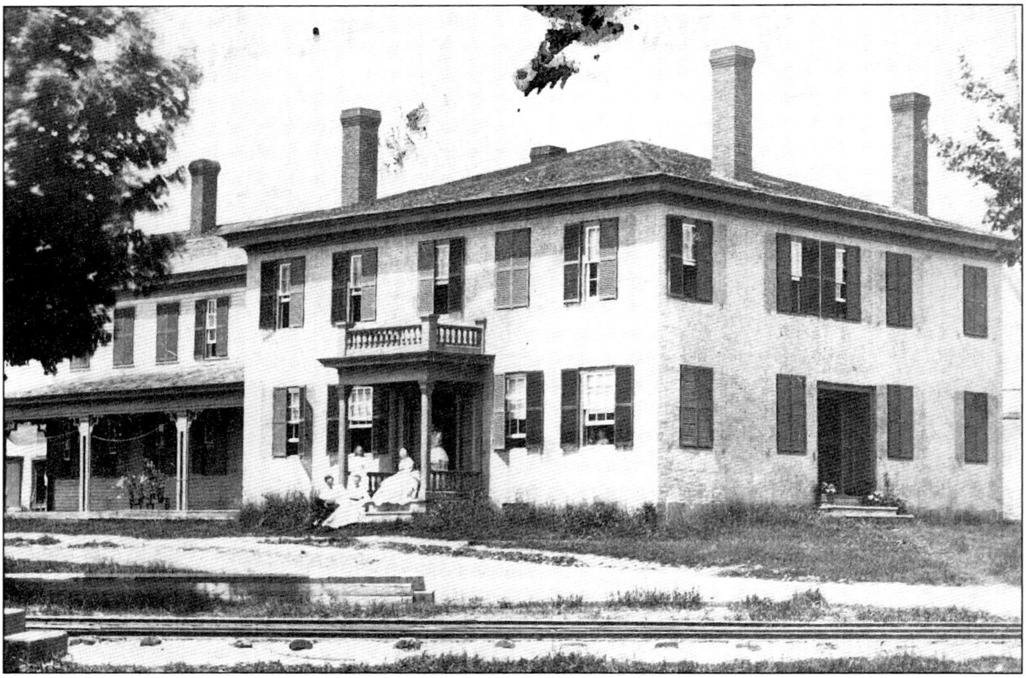

This brick house was owned by Stephen Wing when this photograph was taken, *c.* 1890s.

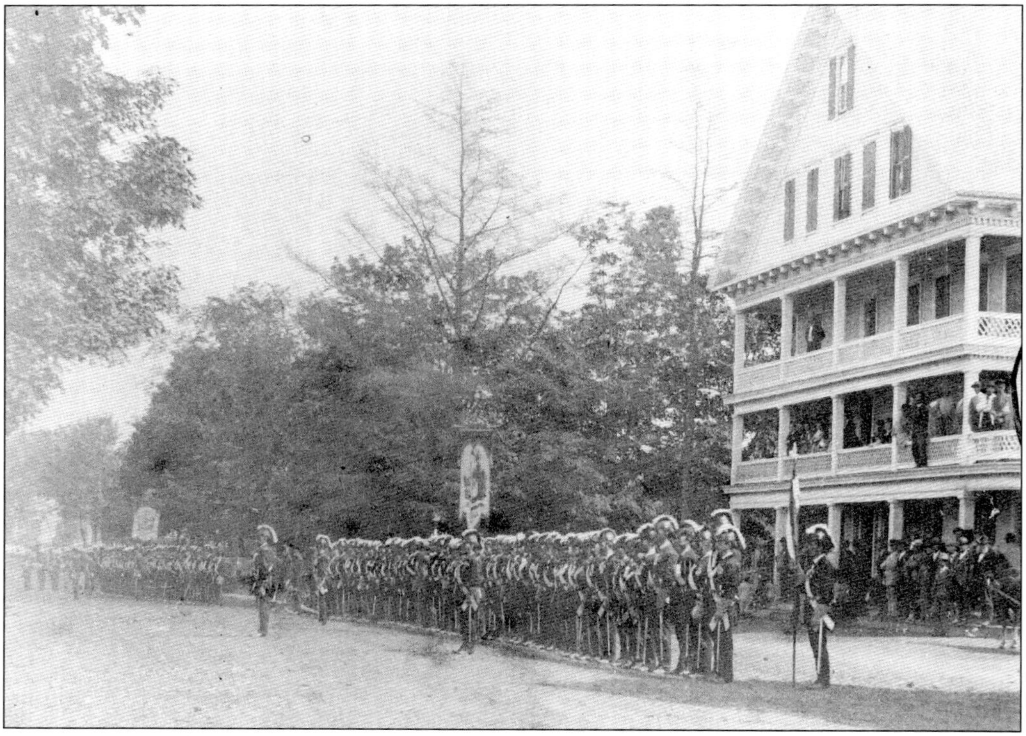

A Masonic parade in front of the Turner House. The hotel burned May 28, 1881, with an $80,000 loss.

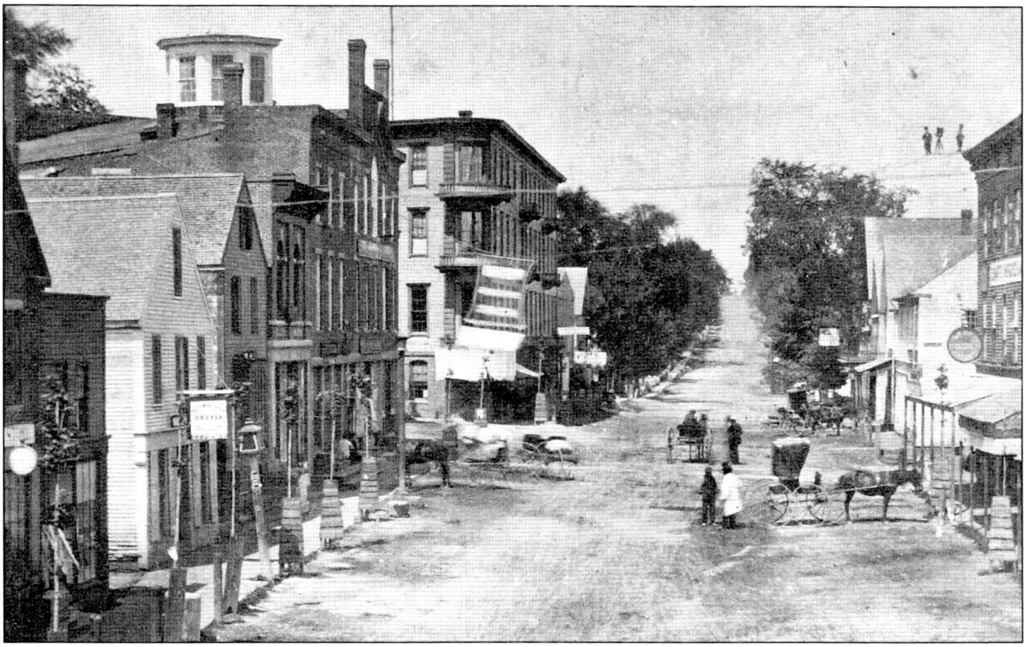

Dr. Mann in a white duster stands in back of his team. Amos Angier Mann was a character. He made his own patent medicines and sold them at a Skowhegan drug store in which he had half ownership. He often was called in when his remedies failed.

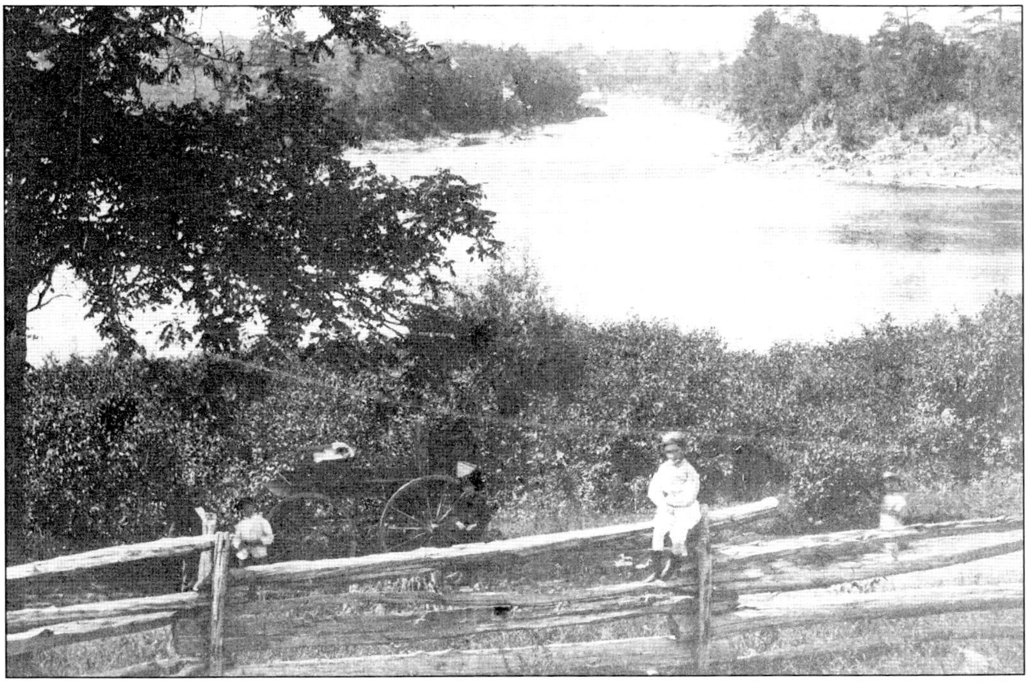

A boy sits on a fence before the turn of the century, looking over the Kennebec River. Like other Maine communities on rivers, Skowhegan was started in large measure because of the availability of water power.

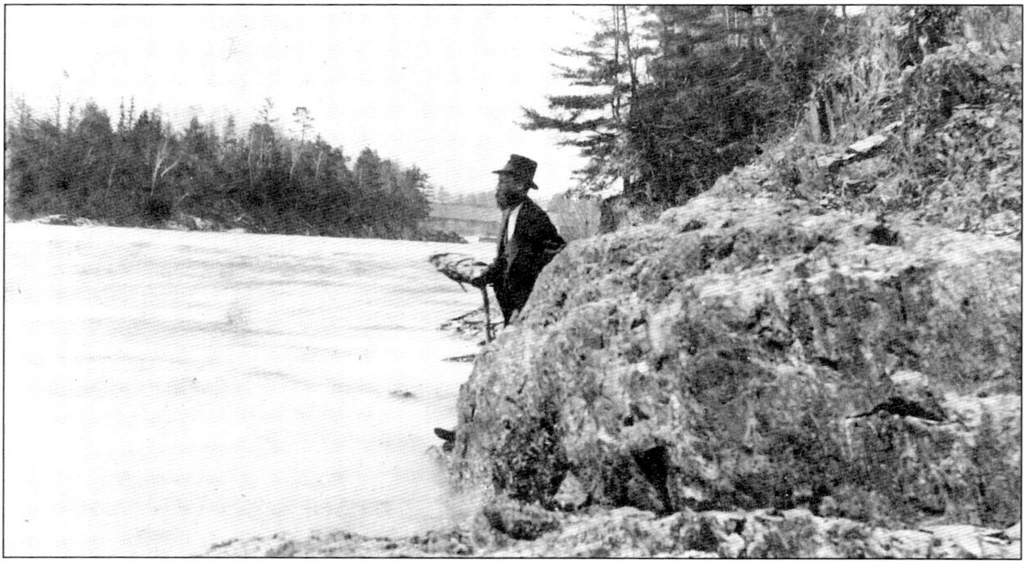

A man in a top hat also looking out over the Kennebec.

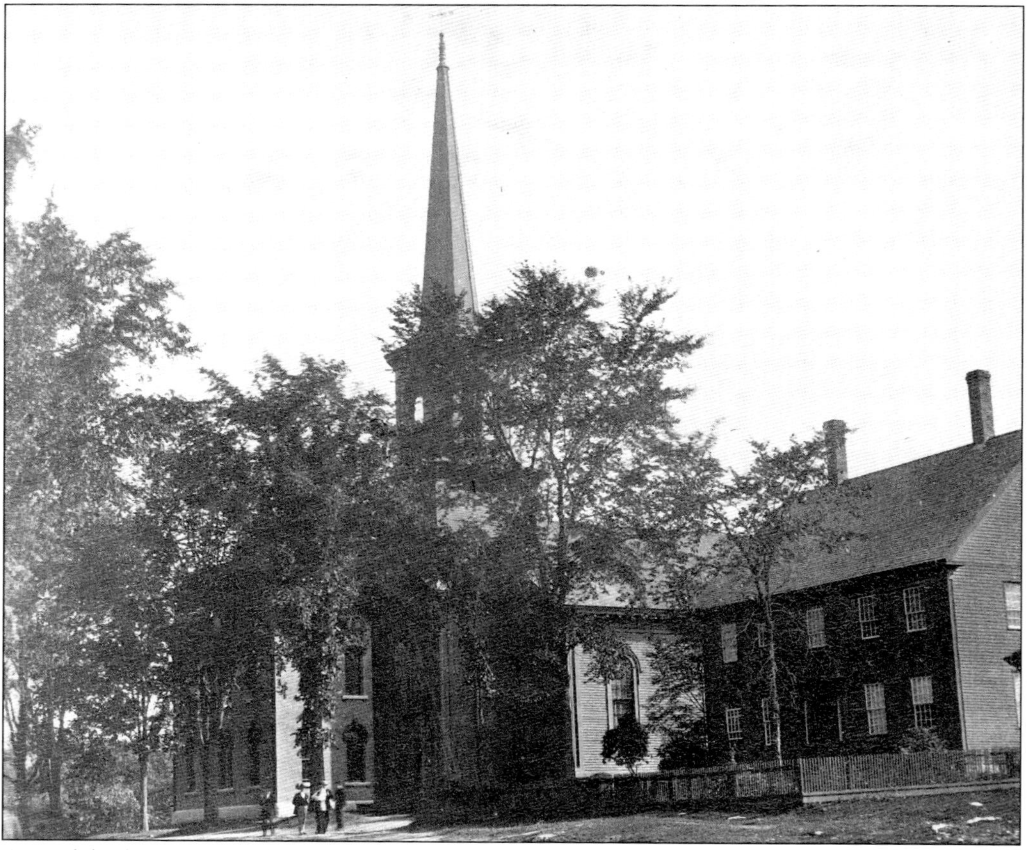

A quick look at some of Skowhegan's churches about the turn of the century. The Congregational church was on Island Avenue.

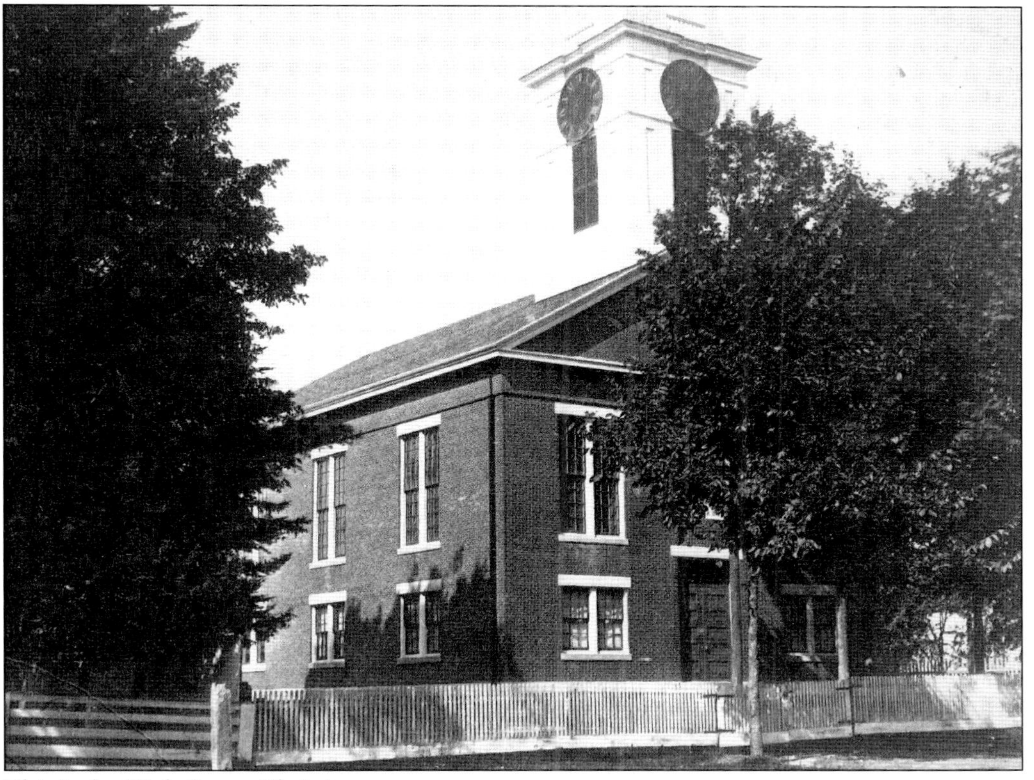

This is the High Street Christian Church.

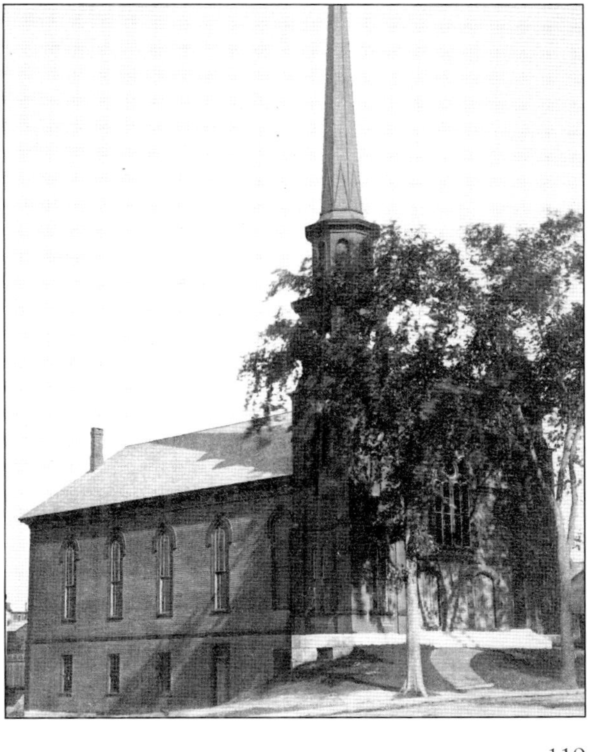

The Methodist Episcopal Church is on Skowhegan Island.

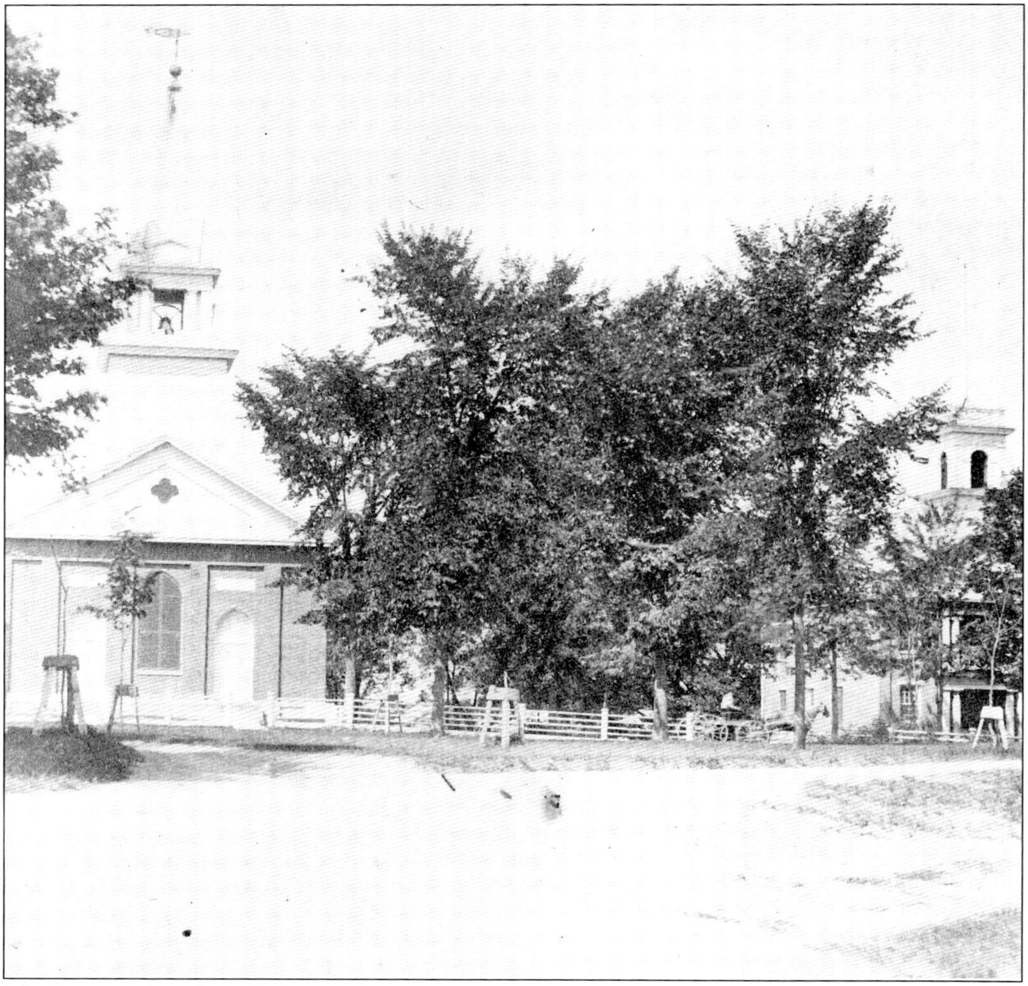

The Baptist church and Bloomfield Academy on Baptist Hill, an area that could well be made into an historic district.

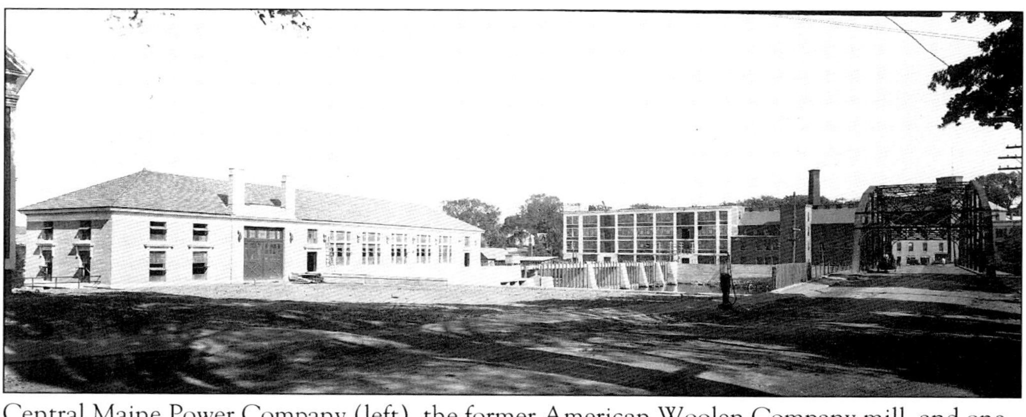

Central Maine Power Company (left), the former American Woolen Company mill, and one of the bridges over the Kennebec River.

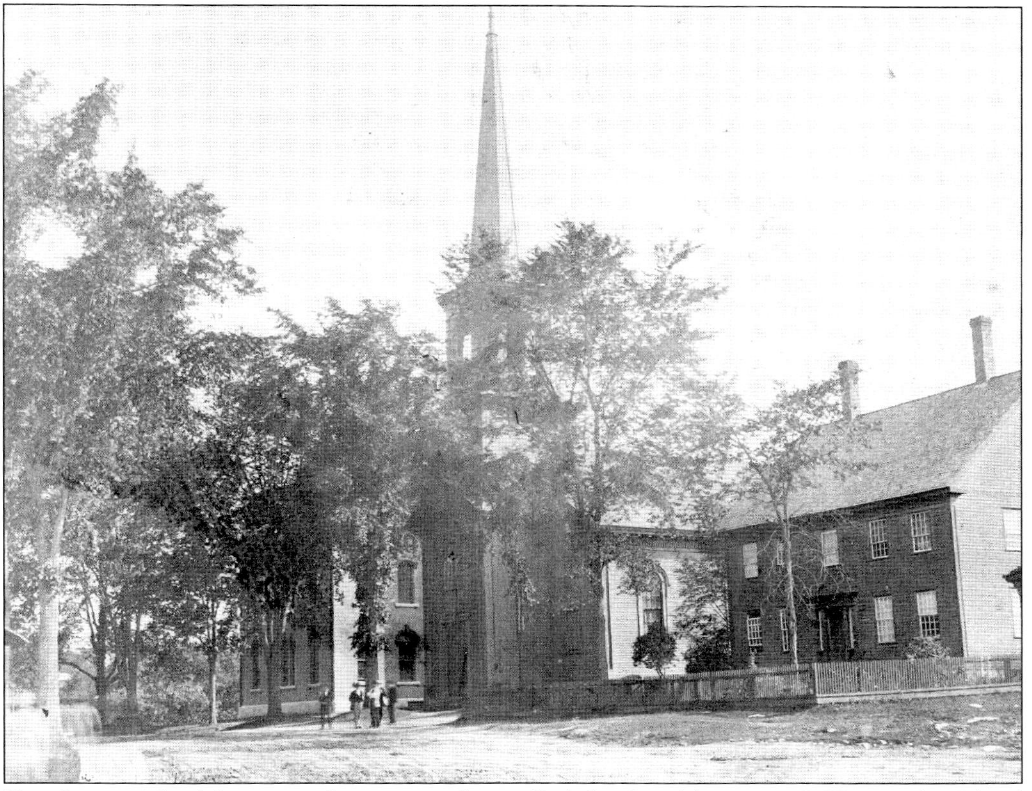

Skowhegan Island became what one author called "a churchly center." This is the Island Avenue church.

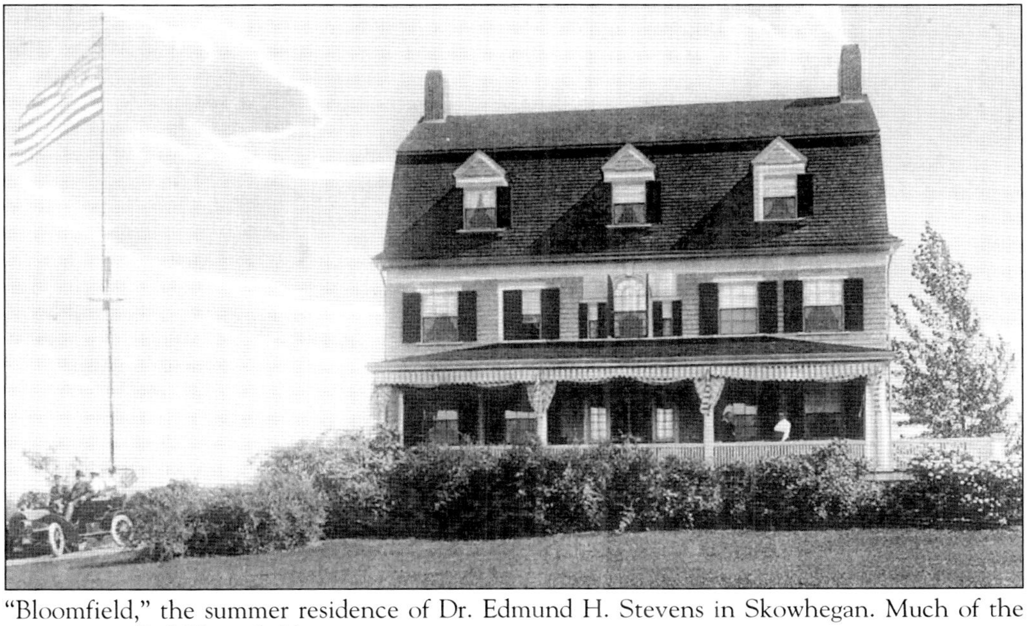

"Bloomfield," the summer residence of Dr. Edmund H. Stevens in Skowhegan. Much of the town was called Bloomfield at one time.

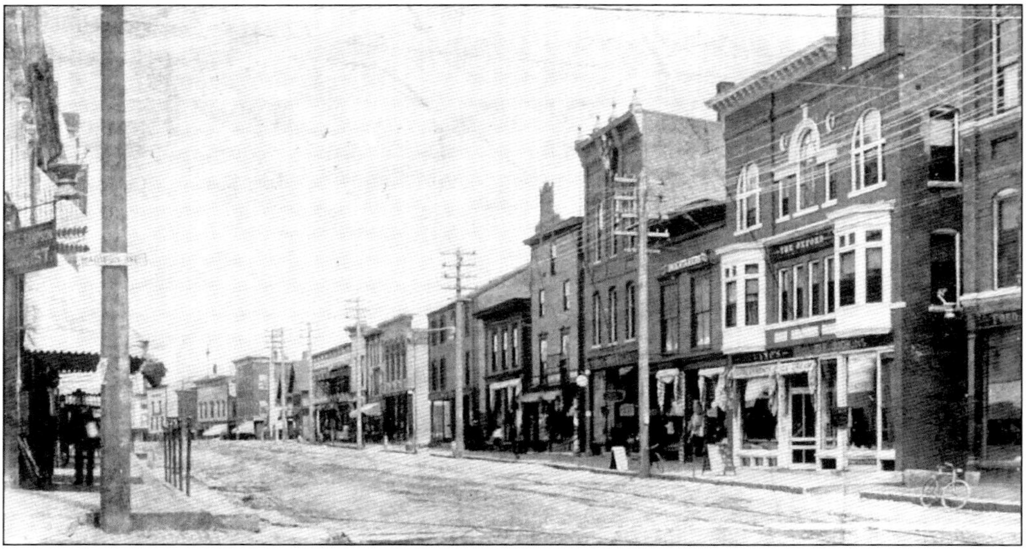

Water Street about the turn of the century.

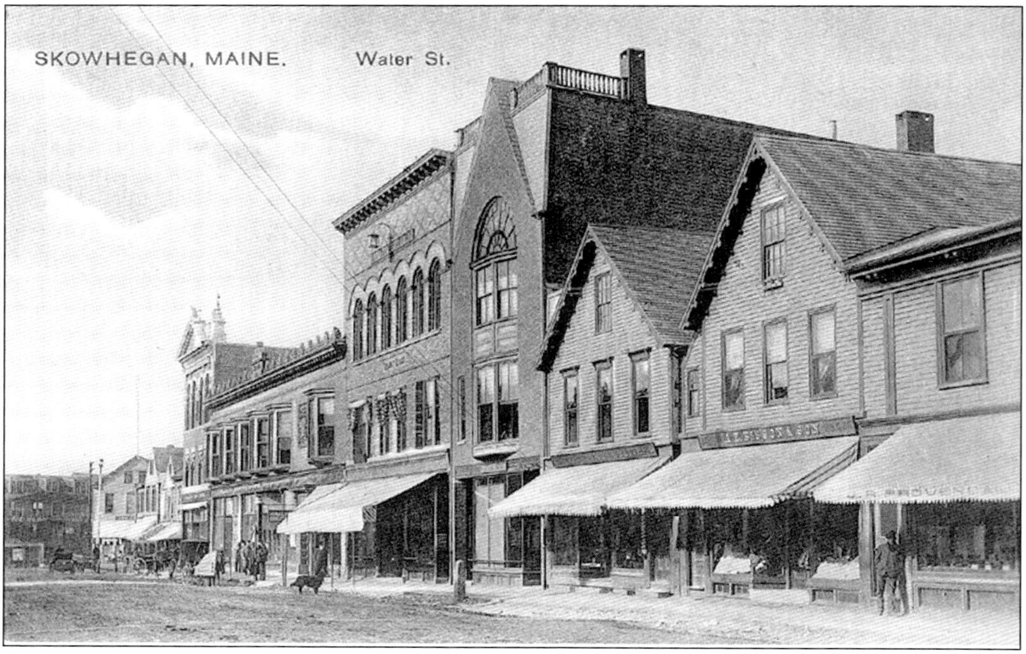


Another view of Water Street, a core of Skowhegan's downtown area.

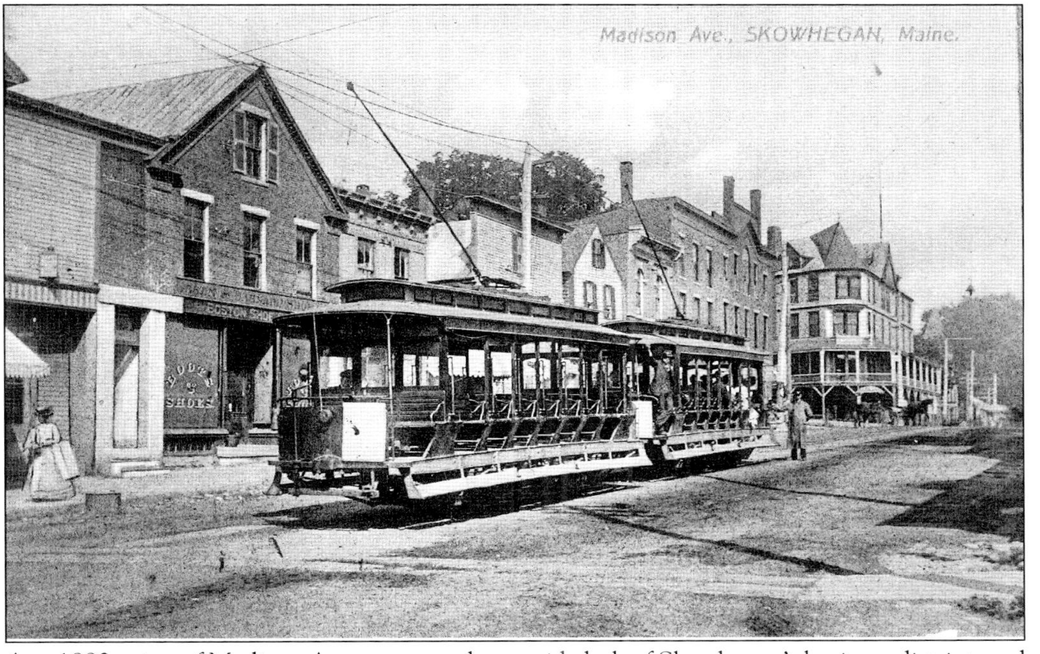


A c. 1880s view of Madison Avenue, now the outside hub of Skowhegan's business district, and a trolley car.

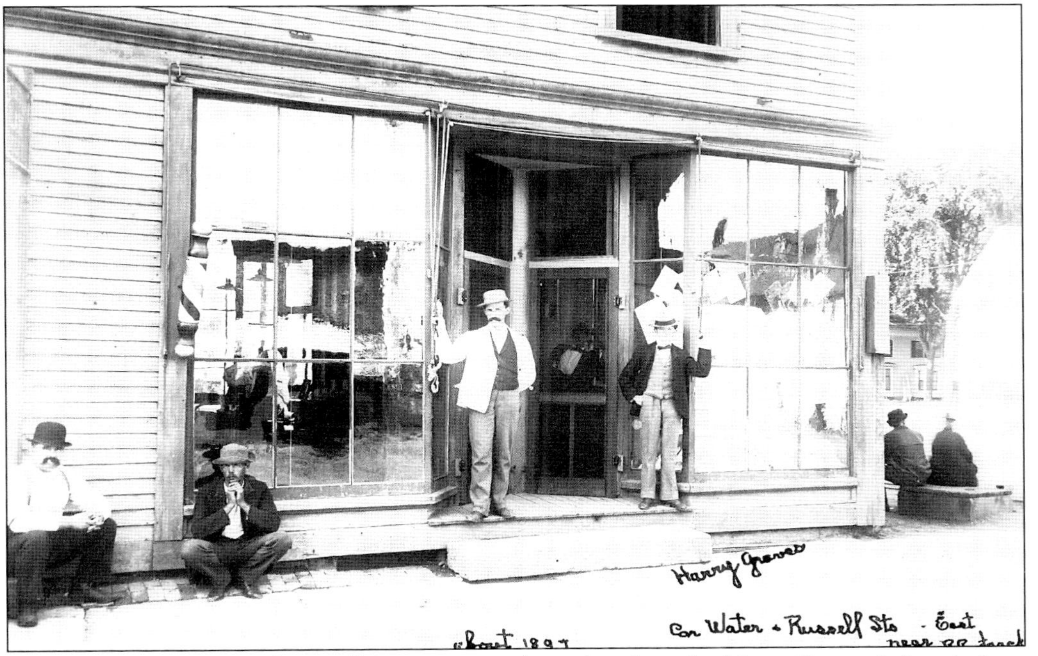


The corner of Water and Russell Streets, near the railroad tracks. Harry Graves is fourth from left. This photograph was taken around 1897, the year Margaret Chase Smith was born.

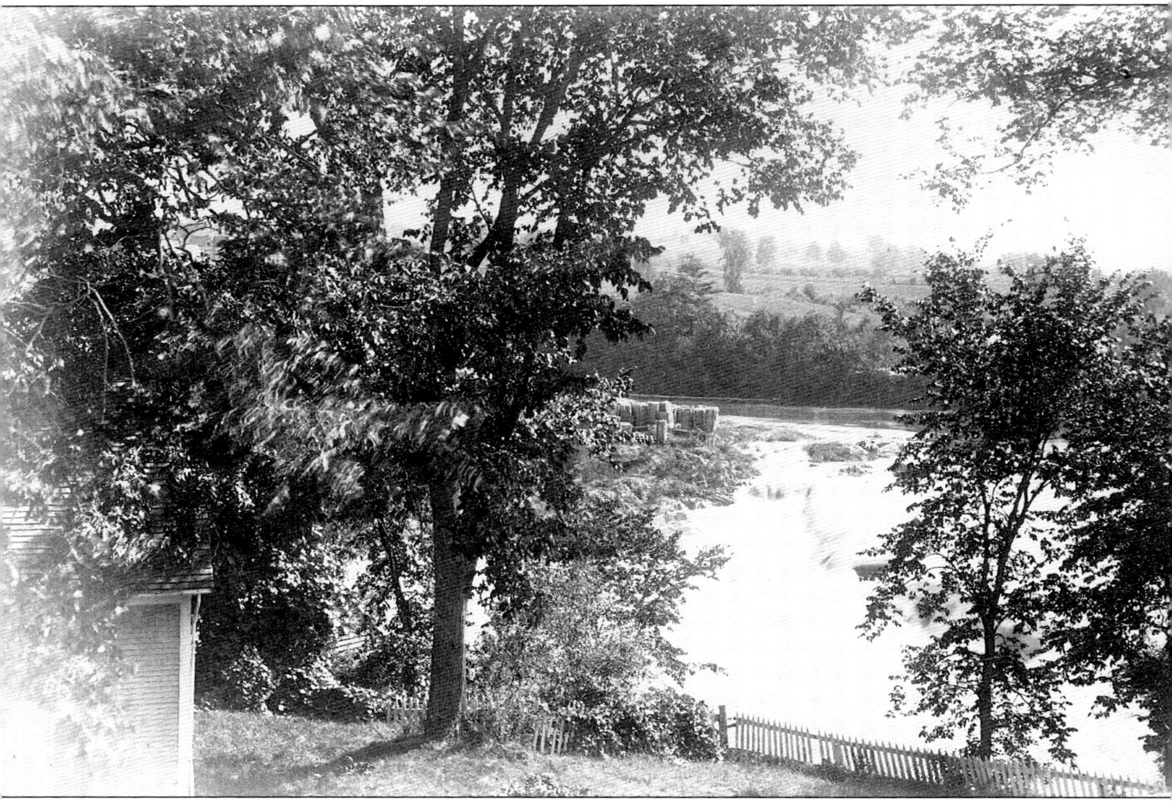

An excellent view of Skowhegan Falls, where much water power was generated, from the west side of the home at 6 Elm Street, which owned by Myra R. Arnold at the time. The photograph was taken in 1886.

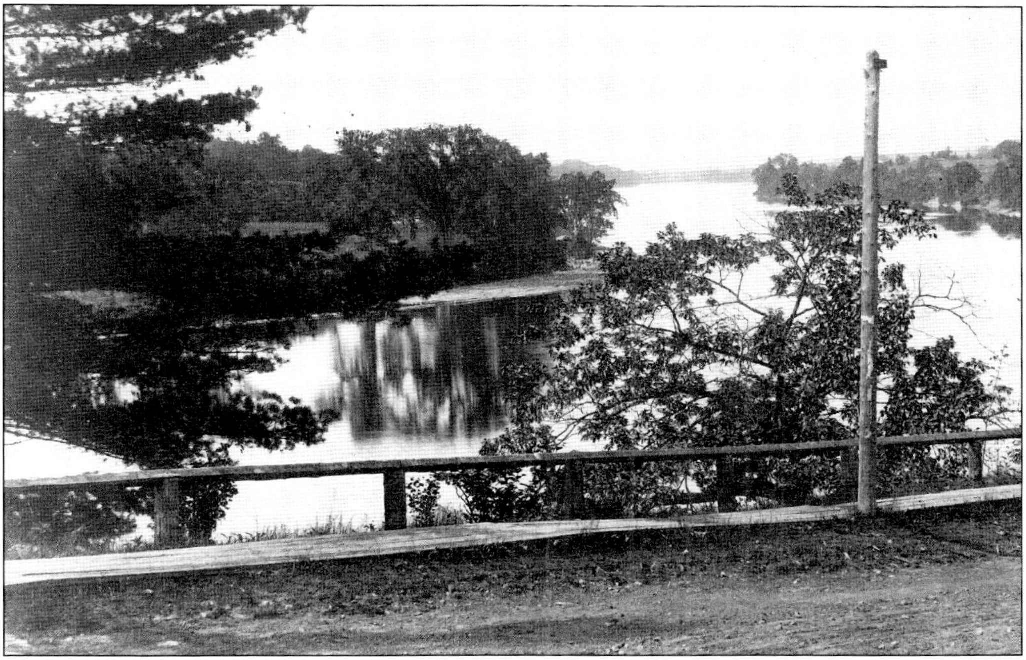

We fade out with views of the mighty Kennebec. This was also taken from Elm Street, in the 1870s or 1880s.

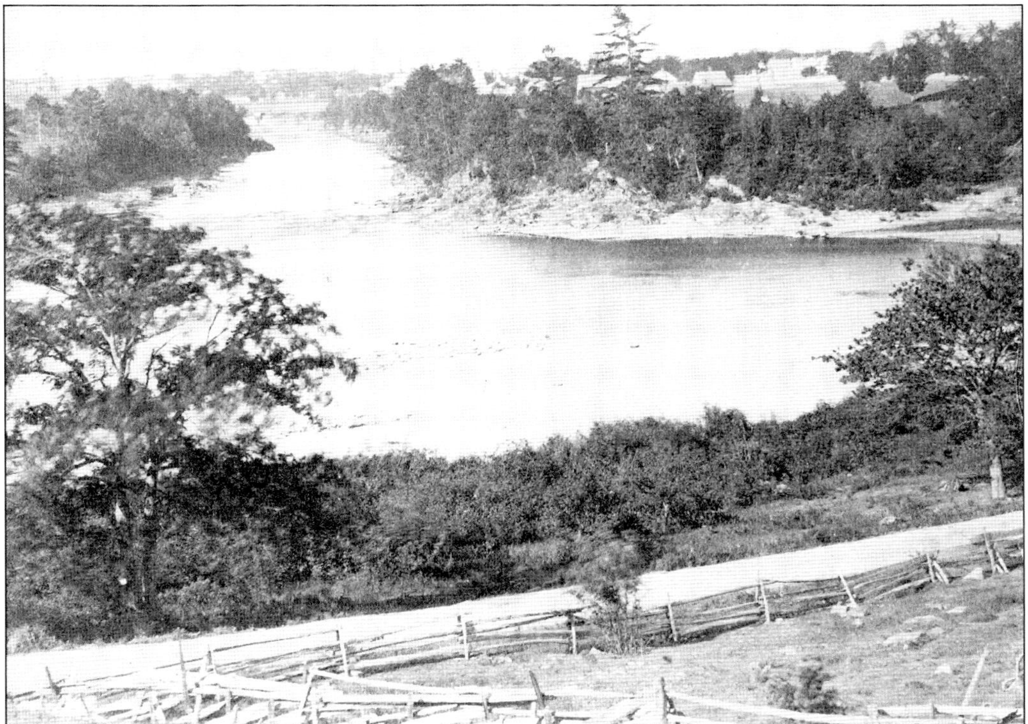

The Kennebec as seen from below the Great Eddy.

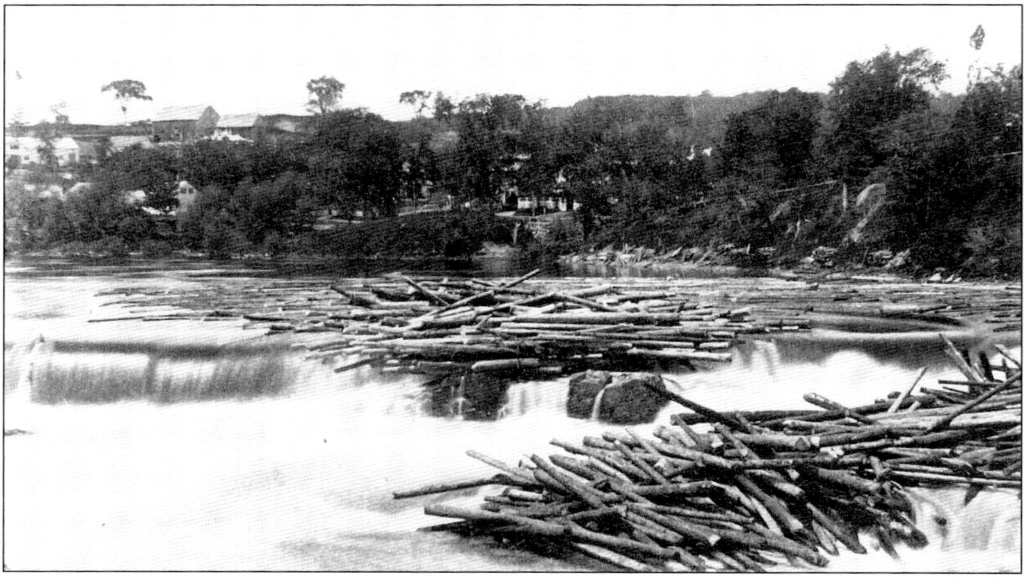

The falls at Skowhegan with many logs in the Kennebec, a sight no longer possible.

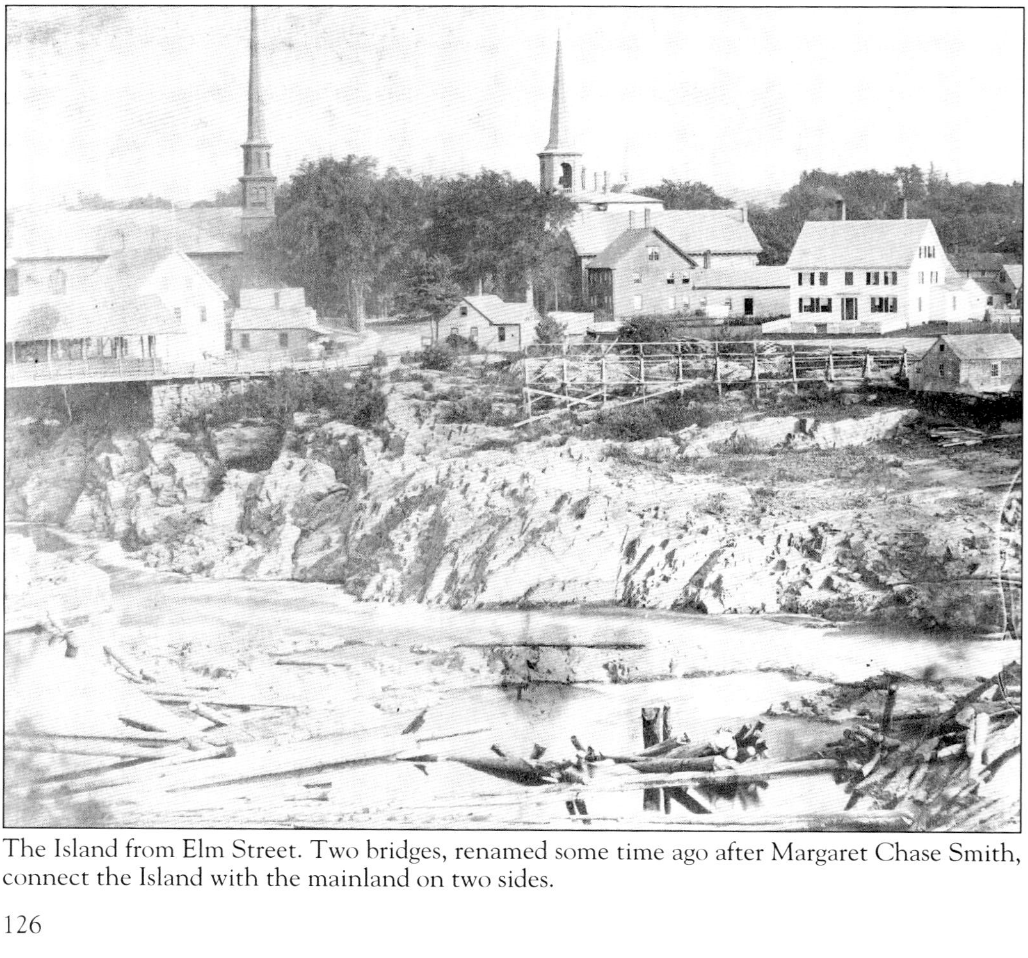

The Island from Elm Street. Two bridges, renamed some time ago after Margaret Chase Smith, connect the Island with the mainland on two sides.

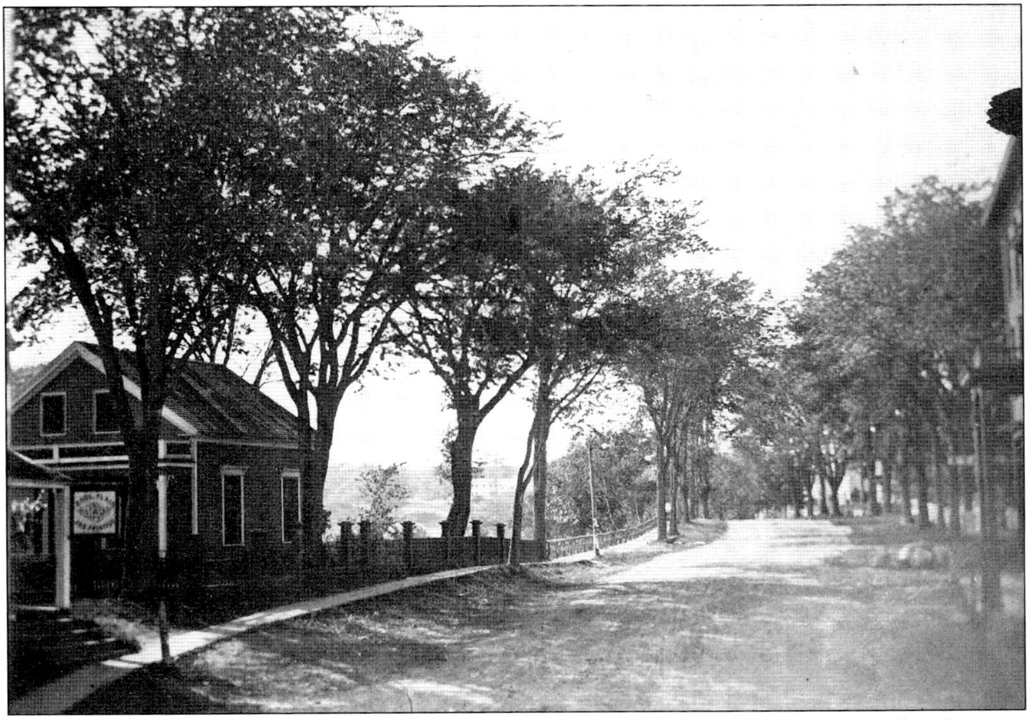

Elm Street looking west about 1863. The old Neil homestead can be seen in the distance between elm trees. The Farwell place is on the left; Brewster House, which burned in December 30, 1872, is on the right.

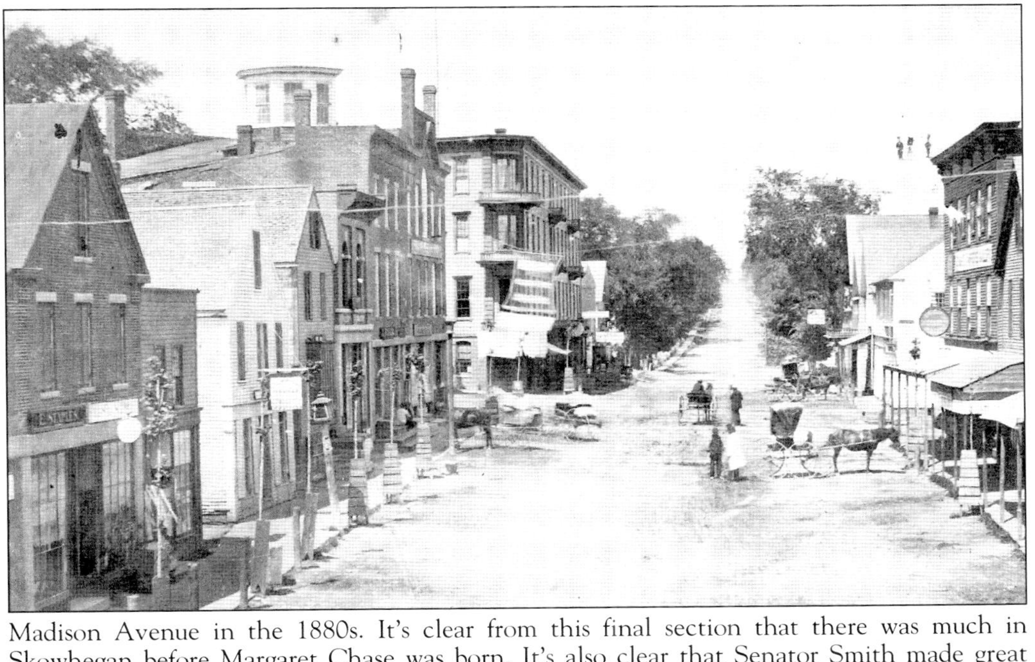

Madison Avenue in the 1880s. It's clear from this final section that there was much in Skowhegan before Margaret Chase was born. It's also clear that Senator Smith made great contributions to this town, and continues to do so with her library.

# Acknowledgments

My greatest thanks must go to Dr. Gregory Gallant, director of the Margaret Chase Smith Library in Skowhegan, for the wonderful help and cooperation shown me. I'd also like to thank Angela Stockwell and Reginald Collins of the library staff and especially that Caron girl out front who was everlastingly kind.

Once again Earl Shettleworth, director of the Maine Historic Preservation Commission, gave material—postcards, stereoptic slides, and photographs which provided a base for all the other work. Richard J. Warren, publisher of the *Bangor Daily News*, gave permission to use the photographs from the folio prepared for Senator Smith on the Eisenhower visit.

Two high school history teachers, one retired and one not, provided help. I want to thank especially David Harville, who teaches at Nokomis High School in Newport, for letting me use his collection of photographs (he has many more artifacts) of the Skowhegan boys who died in World War II. To Erland F. Penley, retired now after teaching for more than thirty years at Skowhegan's schools, I must give bountiful thanks. He allowed me to take my pick of the photographs collected for the Bloomfield Academy Trust. Those photographs are one of the ingredients that will go into making the academy a museum.

Portland attorney Merton Henry is the person who put me in touch with Gallant. Lee Granville, president of the Skowhegan Camera Club, pointed me to Joe Penley. One of Senator Margaret Chase Smith's nieces, Ann Herrin, was more helpful than she probably knew. Judi Inchauteguiz, curator of History House in Skowhegan, did the best she could for me. Greg Gallant provided many, many leads. I was quite amazed with how quickly much of this help was given. I thank you, one and all.

And, once again, I'd like to thank the people at Arcadia, my publishers. Included are Sarah Maineri, now my editor, Jim Burkinshaw, Michael Guillory, and Aaron Faulkner. After my campaign is over, I'll be back again, hopefully, as quickly as possible.

Frank H. Sleeper